Pâtés &
Terrines

Pâtés & Terrines

Friedrich W. Ehlert · Edouard Lonque · Michael Raffael · Frank Wesel

Hearst Books

New York

English edition published by
The Hamlyn Publishing Group Limited,
Astronaut House, Hounslow Road, Feltham, Middlesex, England.
Copyright © The Hamlyn Publishing Group 1984.
Original edition published under the title *Das Grosse
Buch der Pasteten*, copyright © by Teubner Edition, Germany.
First published in the United States by Hearst Books 1984.

Front cover photograph by James Jackson
Phototypeset by Tameside Filmsetting Limited
in 9½ on 10½pt Monophoto Times

Library of Congress Catalog Card Number: 83-83312
ISBN: 0-688-03896-4
Printed in Spain
First U.S. Edition
1 2 3 4 5 6 7 8 9 10

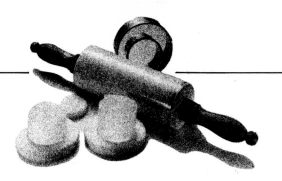

Contents

Introduction

We are happy to be able to bring you a book unique in both content and format, a book on one of the most interesting aspects of the art of cooking. The emphasis is firmly on the word "art," for in fact its subject is more than mere cooking, pâté and terrine making having a long and complex culinary history. Without doubt it is a fascinating, many-faceted subject. The fascination, and to some extent the air of mystery which surrounds pâté making, was one of the main reasons behind this book.

The number of pâté and related recipes from around the world is legion and it would have been impossible to include them all in this book. It was more a case of having to choose from a host of recipes those that truly justified the term pâtés and terrines, and those that closely resemble them in their methods of preparation. Here we had to define our terms of reference exactly because the "pâtés and terrines" which have come down to us from the past include terrines, galantines, ballotines, etc. The differences between these dishes are often confused, not only when transposed from one country to another, but even on a national level. Terrines are called pâtés, or vice versa, and terrines are often referred to as parfaits or galantines. We have tried to bring a little order into this confusion, by setting out certain basic criteria for each type of pâté or terrine to help you identify them with more certainty. In this we have taken into account historical development as well as the opinions of experts both at home and abroad. In each separate chapter we have attempted to explain the individual characteristics of each type.

In choosing the recipes for inclusion in this book we have selected the most representative examples of each group of pâtés. A typical recipe, which we have called a basic recipe, is explained in every chapter with both text and photographs. These are both recipes in their own right which you should be able to follow without difficulty, and at the same time they provide all the information you need to create imaginative new dishes of your own. That is why we have devoted a lot of space to these basic recipes. Regardless of whether it is pastry making, fillings, or how to stuff a galantine that worries you, you will find all these explained in both photographs and text with all the essential information.

Pâtés and terrines have continued to grow in popularity in recent years. Our book celebrates this renaissance and will certainly be indispensable for all cooks intent on scaling the heights of this culinary art. It will also appeal to those who prefer simpler dishes, such as country terrines with all their honest goodness. We have tried to produce a book that will satisfy all the requirements of the professional chef, and at the same time provide the enthusiastic cook at home with a book that is easy to follow. It is to be hoped that we have achieved these aims, that the reader will enjoy the book and find inspiration in it, develop the skill of pâté making and at the same time derive all possible pleasure from a classic work of this kind and from the pâtés and terrines which it contains.

Christian Teubner

Past and Present

PÂTÉ AND TERRINE making has a long and illustrious history, unique in that today it is as prized and practiced an art as it was in the days of Catherine de Medici's banquets. One of the most fascinating things about pâtés and terrines is that, in spite of their well-earned reputation for elegance and sophistication, they started life more as a means of preserving the produce of the autumn slaughtering of pigs. As well as the hams which were salted, and the sausages that were packed into cases, other tasty, meaty morsels were made into pâtés or terrines, sealed with lard and put away for later enjoyment.

For Sidney Smith, renowned eighteenth-century wit and bon viveur and a fine parson too, heaven was "eating *pâté de foie gras* to the sound of trumpets." Certainly, as enshrined, say, in the menus of the three-star restaurants of Paris's right bank, this might not seem too wild a claim. The experience of such a masterpiece definitely ought to make an extra-terrestrial impact on those of us fortunate enough to know it, but there are many, many excellent pâtés and terrines and related dishes more easily made from simple ingredients which give comparable pleasure. And a lot of us would sacrifice the sounding of trumpets for an honest bottle of wine.

Pâtés and terrines are equally at home, as we have seen, whether in picnic basket or on grand buffet table. In fact, they are probably the world's most adaptable culinary form – portable, even-tempered and long-lived. Dressed up and decorated, sparkling with aspic diamonds, garlanded with radish roses and pastry leaves, they make a matrimonial feast. But a simple chicken terrine (the easiest dish in the repertoire now thanks to the food processor) needs only a salad and some bread to make a most satisfying lunch. The selection of recipes in this book covers the entire range, from grand galantine to tiny samosa. They teach the art of making the European classics, but much more than this they remind us too – should it be necessary – of the greatness of the English pies and potted meats, so long a stalwart favorite in that country but deserving of a much wider audience.

Whatever the occasion or the need, there is a pâté or terrine to suit. As a beginning for a formal meal, think of an airy *bouchée*, *parfait* or *timbale*. Some of these, and possibly the lightest of all, the *vol-au-vent*, also make a perfect savory. As a meal on its own, nothing could be finer than a *kulebyaka* or steak and kidney pudding. As you will see, the possibilities are limitless. The only problem is deciding where to begin.

Pastries

Long ago, the inventive Ancient Greeks were already enclosing meat, fish and all kinds of vegetables in pastry and they are thus credited with inventing the pie. It is also an established fact that the ancient Romans followed their example. But no one knows exactly who invented pastry, that crisp crust which encloses the choicest foods, protecting them, preserving their juices and enhancing their flavor. It seems certain, however, that the first pastries were made simply with flour and water and resembled our eggless pasta dough. This has led to the conjecture that the ancient Greeks and Romans left their pastry uneaten out of consideration for their teeth, and indeed it would have required considerable force to bite through this primitive form of pastry to reach the filling.

Easy-to-work pastry

It is clear that early pastry cooks were not slow to discover the advantages of adding fat and eggs to give their pastry a more edible, lighter consistency. But pastry was not always intended for eating. In the Middle Ages it was used to make attractive table decorations, designed to stimulate the appetite. While these could be extremely artistic constructions, sometimes the designs were very simple. However, simple or extravagant, to be eaten or not, a pastry crust has always been an important part of pie making and justifiably so. Pastry was, and still is, an easy-to-work material. The simpler the pastry (that is, the less fat it contains) the more complex the constructions that can be made with it. This is obvious from the exotic pastry constructions of the Middle Ages, the Renaissance, the Baroque and Rococo periods, described in the literature of the time.

The first great pastry cooks were the Italians, who were later imitated by the French. It was they who first improved the flavor of pies by leaving out the pastry altogether, thus inventing the terrine and galantine.

It must be light, and rich in fat

The most important pastry, and the first in the history of pie making, is the pie or kneading pastry, known in grandmother's day and even earlier as rub-in pastry, after the process of rubbing the fat into the flour with the hands to form crumbs before adding the other ingredients. It is still made in the same way today, or alternatively all the ingredients can be worked quickly together to give a good pastry which is rich in fat. Most pies intended to be eaten cold, and some small pies to be eaten hot, are made with pie pastry. It can also be used for old-fashioned English pies, even though suet pastry is more often used – and for good reason, because beef suet makes pastry flaky and light.

Pies to be eaten hot

Puff pastry piecrusts are invariably eaten hot, as in the case of *bouchées à la reine* and *vol-au-vents* or patties. There are, of course, sweet cakes made with puff pastry which are eaten cold, but in the case of savory pies puff pastry is, without exception, eaten hot, since the pastry loses its flaky consistency when it cools and the moist filling makes the pastry heavy. This moves puff pastry into second place in the order of importance of piecrusts.

Puff pastry is a delight to eat when it has been expertly prepared. Although there are several ways of making it, the principle remains the same: the thinnest and finest possible layers of a water-based dough and butter give this pastry its airy consistency. Contrary to general opinion, puff pastry is not particularly difficult to make, but it is extremely time-consuming. To save time you can use one of the frozen varieties, for these are generally excellent, but if you particularly want a puff pastry made with butter you will have to make your own.

We still have not mentioned the third type of pastry used for pie making: yeast or brioche pastry. This plays only a minor part in classic pies, but some chefs, such as the famous Maître Haeberlin of Alsace, make a superb foie gras in yeast pastry. Yeast dough is better known, however, in connection with Russian *pirozhki*, Galician and South American *empanadas* and a number of specialty dishes.

As far as pie making is concerned we can ignore pasta and choux pastry, although there are a few specialties in which they are used.

Pie pastry

Pie pastry is usually associated with sweet tarts, but pastry for savory pies naturally contains no sugar. In France and Switzerland the term pie pastry or *pâte brisée*, refers exclusively to piecrust which contains salt rather than sugar.

Of all the pastries used for pie making simple pie comes top of the list because almost all savory pies are made with it. The quantities of its basic ingredients – namely flour, fat and liquid – vary according to the type of pie. More fat and less liquid gives an extremely crumbly pastry which is quite difficult to handle. It does not cling well together and falls apart easily when rolled. If the liquid content is increased the pastry holds together better and is easier to handle. The quality and quantity of flour is also crucial, the most important thing being for the flour to be fresh with a pleasant wheaty smell.

Flour that has been stored for a long time becomes more elastic in use and can make for brittle pastry. The quality of the flour also influences the amount of water needed, so if you are making a pastry crust for the first time, don't add all the flour initially, but keep some back to work into the pastry if it does not hold together well. If the pastry is too firm you will have to work in a little more water. It is essential for the pastry to hold together if it is to line the pan properly. It is better to use a firmer pastry for cutting into decorations.

Don't think you are restricted solely to salt for seasoning pastry. You can use other seasonings too, sprinkling them into the pastry once you have decided on the character of the filling; a country-style filling, heavily flavored with garlic, for example, goes well with a sprinkling of pepper and nutmeg. For fish and veal pies a touch of ginger will complement the flavor. After mixing, the dough must be left to stand in the refrigerator for at least an hour. This will allow it to settle and to take on a slightly softer consistency (a point to bear in mind when mixing the pastry) and easier to roll. To work together any leftover pastry, knead it as little as possible on as little flour as possible and reroll. Overworking the pastry can easily make it brittle so that it shrinks during cooking.

The following recipe for a good all-round pastry should give excellent results:

> 4 cups flour
> 1 cup butter
> 1 teaspoon salt
> $\frac{1}{2}$–$\frac{3}{4}$ cup water
> 1 egg

Pastry made with shortening is also recommended. It is easy to work and gives a crisp result.

Sample recipe:

> 4 cups flour
> $\frac{3}{4}$ cup shortening
> 1 teaspoon salt
> $\frac{1}{2}$–$\frac{3}{4}$ cup water

1 **Sift the flour onto the worktop.** Make a well in the center; cut the butter into cubes and place it in the well. Sprinkle with the salt. Professional chefs can estimate the quantity by eye, but it is advisable to measure it if you are unsure.

2 **Pour the water onto the butter.** You can add all the water at once, or add it gradually if you prefer. The latter method would be easier for beginners because if the water is added gradually it binds easier and quicker with the butter (or other fat).

3 **Add the egg.** Make sure that it is the same temperature as the butter, otherwise it will be difficult to work in. It is a good idea to break the egg into a cup initially to test for freshness. Mix the butter, egg and water together.

4 **Gradually work in the flour.** Work the butter with one hand, adding small amounts of flour with a dough scraper in the other hand. Work as quickly and carefully as possible, mixing the ingredients thoroughly together.

5 **Knead the dough together as quickly as possible.** The faster you work, the better the dough will hold together; it may nevertheless become dry and cracked, but you can remedy this by adding a little more cold water.

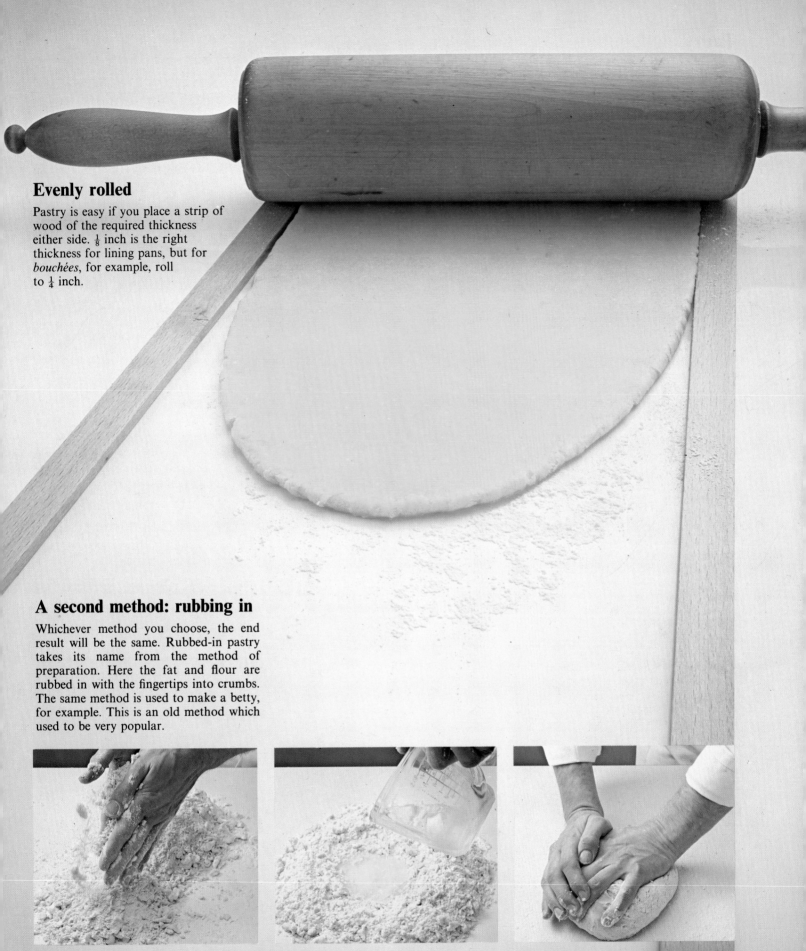

Evenly rolled

Pastry is easy if you place a strip of wood of the required thickness either side. $\frac{1}{8}$ inch is the right thickness for lining pans, but for *bouchées*, for example, roll to $\frac{1}{4}$ inch.

A second method: rubbing in

Whichever method you choose, the end result will be the same. Rubbed-in pastry takes its name from the method of preparation. Here the fat and flour are rubbed in with the fingertips into crumbs. The same method is used to make a betty, for example. This is an old method which used to be very popular.

1 **For the rubbed-in method, sift the flour** onto the worktop. Add the butter in small pieces. Rub in carefully with the fingers, working the butter into the flour to form a crumbly mixture.

2 **Make a well in the mixture.** Sprinkle with the salt and pour in the water. Then add the egg. Work the liquid into part of the flour-and-fat mixture, then blend in the remaining mixture working from the outside inward.

3 **Using both hands, shape the dough quickly** into a ball and knead firmly, so that the dough clings together well. Like dough made by the previous method, rubbed-in dough also needs to be covered and left to stand in the refrigerator for 1 hour.

How much pastry do you need?

Recipes are sometimes extremely comprehensive and this can make them appear complicated. To avoid this the recipes in this book have been kept as simple as possible. For pies, the quantity of pastry required is given in weight. This may be confusing to anyone who is not used to baking, so, to avoid any problems we have compiled the table on the right: this tells you what ingredients you require to make a given weight of pastry. It may also tempt you to try variations of your own on any given recipe. By altering the egg or fat content, or the quantities of flour, many such experiments have inspired new ideas which have been successful enough to become standard recipes. In the same way

you can experiment with the kind and quantity of seasoning, thus creating your own individual recipes.

It is always advisable to make more dough than you actually need, for it is easier to roll out a larger sheet of dough and cut it to size than to try to roll the dough to fit the

pan exactly. You can use any leftovers to make decorations or make them into savory sticks sprinkled with poppy seeds and caraway.

For about $1\frac{1}{2}$ lb dough	For about $3\frac{1}{2}$ lb dough	For about $2\frac{1}{4}$ lb dough	For about $3\frac{3}{4}$ lb dough
4 cups flour 1 cup butter 1 teaspoon salt 1 egg white 10–12 tablespoons water	7 cups flour $1\frac{3}{4}$ cups butter 2 teaspoons salt 1 egg 1 egg white 1–$1\frac{1}{4}$ cups water	5 cups flour $1\frac{1}{4}$ cups butter $1\frac{1}{2}$ teaspoons salt 1 egg $\frac{3}{4}$–1 cup water	9 cups flour 1 lb (4 sticks) butter $2\frac{1}{2}$ teaspoons salt 2 eggs $1\frac{1}{2}$–$1\frac{3}{4}$ cups water

Suet pastry

There is no reason to turn up your nose at the thought of pastry made with beef fat, i.e. suet, especially if it is the best beef fat, kidney suet.

Suet makes pastry rise well and gives a consistency like that of puff pastry, but it should only be used for pies that are to be served hot.

$\frac{1}{2}$ lb (1 cup) beef suet
4 cups flour
1 teaspoon salt
$1\frac{1}{4}$–$1\frac{1}{2}$ cups water

1 **Prepare the suet.** If you leave it to chill in the refrigerator for a while it will come out of the skin easily. You can also buy suet skinned and chopped, but the best kidney suet is that bought in one piece.

2 **Finely chop the suet.** This is easiest with a large, sharp knife held in both hands like a chopping knife. Sprinkle lightly with flour to prevent the suet sticking together.

3 **Initial mixing.** With the fingertips thoroughly mix the flour, fat and salt in a bowl, crumbling the suet as you mix. Do not completely crush the pieces of fat or the pastry will not rise as well.

4 **Add the water a little at a time** – $1\frac{1}{4}$ cups will usually be enough. Add more only if necessary. Stir briskly while adding water to bind the flour and fat well together.

5 **Knead the dough,** as quickly and firmly as possible. Fat, flour and water must form a homogenous mixture. Suet pastry does not keep, but should also be left to stand or chilled for a while before baking.

Yeast pastry

Yeast pastry is seldom used in piemaking, but it is worth a mention as it is used in a few specialty dishes, in Russian *pirozhki*, or Spanish *empanadas*, for example. It is important to use fresh compressed yeast if you can, because of its pure yeast cells which multiply rapidly in the right environment. And the right environment for yeast consists of food and moisture – provided by the dough – together with warmth. By a process of fermentation the yeast cells change the starches present in the flour into glucose, which in turn changes into alcohol and carbon dioxide. It is this gas which makes yeast pastry so light, quite apart from the typically fresh and pleasant taste which the yeast gives. There are two ways of making yeast pastry. The first method, the one illustrated in the photographs, is the

warmth method. The second method, the cold method, consists of dissolving the yeast in milk and mixing the pastry without allowing time for fermentation. This sort of dough is particularly suitable for fillings which are extremely sensitive to heat. Whichever method you choose, yeast pastry is much easier to make than many people think.

Basic recipe:

4 cups flour
2 (.6 oz) cakes
compressed yeast or 2
packages active dry yeast
1¼ cups lukewarm milk
3 tablespoons butter
2 eggs
1 teaspoon salt

1 **Sift the flour into a bowl.** Make a well in the center. Crumble the compressed yeast into the well or sprinkle over the dry. Pour on the lukewarm milk. Stir to dissolve the yeast in the milk. Sprinkle a fine layer of flour over this mixture.

2 **Cover the bowl and leave the mixture to rise** for 15 minutes in a warm, draft-free place. Cracks on the surface of the yeast mixture appearing in the covering flour are a sign that the mixture has risen sufficiently.

3 **While the mixture is rising,** melt the butter in a saucepan. Add the eggs and beat them into the butter. Stir in the salt and leave to cool slightly until lukewarm.

4 **Pour the egg and butter mixture over the yeast mixture** in the bowl. Stir all the ingredients together with a spoon and beat for a time until the dough becomes lighter and the ingredients are thoroughly mixed.

5 **Knead the dough with your hands** until dry and smooth. This stage can be done with a spoon, but you will get better results if you do it by hand. If the dough is too soft you can add a little more flour at this stage.

6 **The dry, kneaded dough** is now shaped into a ball. Place in the bowl, sprinkle with flour and cover the bowl. Leave to rise for 15 to 20 minutes to give the yeast cells sufficient time to ferment fully.

7 **When fully risen the dough** should at least have doubled in volume. Then it has risen fully. To give a finer texture, knead once more, and leave to rise for a further 15 to 20 minutes in a covered bowl.

Puff pastry

This is the lightest pastry of all, and is particularly suitable for crusts which are to be baked unfilled and filled later with a hot mixture. It takes some time to make, but is quite easy if you stick to the rules. Alternate fine layers of flour-and-water dough and butter cause the pastry to rise during baking. There are two methods of preparation; you can either wrap the butter in the water dough, or instead work the butter with a little flour, roll it out and wrap the water dough in the butter.

9 cups flour
1¾–2 cups water
2½ teaspoons salt
2¼ lb (9 sticks) butter

1 **To make the flour-and-water dough,** sift 7 cups flour onto a pastry board and make a well in the center. Add the cold water and salt and work together quickly with your hands, working from the center outward.

2 **Knead the dough** until the surface is smooth and shiny. Shape into a ball, cover and leave in the refrigerator for at least 15 minutes. A cross cut in the top will help the dough to settle.

3 **Next prepare the butter.** The butter should be as cold as possible. Cut up the butter, place on the pastry board, sift the remaining flour over and work them together. Shape into a ball, cover and again leave to chill in the refrigerator.

4 **Roll out the butter.** It should not stick to the board if it is thoroughly chilled and the board liberally sprinkled with flour. Roll the butter into a rectangle about 18 × 30 inches.

5 **The flour-and-water dough goes inside the butter.** The dough should be rolled to 16 × 14 inches and placed over one half of the butter. Fold over the other half of the butter sheet.

6 **Place the edges together** and press firmly together with the fingers to seal the dough completely inside the butter. Sprinkle the work surface lightly with flour.

7 **Roll from bottom to top.** It is essential to maintain an even pressure with the rolling pin to get even layers of pastry. Then roll alternately from left to right.

8 **Roll from left to right.** By continually changing direction you will keep the layers even as the dough becomes thinner and thinner. Roll out the dough to about 18 × 30 inches and chill for 15 to 20 minutes.

Puff pastry

an alternative method

Experts could spend many happy hours discussing which of the two methods of making puff pastry is the correct one – or whether perhaps a combination of the two would give the best results. In fact the results are almost identical. The pastry described in the photographs is made with an outer layer of butter and flour. The advantage of this method is that it will not dry out and can be stored for a few days before use. It has a tendency to stick to the work surface during rolling out, but you can usually prevent sticking by sprinkling the surface generously with flour.

The second method also has its advantages: with the dough on the outside you can use unadulterated butter, that is without flour, whereas in a warm room you will have to add up to 10 percent flour to the butter to make it easy to handle by the first method. But it soon dries out and then cracks during rolling, allowing the butter to escape. You can avoid this by wrapping the dough in foil before chilling it in the refrigerator.

9 cups flour
$2\frac{1}{4}$ cups water
2 teaspoons salt
$2\frac{1}{4}$ lb (9 sticks) butter

or

9 cups flour
2 cups water
2 teaspoons salt
$2\frac{1}{4}$ lb (9 sticks) butter

Cut a cross in the top of the flour-and-water dough. Work it into a smooth dough in the usual way, shape into a ball, flatten slightly and cut the top. Cream the butter until smooth and shape into a slab, or work in with the 1 cup of flour.

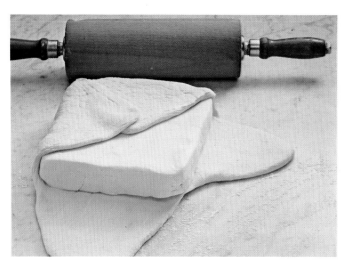

Wrap the butter in the dough. The cross in the top will make it easy to roll four pieces outward from the center. Place the slab of butter in the center and fold over the four corners of dough, sealing the edges. You will get a better seal if you first brush the edges with water. Roll and make your turns as described for the first method.

9 **To make a single turn,** fold one third of the dough into the center and fold the remaining third over it like an envelope. You now have three layers of dough one on top of the other. Wrap in wax paper and leave to chill in the refrigerator for 15 to 20 minutes.

10 **To make a double turn,** fold the left and right edges into the center, so that they meet. Then fold the dough over again lengthwise to give four layers, one on top of the other. Again, leave to chill.

11 **How many turns was that?** A simple way of remembering is, after each turn to make the appropriate number of fingerprints in the dough. You will need four turns altogether, two single and two double.

Seasonings

It is difficult for us to imagine the immense variety of seasonings used by cooks in the past, but literature provides us with several examples.

We tend to forget that a knowledge of seasonings was indispensable to the medieval cook. In the days before refrigerators seasonings were used liberally to hide the taste and smell of foods which were no longer fresh. Pepper, for example, not only masked such flavors – it also delayed the process of decay by up to 24 hours. Pies, however, required a profusion of seasonings for other quite special reasons. Seasonings were both rare and expensive: pepper, for example, was worth its weight in gold and some businesses made their profits in dealing in spices alone. One pound of nutmeg cost as much as seven fatted oxen, according to a price list of 1393. So spices became a status symbol and were most used where they created the maximum impression – that is, in pies, the most showy of all the dishes brought to the table. At the wedding banquet of a sixteenth-century Burgundian nobleman 190 pounds of pepper alone was used.

Explorers like Columbus, Magellan and Vasco da Gama had a lot to thank the cookery business for: when they landed on foreign soil they did not only look for gold, because astronomically expensive spices were even more in demand in Europe. It was at this time that the special association of individual herbs and spices with a particular geographical area was established: cloves from the Moluccas, ginger from India, chili from America, allspice from Jamaica and Cuba. You can see from this small sample of countries which produce the spices used in pâté and terrine making that you can almost imagine yourself following in Columbus's footsteps. You can imagine, too, the amount of international wheeling and dealing which went into producing a good meal – and it was a long time before spices became any cheaper. To keep prices high the Dutch restricted planting of nutmeg trees in their spice islands to the few that they needed for their own requirements. And finally, there were also those herbs and spices which were native to Europe. The more inventive cooks replaced foreign spices with imaginative combinations of fresh or dried herbs, a form of economy which was to appear over and over again in times of need.

But less imagination is required in today's commercial world where you can buy mixtures of pie seasonings. No one could object to them on the grounds of their quality, but what a comedown from the time when seasonings were an opportunity for creativity and a means of self-expression! Ready-mixed herbs take away the greatest pleasure in pâté and terrine making: the chance to give these culinary works of art their own, quite individual flavor.

The art of mixing herbs and spices

It is not as difficult to use herbs successfully as is often thought. With 15 ingredients, which you probably already have in the kitchen cupboard, you can make a "basic seasoning" with which to experiment. You can use these ingredients to mix enough seasoning to keep some in stock, but no more than you are likely to use within six months, for herbs soon lose their aroma, especially when mixed with other herbs. That is why it is important to stick to the quantities given in the recipe, or to what you think you can use. This mixture forms a basis on which you can experiment. You may make mistakes – but you may also make the most delicious discoveries.

While you can give your imagination free rein, do not totally ignore the experience of generations of cooks who have learned what goes well with what – and what does not. Wild boar and juniper, for example: these bitter berries can be added to the basic seasoning to complement any game dish. A little marjoram and garlic also bring out the flavor of game very well. But avoid strongly flavored herbs with a delicate venison pâté, where grated orange or lemon peel are better than marjoram. Rosemary and sage go well with poultry, and concentrated fresh orange juice goes well with duck. Another idea for duck is to add coarsely chopped green peppercorns, as in one variation on foie gras. You can see that there are no limits to the possible variations. But you need to feel your way carefully to avoid gross and possibly expensive errors of judgment: a goose liver pâté seasoned with garlic might make your dinner guests beat an immediate, hasty retreat.

Alcoholic flavorings

Labels such as "cooking wine" or "hotel quality," which are synonymous with second-rate, should serve as a warning. Despite the assertions made in many cookbooks, you should use only the best for cooking, the wine with the best bouquet, the brandy with the best aroma. Alcohol content is unimportant, only the flavor counts. The alcohol evaporates of course and you can't get drunk from eating pâté.

Alcohol should never be mixed directly into the filling, for it expands and could cause the pastry to crack during baking. So it is best to use liquor in food in the following way: use it to dilute the juices left in the pan after cooking the main ingredients and reduce it, where possible adding a little broth made with leftover bits of the meat used for the pâté. The sauce obtained can be added to the filling or used to moisten the other ingredients. It is obvious that a sauce of this kind is always better than barbarically sprinkling a filling with some kind of cheap spirits.

Allspice

Pimenta officinalis

Often called Jamaican pepper, allspice is the dried berries of the Jamaican pepper tree, from the myrtle family. Its name exactly describes its flavor, which combines those of several spices. Allspice is particularly good in meat, poultry, and even fish, fillings and is included in most spice mixtures for pâtés. Its flavor is not overpowering so it is seldom used as an individual seasoning.

Aniseed

Pimpinella anisum

A spice known for thousands of years from the *umbelliferae* family. The dried seeds taste and smell extremely spicy and fresh. Aniseed is typical of the spices best used in isolation and should be used in very small quantities in mixtures. Yeast dough *pirozhki* can be sprinkled with whole seeds. The flavor goes well with hot-and-sweet meat fillings.

Star anise *Illicum verum* is unrelated botanically to *Pimpinella anisum*; it is nonetheless very similar in flavor.

Cardamom

Elettaria cardamomum

This is the dried fruit of the Indian cardamom plant. The three-sectioned seed pods range in color from white (bleached) to brown-black, depending on the degree of drying. The most common is the light brown, bought ground or as whole seeds. It smells and tastes pleasantly spicy, is slightly hot and is ideal for spice mixtures. It is a must in a variety of curry powders or pâté seasonings for a truly spicy flavor.

Chili peppers, Cayenne

Capsicum frutescens

This, the hottest of all spices, is grown in its American homeland in various sizes, colors and strengths. The name cayenne pepper is confusing, for botanically the plant belongs to the paprika, and not the pepper, family.

In its dried, ground form it is the ideal seasoning to give hotness with neutral flavor, best used in small quantities with fish and shellfish and in more generous quantities in hot meat fillings and stews.

Coriander

Coriandrum sativum

A spice dating from the time of the Old Testament. The dried seeds have a pleasant, mildly spicy taste. Its main use is in combination with other spices, which makes it one of the main ingredients of curry. It goes well in spice mixtures for coarse pâtés.

The green leaves of the coriander (cilantro) are an aromatic herb, although the flavor is oily and pungent, for which reason they should be used sparingly.

Cumin

Cuminum cyminum

This is not to be confused with *Carum carvi*, a member of the Mediterranean parsley family. The golden brown seeds look very much like caraway and have a highly aromatic and slightly bitter flavor. Cumin is a spice long neglected in northern climes, although it makes an ideal seasoning for strongly flavored meat and is suitable for inclusion in spice mixtures – use it in spice mixtures for pies or curries. Excellent too for chutneys and other accompaniments, or sauces.

Ginger

Zingiber officinale

Ginger is the rhizome root of the reed-like ginger plant of the spice lily family. Whole roots keep their flavor over long periods and, freshly grated, are always preferable to ground ginger. They have a burning hot, slightly sweet flavor and will go excellently as part of a mixture of seasonings for meat fillings, game, poultry and fish.

Fresh ginger roots are usually one of the milder varieties and should be used more generously.

Green peppercorns

Piper nigrum

This is a newcomer from the pepper family, used freeze-dried or available preserved in its raw state. Both varieties have a mild, aromatic pepper flavor, which is excellent where pepper is used as the only seasoning. The dried form is stronger, but still relatively mild. Despite accepted practice, the green variety should never be used as whole seeds. Its full aroma comes out only when crushed.

Paprika

Capiscum annuum

The most widely used types of paprika are mild paprika, sweet paprika, which is medium-hot, and rose paprika, the hottest of the three. All three come from pimientoes. The degree of hotness is determined by the amount of capasaicin, found around the seeds and membrane of the pod. The more of this section of the plant included in the powder, the hotter it will be. It is best in stews, sauces and highly flavored meat mixtures.

Pepper

Piper nigrum

Pepper only retains its full spiciness and hotness when freshly ground. White and black pepper come from the same plant. Black pepper is originally green, becoming brown-black and shriveled during drying. It is hot and quite direct in taste. For white pepper the fully ripe seeds are used; they are soaked, the skins removed, and then dried. It is less hot and milder in flavor. When buying whole peppercorns remember: the larger the corns, the better the aroma.

Bay

Laurus nobilis

This is a pâté seasoning par excellence, and often used as a decoration for terrines. The leaves of the evergreen bay tree can be used fresh or dried. Fresh leaves are more aromatic, but have a slightly bitter taste, which disappears after drying for 2–3 hours. Chopped or crumbled bay leaves give an appropriately spicy flavor to meat fillings, and are especially good in liver and poultry pâtés.

Caraway

Carum carvi

Caraway, the dried dehiscent fruit of the caraway plant, grows wild throughout Europe and is also widely cultivated. An unusual spice with an indefinable flavor, used in all types of recipes from bread to baked cabbage. Its strong taste makes it a spice best used on its own with meat, cheese, cabbage or bread. Nevertheless it can be blended with other spices, in curries for example, or in mixed seasonings for country-style pâtés.

Cinnamon, Cassia

Cinnamomum zeylanicum/cassia

There are two types of cinnamon, which are rarely available separately in the stores. Cinnamon and cassia are both the dried inner bark of the cinnamon tree, but their flavors are quite different. Ceylon cinnamon is aromatically spicy, sweet and mild and light in color. The thinner the bark the better the cinnamon. Cassia has a highly spiced flavor, is sweetly hot, and darker, and the bark is thicker. Because of the difference in flavor, cassia is suitable for strongly-flavored fillings, cinnamon for more delicate ones.

Cloves

Caryophyllus aromaticus

The clove is the dried flower bud of the clove tree. Its unmistakable taste is highly spiced, almost burning. Although a typical spice for individual use, it can also be combined successfully with other spices.

Cloves are essential in most spice mixtures for sausage dishes and pâtés, but are also used on their own to season sauces and stews and, of course, fruit dishes. One point to watch: only buy cloves in small quantities for they quickly lose their aroma.

Curry powder

This is an asiatic mixture of spices, containing up to 30 separate spices. Curry – the word is an anglicization of the Indian *kari* – can be bought in powder or paste form and used with a wide range of curry dishes. Its main ingredients are coriander, pepper, chili, cumin, cardamom, and turmeric which gives curry its distinctive yellowy-green color. When buying spices for curry buy only the best quality, and store in small quantities in light-proof containers. It is an essential ingredient in the preparation of various curries and patty shell fillings.

Fennel

Foeniculum vulgare

A spice from the umbelliferae family, like aniseed and caraway, ripe, dried fennel seeds have a highly aromatic, fairly sweet flavor, slightly reminiscent of aniseed. Native to Asia and the Mediterranean, it is used mainly in dishes from these areas. Used on its own as a flavoring for bread and cakes, it can also be used in spice mixtures in small quantities.

The tender leaves of the fennel plant can, like dill, be used for fish pâtés and terrines.

Juniper

Juniperus communis

Juniper berries – round in shape and $\frac{1}{4}$ inch in diameter, are the ripe berries of the juniper bush, native throughout Europe. They have a strong, slightly bitter and resinous smell and flavor, which makes them the ideal spice for spice mixtures for game. In pie making they are occasionally used for fillings and sauces. The whole berries are often used to decorate game and country-style terrines. When stored be careful that they do not dry out.

Nutmeg and Mace

Myristica fragrans

Beneath the fleshy skin of the fruit of the nutmeg tree lies the hard (when ripe) nut. Within this shell lies the actual nut (nutmeg) surrounded by a seed covering (mace), often wrongly described as nutmeg blossom. Mace has a very pleasant, mildly spicy taste and is an ideal seasoning for any light spice mixture for pies and stews. The nutmeg, on the other hand, has a much stronger flavor and smell and should always be freshly grated.

Saffron

Crocus sativus

The name saffron comes from the Arabic *Za'fran*, meaning yellow. The spice is something of a hybrid as it is a spice and coloring at the same time. It is the dried stamens of a type of crocus, and it takes 80,000 stamens to produce $2\frac{1}{4}$ pounds saffron, which explains its high price. Its taste is unmistakably bitter-sweet. It is also highly colored: 1 gram of saffron is sufficient to give 3 quarts of water a deep yellow color.

Yeast pastry colored with saffron gives a beautiful golden-brown crust.

Vanilla

Vanilla planifolia

This is the fully ripe pod of a climbing orchid native to Mexico. By drying in the sun, soaking and fermentation the flavor is allowed to develop fully in the pod. Vanilla, actually a "sweet seasoning" with an unmistakable scent and aroma, can also be used to vary spice mixtures for pâtés. It is particularly suitable for delicately-flavored meat or poultry or fine liver pâtés. Vanilla should be stored in an airtight container, for it easily absorbs foreign smells.

Pâtés and Seasoning

These are two words which might cause a problem, for if we omit the "and," we are left with the old, vague phrase "pâté seasoning." It is difficult to believe that this term has featured in cookbooks for the last 300 years, with its constituent parts seldom listed. Even famous cooks used to refer in their recipes for lobster, sweetbreads and goose liver pâté to "pie seasoning." When you attempted these recipes you were left to guess what such a mixture might contain. Today you can devise your secret formula, or simply buy a spice mixture.

Your own basic mixture

It is generally assumed that it is simpler and safer to use a bought pâté seasoning than to try and make your own with the limited selection of spices at your disposal. Nevertheless the inventive cook will welcome the opportunity to blend various seasonings to produce an individual, unmistakable flavor. Naturally the spices used should be fresh and of the best available quality. Whole seeds are preferable to the ground variety, as they will generally have more flavor. You can grind your spices in an electric spice or coffee grinder or a food processor. The minute quantities of 8–10 separate spices required for one recipe cannot be measured accurately, so you should be prepared to make enough for several pâtés. This still leaves room for variation, for you can alter the flavor of the basic mixture by adding different spices, or even fresh herbs, each time you make a pâté.

Highly accurate scales are essential for weighing the minute quantities involved, to guarantee the same flavor every time. The most accurate scales are pharmacist's scales with a range of weights.

For delicately flavored meat fillings

¾ oz white peppercorns
½ oz coriander
1 oz thyme
1 oz basil
¼ oz cloves
¾ oz nutmeg
½ oz bay leaves
¼ oz allspice
¼ oz mace
1 oz dried mushrooms

An all-purpose spice mixture

½ oz white peppercorns
½ oz black peppercorns
½ oz mild paprika
¼ oz hot paprika
¼ oz marjoram
¼ oz thyme
¼ oz basil
¼ oz nutmeg
¼ oz mace
½ oz bay leaves
½ oz cloves
¼ oz ginger

For highly-flavored country-style pâtés

¾ oz dried green peppercorns
¼ oz ground allspice
¼ oz ground mace
¼ oz mild paprika
¼ oz ground coriander
¼ oz fresh thyme
¼ oz fresh rosemary
¼ oz fresh basil
¼ oz fresh marjoram
1 heaped teaspoon ground cloves
6 bay leaves

Special seasoning for game

½ oz white peppercorns
½ oz black peppercorns
¼ oz mild paprika
¼ oz hot paprika
¼ oz fresh marjoram
½ oz fresh thyme
½ oz fresh basil
½ oz ground nutmeg
½ oz ground mace
10 bay leaves
½ oz ground cloves
½ oz lovage
½ oz ground ginger
1 oz juniper berries
2 oz dried mousseron
(pickled mushrooms)

Pâté salt, a mixture of pâté seasoning and salt, should not be made up without first checking for flavor. A mixture of this kind has two advantages: it stores well and involves only one batch of weighing. Depending on the mixture, you will need ¾–1½ oz spices to 18 oz salt, and ½–¾ oz pâté salt per 2¼ lb filling.

Ready-made pâté seasoning

With all due respect to homemade seasonings, a really good (and here you will have to rely on the reputation of the manufacturer) store-bought pâté seasoning has several advantages, even for the most creative cooks.

The consumer cannot expect to be aware of the variable quality of individual spices, caused by variable harvests, but the manufacturer can balance out this factor. Commercial grinding techniques preserve more of the flavor than the kitchen spice grinder and modern packaging guarantees freshness. This may be little compensation for uniformity of taste but, as with homemade mixtures, there is opportunity for a host of individual variations. You can use a store-bought mixture as a base and add a personal touch with fresh herbs or dried juniper berries, garlic, dried mushrooms or grated citrus fruit peel.

Testing your seasoning

Regardless of whether you choose store-bought or homemade seasoning, you should always cook a trial sample before using your mixture for the first time (break off a small piece of the filling, shape into a ball and sauté for a minute or two). Only in this way can you ascertain the effect of your seasoning and salt. If you always make the same quantity of filling for the same container, it is a good idea to wrap the pâté salt in individual foil packages, each containing enough for one pâté.

Other types of seasoning have an important part to play in the flavor of pâtés and terrines. Orange and lemon peel, for example, dried mushrooms, or the famous truffle. Finely chopped truffles give a wonderful flavor to pâtés.

Liquid seasonings, i.e. any alcohol, should be of top quality. Quality is particularly important with drinks of high alcoholic content, for alcohol should never be added directly to a filling, but slowly reduced with a broth to give a syrupy consistency. The alcohol evaporates during reducing, leaving only the flavor of the spirit. This is why you should use only the best. The same is true of wine which is often used to improve the flavor of the broth.

Quality is important, particularly with spirits whose alcohol content is evaporated by reducing to leave only the basic flavor. It is clear that this makes it essential to use only the best brands. The quality of the wine used (Madeira, port or sherry for example) is an important factor in the flavor of aspic.

The onion – seasoning or vegetable?

There is no clear answer to this question when it comes to pâté making. In some types of gourmet pâté the rather ordinary flavor given by onion would be inappropriate, and garlic should never be used. The delicate flavor of shallots is better suited for such dishes. However, it is quite a different matter with strongly-flavored country-style pâtés and terrines. Here the strong flavor of the onion, and occasionally garlic, is quite suitable. But they are still a seasoning and should be used in relatively small quantities. In fillings for meat pies, and even puff pastry patties, onion is often an essential part of the final flavor.

1. White onions, usually hot and highly flavored, are used where a strong flavor is required.

2. Red onions, ranging in color from purple to violet, are milder and can be used in larger quantities.

3. Scallions are picked before reaching maturity, and are particularly mild and flavorsome.

4. The shallot, the mildest of the onion family is a real seasoning onion, with a delicate, highly aromatic taste and little of the typical onion flavor.

5. Garlic, whose flavor is as popular as its smell is unpopular, is mainly used in highly-flavored pork and lamb fillings.

Seasoning with herbs

Leaving aside Mediterranean cooking, which has always shown a predilection for herbs, the use of herbs has for centuries past tended to go in phases. People were inclined to turn to native herbs when times were hard and money in short supply. The reason for the present popularity of herbs is, hopefully, not a passing phase, but recognition of the fact that herbs (particularly fresh ones) can complement more exotic spices to give added variety to the number of possible seasonings.

Fresh herbs for pâtés and terrines

For a long time now ready made seasoning mixtures have included dried herbs. Replacing dried thyme with fresh when you make up your own mixture does not considerably alter the outcome. Fresh herbs should be used, however, where their qualities can be fully appreciated – in fish pâtés and terrines, for example, in aspics or the various sauces for hot pies. Indeed, you should try to experiment with the full range of herbs and not stick merely to parsley and chives. Fresh herbs have become so popular that they are now often sold in supermarkets during the summer months at least. They will keep for up to a week in the refrigerator if you stand them in water, or sprinkle them with water and wrap them in a plastic bag.

The best thing of course is to have your own herb garden, but even a window box on a balcony can provide fresh herbs throughout the summer. Grown from seed or cuttings, you can always have a fresh supply of your favorite herbs. And if you grow more than you can use there are two ways of preserving herbs: the old-fashioned drying method (not all herbs can be dried however) and freezing, which preserves the qualities of the herbs excellently. It is worthwhile chopping herbs before freezing and freezing them in individual portions. But you can also freeze whole leaves (rosemary and basil are particularly suitable) and use them for decorating terrines.

1 Basil

Ocimum basilicum

Almost a universal herb, it has a strong, hot taste and should be used sparingly in delicately-flavored dishes. Its slightly peppery taste goes with almost every type of meat, and also with vegetables and mushrooms.

2 Mugwort

Artemisia vulgaris

This is a traditional European herb for poultry, especially duck and goose. Its pleasant but slightly bitter taste is similar to that of vermouth. Cut before flowering, it is milder and less bitter.

3 Savory

Satureja hortensis

Its German name *Pfefferkraut* (pepper herb) indicates that this is a hot herb. Its true flavor is only fully brought out by boiling. It is equally good fresh or dried.

4 Borage

Borago officinalis

Its individual flavor does not go well with all ingredients. Fresh, young leaves have a delicate flavor and go well with strongly-flavored cold meat dishes, vegetables and sauces. It loses its flavor if dried.

5 Dill

Anethum graveolens

A real fresh herb, dill should never be cooked. Its refreshing flavor complements various salads and sauces, but it is best with fish. Ideal for freezing.

6 Tarragon

Artemisia dracunculus

This slightly bitter herb only retains its full flavor if used fresh. Recommended for hot and cold poultry and fish dishes, it also is very effective in combination with dill and lemon balm.

7 Lovage

Levisticum officinale

This herb is mainly used in strongly-flavored pâtés or meat stews, but use sparingly to keep the rather strong celery-like taste in check.

8 Marjoram

Majorana hortensis

Too often associated with sausages and earthy dishes, in small quantities it is recommended for even the finest fish, game and poultry pâtés. It has the most flavor while in blossom and dries well.

9 Oregano

Origanum vulgare

Also known as wild marjoram, this is best known as a seasoning for pizza. It goes particularly well with strongly-flavored fat meat. Cut it while still in blossom. Oregano is milder dried than fresh.

10 Parsley

Peteroselinum crispum

Both curly and flat-leaved varieties are used for seasoning and garnishing. Together with the root, it is part of a bouquet garni. Use with meat dishes, mushrooms and vegetables. Freezes well.

11 Mint

Mentha piperita

The leaves have a strong, refreshing smell, warming at first, and then cooling. Recommended for any dish where its refreshing flavor would be suitable, mint is also good dried, and freezes well.

12 Burnet

Pimpinella saxifraga

This aromatic little herb, with a slightly hot flavor, has a very pleasant taste and goes best with cold meat, poultry and fish. Burnet should not be boiled. It is unsuitable for drying.

13 Rosemary

Rosmarinus officinalis

This is a highly individual herb with a refreshing, camphor-like taste. Used in small quantities, rosemary goes well with meat, game, poultry and even fish. It loses none of its flavor when dried.

14 Sage

Salvia officinalis

Its strong, slightly bitter flavor goes equally well with all types of meat, poultry, game, and also eel or fish from the sea. It loses none of its flavor when dried.

15 Chives

Allium schoenoprasum

This is a herb from the onion family, with a similar taste. Chives are recommended whenever you want a fresh onion flavor. Cooking destroys most of its flavor.

16 Thyme

Thymus vulgaris

Its pleasant, slightly hot taste makes it an ideal partner for many types of meat, as well as fish and vegetables. It is equally good either fresh or dried.

17 Hyssop

Hyssopus officinalis

This is an extremely versatile, but little known, herb with a strong, slightly bitter smell and taste, but not an overpowering flavor. Recommended for strongly-flavored meat pâtés, it loses flavor when dried.

18 Lemon balm

Melissa officinalis

The name says it all – it has a lemony taste and smell. Use this herb to flavor wherever lemon would be appropriate, particularly in fish dishes, but also with veal, game and poultry. It loses much of its flavor when dried.

Forcemeats

DELECTABLE FILLINGS FOR PÂTÉS

The French word *farce* (forcemeat) means "practical joke, prank" and demonstrates the common origin of eating and display. At one time it was common to play a joke on the guests by filling a hen, fish or some other small animal with a *farce*. It was much later that forcemeat was improved and made more appetizing to enhance the taste of the food that was stuffed. Eventually the preparation of stuffings became one of the highest achievements of the art of cooking.

Whereas the stuffing was only an interesting addition to stuffed meat dishes (galantines), the pie was created to show off the filling, and finally the stuffing alone sufficed to form the terrine. These contain either the finest ingredients or alternatively simple, strongly-flavored meats, as, for example, in the case of a homely liver pâté or a French country-style terrine.

There are many different methods of obtaining excellent results, but a good stuffing must be light and airy; it must release its flavor as it melts on the tongue. This is equally true of a stuffing made entirely with meat, or one which includes egg, bread, or even flour. Purists who make their pâtés and terrines strictly with meat alone, and only include pork fat where necessary, will no doubt stop reading at this point. But in some situations we all have to compromise, to save time maybe, or to make expensive ingredients go further, regardless of the fact that good home cooking will always be more welcome than a continual diet of gourmet specialties. This is in no way to detract from haute cuisine, but rather to underline the value of simple pâtés (and fillings).

The pure, classic forcemeat

This consists of three elements: firstly, the main flavoring ingredient, which gives the pâté its dominant flavor and usually its name too – for example, veal, game or poultry. Secondly, the pork, which is not absolutely essential, but which gives a good pâté its smoothness. Thirdly, the pork fat which, in the right quantities, makes the pâté light, gives it its individual, melting consistency, and is unrecognizable as fat. Added to these we have seasoning with possibly other meat, nuts or mushrooms. It is an extremely simple recipe.

Success in making forcemeat depends on the binding agents, which, in other types of forcemeat, would consist of eggs or bread crumbs. In a pure meat forcemeat the binding agent is the meat's natural protein which holds the other ingredients together. But at high temperatures it tends to coagulate which makes it useless as a binding agent. As a result any preparation of fillings must be done at the lowest practical temperatures, and the mixture never allowed to reach room temperature. This would be enough to risk ruining the filling. Cold, cold and cold again must therefore be the watchword throughout the whole process of preparation.

Questions of quality

A point which is often disregarded in cooking becomes of the greatest importance in all fillings or pâtés: the finest meat, the freshest fish, the best game, only these are good enough. There are few problems with game and game birds which live in their natural surroundings and feed from natural foods. There is more of a problem with fish. If you live on the coast fresh fish should prove no problem, but for anyone else, always buy from a reputable fish merchant where you can be sure the fish will have been properly refrigerated before it reaches him.

To sum up: regardless of whether you are making a simple, country-style terrine, or an exotic quail pâté with truffles, pay attention to quality. It is sad that the wide choice in the stores today makes this more important than ever before, but there is a solution to the problem, organizing your menu around foods available fresh on the market. This is not a new idea, but it guarantees quality and is essential to a good stuffing.

One disadvantage of forcemeat is its richness, so do not eat excessive quantities of pies or pâtés: they should be eaten as carefully as they have been prepared.

Basic facts about forcemeats

There are just about as many fillings as there are different kinds of pâtés, terrine or galantine. Every filling is unique, if only by virtue of slight variations in composition or seasoning. Nevertheless there are only a limited number of very similar ways of making fillings, the main variations consisting primarily of the various binding agents.

A filling should, as far as possible, hold together – bind – without any other help. The natural protein in the main ingredient should bind sufficiently, thus retaining all

A triumph of the art. A selection of gourmet terrines in the chilled cabinet at Fauchon's, the famous Paris food store, which offers an unrivaled selection of pâtés and terrines, all made from the finest ingredients.

the full flavor of meat or fish.

Protein binding is thus the only form of binding when lean meat and pork fat are used. Other binding agents which give a deliciously smooth filling when used correctly are: white bread with milk or cream, whole eggs, flour panada or rice.

Heat-sensitive protein

It is essential to release as much protein as possible from the meat by careful chopping. But heavy work, with any implement, produces heat and this in turn coagulates the protein and diminishes its binding qualities. This seems to be a vicious circle, but can be overcome easily if a few basic rules are observed.

1. Chill all ingredients thoroughly. Even the utensils, for example the grinder, should be cold.

2. Season the meat as you cut it: salt helps release the protein.

3. When chopping meat make sure your equipment is in perfect condition. The blade of the grinder, food processor or knife must be sharp, so that they actually cut the meat rather than crush it.

4. Chill the ingredients after each stage of the recipe, regardless of whether the stuffing relies on natural protein for binding or includes some other binding agent.

5. Depending on the ingredients and method of preparation of the recipe, some ingredients such as fat or cream can be frozen, and the frozen pieces of fat and frozen crushed cream will help keep the other ingredients cool during the chopping or grinding process.

In the end it is not half as difficult as it seems at first, when you consider the variety of utensils and the basic rules you must follow. But these rules *must* be followed if you are to get good results, no matter how small the quantities you are handling.

These basic points provide a framework within which you can give rein to your imagination when making pâtés, pies, galantines and terrines. A stuffing offers unparalleled opportunities for experimentation; different seasonings alone can provide a host of alternatives. You can devise new harmonies of taste by using the same filling in various forms. Binding agents can be varied by the use of either eggs, protein, white bread, flour panada or rice.

Sharp tools are essential if the ingredients for a forcemeat or stuffing are to be ground correctly. Regardless of whether you are using a simple hand-operated grinder or an electric machine, the blade must be sharp, to ensure that the meat or fish is cut rather than crushed. The same is equally true of the blades on domestic food processors. Since these work at very high speeds you might not notice that the blade is blunt, but it can have a particularly harmful effect, for the forcemeat or stuffing can overheat in a matter of seconds and rather than the protein being released it may coagulate.

Binding and lightening

1 **A pure forcemeat,** surely the simplest and finest of all. Binding is achieved through the meat's own protein, which is extremely sensitive to heat, so all stages of preparation should be carried out at the lowest possible temperatures. Use only fresh, best quality meat (with all fat and gristle removed) and firm, white pork fatback.

2 **Bread, an easy way to make forcemeat light.** Together with egg white, milk or cream, soaked or – preferably – moist bread provides both lightness and binding at the same time. It is particularly recommended for fish, vegetable or meat stuffings, which are delicate and light.

3 **Egg in the forcemeat.** Eggs are both binding and lightening agents. In contrast to pure meat forcemeat, in which the pork fat is the lightening agent, the fat content can be considerably reduced if you include egg. They act as a neutral tasting binding agent for forcemeat with little meat content, or with a base other than meat, for example fish or vegetable.

4 **A flour panada can be used in any kind of forcemeat** with one proviso. If you add too much, or if the panada is incorrectly prepared, the forcemeat can take on a slightly sticky consistency. Two different methods of preparation should both give good results: the flour panada can be cooked in a saucepan like choux pastry, or boiled and diluted with milk, as for a cream sauce.

5 **Rice has a neutral taste,** even after boiling (in meat, fish or vegetable broth, or simply in water). Rice is a particularly good way of lightening delicate forcemeat, for example fish and fine vegetable. Take care not to add too much rice or the stuffing can take on a slightly greasy consistency.

Classic forcemeat made principally from game

This gourmet forcemeat is prepared according to a set of basic rules which should be followed whichever type you are preparing. Once this method is mastered you can devise a wide range of variations on the theme.

The flavor and success of a forcemeat or stuffing depends above all on the quality of its ingredients, particularly the main ingredient. The main ingredient gives it its dominant flavor and also determines the name of the pâté, galantine or terrine – as in venison pâté, for example. In the following example game, in this case venison, is the main ingredient. The same method also applies to poultry or meat.

A decisive factor in the smoothness and binding of the stuffing is the temperature at which it is prepared. The protein which acts as binding agent soon coagulates at normal room temperatures and loses its binding qualities. Do not ignore any of the instructions on chilling if further stages are to be completed successfully and you are to get a good end result.

The main requirement for the classic forcemeat is that only fresh ingredients of best quality should be used. The second requirement is that the meat must be completely free from fat and gristle.

The third requirement is: cold, cold and cold again. The ingredients should be chilled after each stage, and your utensils should also be cold.

The ratio of ingredients for a classic forcemeat:

$\frac{2}{5}$ main ingredient (game, poultry)
$\frac{1}{5}$ pork (moistening agent)
$\frac{2}{5}$ pork fatback (lightening agent which also provides smoothness)

or

$\frac{2}{3}$ main ingredient (game, poultry) and moistening agent (pork) together
$\frac{1}{3}$ pork fatback

1 **Skin the venison.** Wipe the piece of venison (in this case a haunch) with a damp cloth or paper towels. With a sharp knife lift away a strip of skin, $1–1\frac{1}{4}$ inches wide, then peel away the skin with the back of the knife.

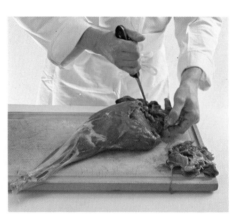

2 **Bone the meat.** Cut out the joint bone. Cut off the skin and meat from the top of the meat. Loosen the knee bone at the joint and remove. Cut along the leg bone, dividing the meat along the natural joins in the skin.

3 **Remove the hollow bones.** Keep the bones and any trimmings (skin, gristle, small pieces of meat) to one side for the broth. Carefully cut out all veins and ligaments. Even after grinding these could cause the pâté to fall.

4 **Trim the pork** (remove skin and ligaments). For the forcemeat it is best to use loin of pork. Hold the bones firmly in the left hand and cut along the bone as far as the vertebrae. Turn the meat over and cut the bone free.

5 **Cut off the strip of meat** which runs along the outside of the loin – also known as the saddle – together with its fat. This is not used in a forcemeat or stuffing, but if chopped will make a good stew.

6 **Remove the ligaments.** With a very sharp knife cut off the fat from the back of the meat and any ligaments you can see. The meat should be completely free from fat and ligaments. A good butcher will of course bone the pork for you on request.

7 **The lean trimmed meat,** divided along the natural joins and with all skin and ligaments removed. Here we have the fillet from a pork loin, and venison flesh from the upper and lower leg.

8 **Cut the meat into strips.** Cut the meat into finger-length strips, about ½ inch thick. The spiral movement of a grinder works better with strips than cubes.

9 **Cut the pork fat into strips.** Use fresh pork fatback. Cut off any rind cleanly and cut into strips as for the meat. Pork fat is easier to cut and handle if chilled in advance.

10 **Mix the salt and pâté seasoning.** The best way is to sieve them together. With store-bought pâté seasoning, mix in the ratio given on the package. This will be given either in relation to the amount of salt or the quantity of stuffing.

11 **The right time to season.** Sprinkle the seasoning evenly over the meat. Salt helps release the protein in the meat.

12 **Orange and lemon suit the flavor of game very well.** In the venison pâté recipe illustrated here grated orange and lemon peel and juniper berries are used as extra seasoning. They should be sprinkled over the strips of meat. Return the meat to the refrigerator and chill it thoroughly.

13 **Grind the meat.** Grind the chilled, seasoned meat – alternating between venison and pork – through the finest blade ($\frac{1}{16}$ inch) of the grinder. Chill the ground meat thoroughly once more.

14 **Repeat the process.** Grind the meat a second time. It is important that the grinder is in perfect working order so that the meat is ground rather than crushed.

15 **Finally, grind the pork fat.** One tip: to get the last remnants of fat out of the grinder, run a piece of wax paper through the grinder. It will not go all the way through and is easy to remove.

16 **Mix together the fat and meat by hand.** This is a rather messy method, but one that gives a particularly good texture. Place a bowl in a larger bowl filled with ice cubes. Place the chilled meat in the bowl and, with cool hands, work in the fat. NB: never allow the stuffing to become overwarm. A simpler way is to grind the fat with the meat. This will give excellent results, but not as good as by the first method.

17 **The final sieving of the pâté,** which is worthwhile, for even perfectly trimmed meat will leave a lot of fiber behind in the strainer. To push the pâté through use a metal scraper or, better still, a dariole mold.

Quick forcemeat made in the food processor

Experience has shown that the job is done much quicker with a food processor, with equally good results. This method does have its disadvantages, however: you can only make small quantities ($1\frac{1}{4}$–$1\frac{3}{4}$ pounds meat), otherwise the machine becomes too hot. In addition you must pay just as much attention to preparing the ingredients, trimming the meat just as thoroughly. But if the basic rules are followed, pâté making becomes easier and quicker. The food processor grinds and mixes the ingredients in one process and this makes for considerable savings in both time and energy. Of course the food processor must be in excellent working order. The blade must be very sharp, so that the meat is ground and not crushed, releasing the important proteins which are to bind the pâté.

Effective cooling is essential. The food processor should be chilled in advance. The meat should be as cold as possible, but not frozen, and cut into cubes about $\frac{1}{2}$ inch in size. The pork fat should be frozen in advance and cut into similar cubes. This helps keep the meat cool during processing. The ingredients should be salted and seasoned in advance. Keep your quantities small, between 3 and 5 ounces depending on the size of the machine. When you make the first batch check how long it takes for the mixture to become smooth and of uniform consistency. To prevent overheating, never let the machine run for longer than necessary. If one batch of pâté feels warm in spite of these precautions do not use it, for it could ruin the whole pâté. Chill the machine between batches.

You can improve the quality of the pâté by passing it through a sieve to remove any bits of skin or ligament.

Meat and frozen pork fat are salted and seasoned in advance and processed together in one step. Process small portions at a time; in this way the machine will run only for short periods and the pâté will remain cool.

The pâté should feel light, homogenous and cool. The food processor will make pâté in a matter of seconds, provided you obey to the letter the rules on chilling, no matter how exaggerated they may seem.

Forcemeat made with egg white and bread Salmon pâté

A combination of egg white, cream and white bread makes an ideal binding and lightening in any pâté whose main ingredient is very light in flavor, for example fish, shellfish, veal or poultry.

As with all pâtés and pie fillings, freshness and quality are especially important with fish and shellfish. If possible, fish should always be used on the day it is caught; to exaggerate slightly, they should add a bit of fresh sea air to the pâté. Of course this is not always possible, for if you live inland it is difficult to buy freshly caught fish, although modern refrigeration and transport help preserve freshness. The best solution is to use freshly caught freshwater fish. Only as a

last resort should you use frozen fish, for only the very best is good enough for a pâté.

The white bread should be fresh, fine textured but not too soft. It is best to use a regular-shaped loaf because this makes for little wastage when you remove the crust. The bread is moistened with fresh light cream and egg white before grinding. Here again, as with any pâté, the ingredients should be chilled after each stage.

A decisive factor in how the pâté binds is the thorough stirring with a wooden spoon. The cream is stirred into the pâté mixture a spoonful at a time until it has a silky sheen. This gives the pâté its smoothness and helps it to bind. This stirring process will take as long as an hour, but a pâté can't be rushed if it is to turn out well.

The illustrations opposite show a salmon pâté in the making but are equally applicable to any fish or shellfish pâté.

Quantities given for fish or meat always refer to filleted fish and trimmed meat.

Basic recipe for fish pâté:

1¼ lb fish
6 oz (5 thick slices) white bread
3 egg whites
¾ cup light cream
1 small onion (¼ lb), sliced
seasoning
2 cups whipped cream

Only fresh fish should be used in pâtés. Filleting fish calls for quite a bit of skill and it is advisable to ask the fish merchant to do this for you. Don't forget that what the fish merchant sees as waste – the bones and head – will make a good fish broth.

1 **Prepare the salmon.** Run your fingertips over the fish to check for bones, and where necessary remove with tweezers. Cut the fillet into long strips and leave to stand in a cool place.

2 **Remove the crusts from the bread.** Cut all the crust from a fresh, but not too soft, white loaf and then cut into ¼ inch slices. It is advisable to use an unsliced, regular shaped loaf.

3 **Moisten the bread.** Lay the sliced bread in a shallow dish. Pour the egg whites over the bread and evenly spoon on the fresh light cream. Leave the bread to soak in a cool place.

4 **Season the ingredients.** Stir the bread into the egg white and cream then place it on a flat dish with the salmon strips. Soften the sliced onion in a little butter and sprinkle all the ingredients with pâté salt and seasoning.

5 **Grind the ingredients together.** After chilling once more, pass the ingredients alternately through the finest blade of the grinder (about 1/16 inch). Chill the pâté, grind a second time and chill again!

6 **Sieve the salmon pâté mixture.** Stand a stable fine metal strainer on a board and push through the pâté, using a metal scraper. This will remove any bones left in the pâté mixture.

7 **Stand the pâté over ice.** Transfer the chilled pâté mixture to a bowl and place this in a larger bowl filled with ice cubes. Stir with a wooden spoon until the ingredients are thoroughly mixed and the mixture takes on sheen.

8 **Work in the whipped cream.** Add 1 tablespoon whipped cream to the chilled pâté mixture and beat in well. Then add the next spoonful of cream. Repeat until you have incorporated all the cream.

9 **The finished, smooth pâté mixture.** The addition of whipped cream and a thorough beating makes the mixture light and airy and as smooth as silk. Sauté a small spoonful to test the seasoning.

Pâté with panada

Pheasant pâté

A flour panada is an excellent way of making all fine forcemeats lighter. Its main use is with very tender meat, for example poultry, but also with fish and vegetables.

The whole quantity of flour panada is seldom required for a pâté. You can use the leftovers to make small dumplings for soup or small choux pastries for savory fillings.

Basic recipe:

1 cup milk
3 tablespoons butter
a little salt, milled white pepper
and a pinch nutmeg
1 cup flour
2 eggs

1 **Bring the milk, butter and seasoning to a boil.** The method of preparing a flour panada is the same as for choux pastry. In a saucepan bring the milk, butter and seasoning to a boil over high heat.

2 **Add all the flour.** Fold a sheet of wax paper in half, open out and sift the flour onto the paper. Tip the flour into the boiling milk and butter mixture all at once.

6 **Pass the flour panada through a fine strainer.** Using a metal scraper, push the chilled panada through a strainer, to remove any lumps formed during the cooking process.

7 **Egg white for extra binding.** Beat the egg white lightly to make it easier to add gradually. Add a little at a time to the meat. Again, the whole mixture should be kept very cold.

8 **Add the panada.** Flour panada is an excellent lightening agent for pâtés, because it rises better than bread during cooking. Stand the bowl in ice and gradually work the panada into the meat.

9 **Pass the pâté through a fine strainer.** When the panada is completely mixed in and the pâté mixture really cold, use a dariole mold or metal scraper to push it through the strainer to remove any ligaments. Chill.

10 **Add cream to give extra lightness.** Stir in the whipped cream a little at a time, making sure that each portion is thoroughly mixed before adding any more.

11 **The finished pâté mixture should be as smooth as silk.** When you have mixed in the cream beat the pâté over ice until it takes on a sheen. Beating makes it smooth and light, the hallmark of a good pâté.

3 **Cooking the panada.** Heat the mixture over a high flame until you have worked in all the flour. This is the most important stage in the whole process. Beat the panada vigorously and continuously.

4 **The finished panada.** The panada, which is soft at first, gradually becomes noticeably firmer. It has cooked sufficiently when it forms a ball which comes away easily from the bottom of the pan.

5 **Stir in the eggs.** Transfer the panada to a bowl. Leave to cool slightly. Add an egg and beat it in thoroughly. Then add the second egg. Cover the bowl and leave the panada to stand in a cool place.

Essential test cooking

You should always cook a sample piece of any pâté mixture to avoid any nasty shocks when you come to eat it. By cooking a test spoonful you can check the seasoning, for experience has shown repeatedly that the flavor of uncooked pâté should always be slightly stronger than the flavor required in the finished pâté or terrine.

Test cooking also checks for binding. If the consistency is too firm and dry add a little more cream.

Place a small amount of pâté mixture in the palm of your hand and take off about half a teaspoon, drawing the spoon toward the ball of the hand.

With the tip of your index finger push the ball of pâté off the spoon into the pan and cook for about 5 minutes. When cooked, the balls should be light and airy in consistency and not too firm. When pressed with the tongue against the roof of the mouth they should feel slightly firm before melting on the tongue.

Pâtés and Terrines

DIFFERENCES GREAT AND SMALL

"A pie is a French dish made from pastry, hollow inside and filled like a fritter." The words of Sebastian Franck, alias Frank von Wörd, who was born in Donauwörth and is best remembered for his religious writings. But alongside his religious tracts he also published in 1534 "Weltbuch," the first popular work on cosmography. It is from this book that his definition of a pie is taken. His definition is more or less correct. Leaving aside several differences for the moment, the general term pie can also be applied to all kinds of terrines, galantines and *bouchées*. As regards his claim that the pie is a "French dish," posterity has shown that Sebastian Franck was wrong. For we know now that even the ancient Greeks and Romans had pies, and that ancient cooks vied with each other to produce new variations on the theme. But it also seems equally clear that for our distant forebears the term pie included any kind of forcemeat, whether cooked in a dish, in pastry or as a stuffing for a roast of meat. Through the centuries, though, as pie making spread throughout Europe, people began to distinguish between these various dishes, introducing appropriate names to describe these different culinary masterpieces. That does not mean that the terms are not still confused even today – indeed they are, even in France. But it is not so difficult to distinguish between the various concepts covered by the general term "pie."

With or without pastry

Basically it is quite simple: anything made from forcemeat and covered in pastry is a pie, whereas terrines are forcemeat alone without pastry, with nothing to detract from the pure flavor of the filling. This simple forcemeat is put into dishes lined with bacon or foil and they are baked in the oven, standing in a water bath. We should add that for centuries experts have been discussing the relative merits of pies and terrines. But since it is difficult to argue on matters of personal taste the question has never been resolved. Today, however, the trend seems to be toward the terrine. This is a pity, for richly decorated pies are a pleasure to behold and their attractive appearance stimulates the appetite admirably – not to mention their effect on the palate. In this respect it is pointless to talk about the higher calorie value of pies over terrines. Neither pies nor terrines were invented with the slimmer in mind, nor should they be considered in this light today. And when *nouvelle cuisine*, which wholeheartedly adopted the terrine, chooses to do away with the traditional pork fat covering, it will be for reasons of flavor rather than nutritional value. Gourmets have never been inclined actually to eat the fat, yet it is a necessary part of the terrine, for it brings out the full flavor and keeps it moist. But even without fat many chefs of the *nouvelle cuisine* school produce pies and terrines which are real milestones in the history of cooking. One has only to think of their fish or vegetable pâtés or terrines.

Spicy country-style terrines

But terrines are not limited to those delicacies cooked in tiny pots (with goose liver pâté the smallest of all). There is another variety of terrine – regardless of whether they are made with goose, duck, hare, venison, pork or liver – which are strongly flavored and highly seasoned. These are the country-style terrines. Despite their name, these terrines can be found throughout the length and breadth of France whether in Paris or the provinces.

So it comes as no surprise to find that even in the smallest village every other household has its own recipe. And even in the smallest family-run restaurant you will never be disappointed with the *Terrine du Chef*. Indeed it is often the highlight of the menu, where it often figures under the alternative names of *pâté de campagne* or *pâté de la maison*. But this does not affect the quality; they may not all be masterpieces, but they are always good honest pâtés.

Pâté, a high-class sausage?

In France and Belgium pâtés and terrines, galantines and ballotines form a basic part of the national diet, like our sausage. In no other country in the world is there a trade specially devoted to the pâté to compare with that of the French *charcutier*. The word comes from *chair* (meat) and *cuire* (to cook), that is, "meat cook," and in France that means pork in particular.

One glance into the window of a French *charcuterie* is enough to prove that it stocks more varieties of pâté than there are sausages in Germany, and this wide variety is by no means limited to gourmet pâtés. In a way they are sausages in a different form, and one can make this assertion without in any way denigrating the outstanding creations of French and Belgian *charcutiers*.

It is true that the consumer is often led by the nose by the term "pâté" which promises so much. But when we come down to it this is a problem that has always been with us and which can be easily resolved. Making your own pies and pâtés with fresh, high quality ingredients is an obvious solution, and a very satisfying one too.

Perfect preparation begins with quality

"The juice of the meat and the flavor of fine herbs, wrapped and baked in a thick pastry, with the enclosed filling cooked in its own juices is a widespread refinement in the art of cooking . . ." A quote from Karl Friedrich von Rumohr. Originally an art historian and writer on art, in 1822 he published his "Geist der Kochkunst" (Spirit of the art of cooking) under the name of his family cook. This was quite remarkable, for he understood a lot about food and realized that natural ingredients, carefully prepared, improved the flavor of food, improved his very poor state of health and gave him great satisfaction. So he was in fact an early prophet of the recent *nouvelle cuisine* movement. An advocate of quality purely and simply.

The quality and freshness of his raw materials are an absolute must for three-star chef Faugeron, for the continuing reputation of his restaurant depends upon it. To him price is of secondary importance.

The need for high quality ingredients, the hallmark of all good food including pâtés and terrines, is thus nothing new. But unfortunately many people forget this – even professional chefs. So, for pastry, the flour, butter and eggs should be as fresh as possible. Pork fat for terrines should be absolutely fresh, snow-white and firm. This is only obtainable from pigs with a good layer of fat. And it is obvious that the forcemeat will only be at its best if fish, meat, poultry, game or variety meats are of top quality. Where vegetables are to be used the best option for the cook is to gather them fresh from his or her own garden. But since this is impossible in most cases, professional chefs try to adopt the standards of the *nouvelle cuisine* chefs in France: many go off to the markets while the rest of us are still sleeping to get first choice of the freshest foods. Or they order certain ingredients direct from Belgium, France and Italy, with delivery by jet if necessary. For this is the only way they can be certain that meat, fish, vegetables, poultry or game are of best quality. Professional chefs have long had their own sources, and some tradesmen have adapted their businesses to suit their specific needs.

This is all well and good, but what options are there for an ordinary person with a sophisticated palate, who would like to make the occasional pâté but is unsure where to get the best ingredients. Let's be honest about this. Foods offered – even in exclusive food stores and leading gourmet shops – are often a disgrace. We are offered limp, obviously old, vegetables. Often we can get only frozen poultry, which is unsuitable for pâtés and pies. Fresh cream is often hard to come by and herbs show their age through their lack of flavor. Only with butter and eggs can you be reasonably sure of quality.

So, unfortunately the cook has no choice but to get up and go to look for fresh sources. Of course, this takes up a lot of time, but it is time well spent. For you can only make a really good pie or pâté from top quality ingredients.

The French, Italians and Spanish are much to be envied. Their markets and shops – even in the smallest villages – offer only fresh goods, and in a variety that would make us green with envy.

The person who can buy whatever he or she needs is really fortunate. Using game and game birds, pork and veal, poultry, fish and shellfish, mushrooms and vegetables, you can make the most interesting pâté variations, find new combinations and invent new dishes.

What about decoration? With special

The choice available in the market should determine the main ingredient of a pie or pâté. Even in the market you will have to check the quality of goods available: not every chicken is slaughtered at the tender age of 6 months.

cutters, for example, you can make pastry decorations in a variety of geometric, fruit or flower shapes. There are no limits to the imaginative ideas possible. There are limits, however, to the ways in which you can decorate a terrine. Here we are generally restricted to sprigs of herbs, bay leaves and seasonings since the decoration is to be cooked with the terrine.

With pies to be eaten cold it is essential to fill them up with aspic, for this is the only way of preserving their freshness and moistness. If a terrine is covered with aspic, this is not an essential part of the process, but just one way of enhancing its appearance. The fact that this keeps the terrine moister is merely a pleasant bonus.

Lining a pie or pâté mold with pastry

While it is true that you can make a pie crust with puff pastry and – less often – yeast pastry, the pastry principally used is, and will remain, basic pie pastry. French pâté chefs, experts in the field, have developed their own methods over years of experience. Many of them maintain that pastry is easier to handle if it is made the evening before, wrapped and left overnight in the refrigerator. One further tip from France: the pastry which covers the bottom and sides of the mold will need to be slightly thicker if the filling contains a lot of fat. This applies, for example, in the case of strong flavored, country-style fillings. The thicker pastry better absorbs the fat, which melts during cooking.

For baking you can use almost any type of container – even earthenware casseroles can be lined with pastry – but thinner metal molds are better. In metal pastry bakes more evenly, crisper and browner.

Here, once more, there is a lesson to be learned from the French, for in France – particularly in the homes, where many more pâtés are baked than here – a lot of time goes into the choosing of the mold. There is even one type available which folds flat. Molds like this make it very easy to remove the pâté or pie. In general, conical molds, those that are wider at the rim than the base, are best. These are also quite good for unmolding.

With a pastry which contains a lot of fat it is generally unnecessary to grease the mold, but experience has shown that pastry dough adheres better to the sides of the mold (an essential requisite) if the sides of the mold are lightly greased with butter first. With narrow molds which are often more difficult to line, this can make the job much easier.

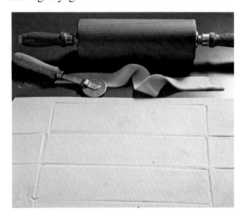

1 Roll out the dough to a thickness of about ⅛ inch. Press the mold into the dough to mark the cutting lines. Three pieces, together with the smaller end pieces, are used to line the mold. The fourth, larger piece forms the lid.

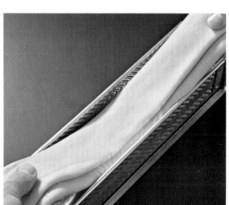

2 Cut off the excess dough with a pastry wheel and set aside to use for decoration. Do not cut off any dough that overlaps at the corners; these will be pressed flat once the dough is in the mold. This is most important if no fat or gravy is to escape.

3 Grease the mold with a little butter. Sprinkle the dough lightly with flour and fold together. Transfer carefully to the mold. Unfold to overhang the sides of the mold. Take care not to compress the dough with your fingers.

4 Make a small ball from the dough trimmings and dip it in flour. Use this ball to press the dough to the sides of the mold. Using a dough ball of this kind has the advantage of being very gentle on the dough; its delicacy of touch is difficult to achieve with the fingers.

5 First using the ball of dough, then the ball of the thumb, press excess dough in the corners up toward the rim of the mold. In this way you will get an even overall thickness and the pie will bake and brown evenly.

6 The dough should overlap the rim of the mold evenly. Use scissors to cut a rim of ½–¾ inch. Wrap the remaining dough for the lid and decoration in foil and leave in the refrigerator until required.

Broth

a fine gravy to complete your pâté

Broth is, so to speak, a flavor concentrate used to enhance the main flavor in a fine pâté or pie. It is made from trimmings, any skin or gristle cut from the meat. The bones are also used and last, but not least, the meat which remains on the bones. Fried with root vegetables, delicately seasoned, and often with wine added this reduced broth gives the perfect finish to any pâté or terrine. It can be incorporated into the filling or brushed over whole pieces of meat which go into the pâté (in this case venison fillets).

Basic recipe for game broth

5 tablespoons oil
$2\frac{1}{4}$ lb game bones and meat trimmings
vegetables (1 medium-sized onion and 1 carrot, diced)
2 tablespoons tomato paste
$2\frac{1}{2}$ quarts water
bouquet garni (1 piece celery with leaves, white of 1 leek, 5 sprigs parsley, 1 bay leaf, 1 sprig thyme)
2 shallots, sliced
1 clove garlic, halved
8 crushed juniper berries
8 white peppercorns
1 teaspoon salt

In a roasting pan, roast the game bones and trimmings in the oil for 15 minutes in a preheated 475° oven. Add the diced onion and carrot and roast for a further 20 minutes. Add the tomato paste and stir in. Dilute with a little cold water, stirring in the sediment from the bottom of the pan. Continue roasting until golden brown. Transfer to a large saucepan, add the water, bring to a boil and simmer gently for 2 hours. Remove the scum from time to time. Add the bouquet garni, shallots, garlic, juniper berries, peppercorns and salt and simmer for a further 45 minutes. Strain the broth, return to a boil and reduce to the strength required.

1 **Roast the chopped game bones in oil.** Heat the oil in a roasting pan. Add the chopped bones and brown all over on the lowest shelf of the oven, stirring from time to time.

2 **Add the vegetables (mirepoix).** Sprinkle the evenly diced vegetables over the bones and brown them. Do not allow them to burn, for this will make the broth bitter. Add the tomato paste and roast until the aroma has developed fully.

3 **Dilute the juices with water.** Add a generous dash of cold water and stir in, incorporating the sediment from the bottom of the pan. When the water has evaporated, repeat the process twice more.

4 **Transfer the roasted bones to a saucepan.** Transfer the mixture of browned bones and vegetables to a large pan and add the cold water. Simmer for 2 hours.

5 **Skim the stock.** Fat from the bones, proteins and any impurities rise to the surface. If you are to get a clear broth it must be skimmed repeatedly.

6 **Add the herbs and seasoning.** For the last third of the cooking time add the bouquet garni and seasonings. Simmer the broth for a further 45 minutes and carefully remove all fat from the surface. Then strain the broth.

Making a reduced essence for venison fillets. Fry the fillets in oil and remove from the pan. Pour off the oil and melt the butter. Soften finely chopped shallots in the butter. Dilute with a generous dash of brandy.

Add the highly jellied broth. Add the strained broth and flavorings. Reduce to a gleaming, thick essence. Strain through a conical strainer over the venison fillets and leave to cool.

Essence for the forcemeat or whole meat

1 tablespoon butter
¼ cup chopped shallots
3 tablespoons brandy
¾ cup jellied game broth

The reduced, jellied broth, further reduced with herbs and alcohol, gives a concentrated essence which, when strained, gives extra flavor to the filling. Alternatively it can be brushed over larger pieces of meat to be included in the pie.

The venison fillets are thoroughly sealed by frying in oil. Frying makes the meat contract slightly so that it retains its shape in the pie or terrine.

Filling and sealing the pâté

In the classic pastry covered pâté the filling must be completely wrapped in the pastry so that it is protected and no juices can escape. Joins in the pastry should therefore be brushed with egg yolk and pressed firmly together to seal.

There are no limits to the imaginative ways in which you can decorate a pie. Possibilities include pinching the edges together with a special tool, marking with a fork or the handle of a spoon, or cutting out or making various decorative pastry shapes which are coated with egg yolk and arranged on the top of the pie.

1 **Add the forcemeat.** Cover the bottom of the pastry-lined mold with a layer of forcemeat slightly less than 1 inch thick. Press it well into the corners with a spoon so that there are no gaps. The forcemeat should be a fraction deeper around the sides of the mold to form a rim.

2 **Add the venison fillets.** Cut the tapering ends from the venison fillets so that they will fit closely together in the mold. Place the fillets over the forcemeat and bang the mold several times on a damp cloth.

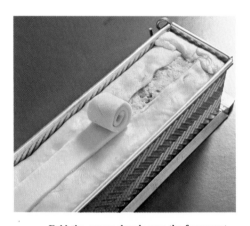

1 **Fold the excess dough over the forcemeat** and press down. If it does not meet at the center, cut a piece of dough to cover the gap, arrange on the pie and press the joins together lightly.

2 **Seal with the dough lid.** Brush the top of the pie with a mixture of egg yolk and cream. Cut a thin layer of dough to the size of the mold, fold into three to make moving it easier and use to cover the pie.

3 **Seal the edges.** Working out from the center, press the lid firmly onto the pie. Press any overlapping edges down inside the mold with the handle of a fork.

4 **Decorate the lid.** Use a jagger or wheel to make a decorative pattern of your own design on the pie. Alternatively, you could use the tines of a fork or two teaspoon handles. NB: take care not to cut through the dough.

5 **Make openings to allow steam to escape** during baking. Use a cookie cutter to cut one or two openings in the top of the pie (the number you need will depend on the size of the pie), or use a small, sharp knife to make the holes.

6 **Add the chimneys.** Brush the pie with a mixture of egg yolk and cream. Place small flower shapes around the openings. Roll a piece of double-thickness foil into a tube and place it in the opening to prevent any escaping juices marking the top of the pie.

3 Sprinkle over the thick, rich essence. With a tablespoon spread the cool, jellying essence evenly over the venison fillets. This will help the flavor of the essence permeate through the pie.

4 Add the second layer of forcemeat. Cover the fillets with a layer of forcemeat, about ¾ inch deep. As this pie is to have two layers of venison fillets you will again have to make a rim with the forcemeat.

5 Add the second layer of venison fillets. Arrange the fillets as for the first layer, again cover with jellying essence, and top with the remaining forcemeat. Do not overfill the mold. Bang it again on a damp cloth to fill any gaps.

Filling and sealing a terrine

Unlike the pie, a terrine is baked in the oven standing in a water bath. In a classic terrine the mold is lined with pork fat. For this fresh pork fatback is cut into thin slices. You can place the slices individually between two sheets of wax paper and pound them until very thin, but be careful not to make any holes or tears. Alternatively, you can line the mold with roasting film or foil: in that case it is important to grease the mold if the terrine is to unmold properly.

1 Line the mold with slices of fat. The slices should be very thin, of equal size and without rind. Place them in the mold, overlapping slightly.

2 The lined mold. Cut the fat slices for the narrow ends of the mold wide enough to turn the corner and seal it completely. It is important for the filling to be completely covered with fat.

3 Seal the filled mold. Fold the excess pork fat into the center and, working in from the side of the mold, press firmly down. Bang the mold several times on a damp cloth, to fill any air gaps.

4 Decorate the terrine. Cut a piece of fat to the correct size to cover the top of the mold. Decorate with the same herbs you have used in the terrine.

Game pâtés and terrines

Were it not for game, pies and their variants, which include terrines and galantines, would be nowhere near as popular as they are. The flesh of game and game birds is a naturally fine product, and needing little embellishment. It is particularly rich in protein, generally low in fat and has a delicious flavor. Nowadays these qualities have come to be even more appreciated when modern rearing and feeding methods rarely produce domestic animals and poultry of suitable quality for pie making. Nevertheless, not all wild game is of the same quality. The pelt or feathers of fresh-shot game show clearly whether the animal is young and tender or old and tough. And to distinguish one from the other you don't need to know a lot about game or to be a hunter yourself. With cut up, or even frozen, meat this is no longer possible and it is advisable to buy from a reputable butcher.

The ban on using frozen meat to make pies or pâtés allows one exception: the consistency of game meat with its low water and fat content means that it freezes better than normal meats. It loses much less liquid during thawing and the quality remains good enough for pâté and pie making.

The choice of a particular cut is the same as for other types of meat: only the best is good enough for a pâté, and then it must be thoroughly trimmed. This of course gives quite a quantity of trimmings, but they can be used to make excellent broth. It goes without saying that for a country-style pâté you can use cheaper cuts of meat, but it should be prepared with just as much care. The meat must be completely free from skin and gristle.

Venison Pâté

Pâté de chevreuil

5 oz lean boneless venison
5 oz lean boneless pork
5 oz fresh pork fatback
pâté salt
10 crushed juniper berries
grated rind of 1 orange and 1 lemon
2 venison fillets (total weight ½ lb)
2 tablespoons oil
1 tablespoon butter
½ cup diced shallot
1½ tablespoons brandy
½ cup jellied venison broth
¼ cup coarsely chopped pistachio nuts
¼ cup diced cooked ham
¼ cup diced cured tongue
¼ cup diced truffle
butter for greasing the pâté mold
1½ lb pie pastry
1 egg for glazing
1-quart pâté mold
Madeira aspic to finish

Trim all skin and gristle from the venison, pork and pork fat, cut it into fingers and sprinkle with ½ teaspoon pâté salt, 5 crushed juniper berries and half the grated orange and lemon rind. Grind the meat twice through the finest blade of the grinder. Grind the fat once only. Transfer to a bowl, stand the bowl over ice and work the fat thoroughly into the meat. Finally put the

mixture through a strainer. With any forcemeat it is important to chill the meat and fat thoroughly after each stage.

Season the venison fillets with pâté salt, and quickly seal in hot oil. Remove the fillets from the pan and pour off the oil. Melt the butter in the pan and soften the shallots. Stir in the brandy and then add the venison broth, and the rest of the juniper berries and grated orange and lemon rinds, and reduce to give a thick essence. Strain over the venison fillets and leave to cool.

Stir the pistachios, ham, tongue and truffle into the forcemeat. Grease the mold with butter and line with pastry dough. Fill 1–1½ inches deep with the forcemeat, slightly deeper around the sides. Place the venison fillets on the forcemeat along the length of the mold and sprinkle with the thick essence. Cover with the remaining forcemeat. Fold the edges of the dough over the top and cover with a sheet of dough. Cut an opening to allow steam to escape, insert a funnel and brush the pie with egg.

Bake for about 40 minutes, first for 15 minutes at 425° then turn down the oven to 350° for the remaining 25 minutes. When the pie is cool fill any gaps with Madeira aspic, poured in through the steam holes.

Tyrolean Chamois Terrine

Terrine de chamois tyrolien

1 lb boneless loin or leg of chamois
¾ lb trimmed boneless pork
1 medium-sized onion
3 tablespoons butter
2 teaspoons salt
1 teaspoon mixed seasoning for game
forcemeat
1 teaspoon thyme · 1 teaspoon basil
¼ teaspoon ground rosemary
1 bay leaf · 8 juniper berries
½ teaspoon dried green peppercorns
1 clove garlic, crushed
⅔ cup brown bread crumbs
3 tablespoons cream
1 egg white · ¼ lb calf's liver
¾ lb fresh pork fatback
1 oz truffles
¾ lb thinly sliced pork fatback
rosemary, thyme, bay leaves and
juniper berries
1½-quart pâté mold

Trim the chamois and pork thoroughly, cut into fingers and place in a large bowl. Cut the onion into rings, heat the butter and soften the onion in it. Leave to cool slightly and then arrange over the meat. Mix the salt with the seasoning, herbs, juniper berries, green peppercorns and crushed garlic and

sprinkle over the meat. Sprinkle the bread crumbs over the meat. Beat the cream into the egg white and pour over the meat. Cover the bowl with foil and chill overnight.

Grind the seasoned meat together with the other ingredients (bread crumbs, egg white and cream) twice through the finest blade of the grinder. Cut the liver and two-thirds of the pork fat into strips and grind twice. Gradually work the liver and fat mixture into the chilled meat and stir thoroughly until the forcemeat is smooth and shiny. Finely dice the remaining pork fat and truffle and stir into the forcemeat. Line the mold with slices of pork fat, fill it and cover with the remaining sliced pork fat. Decorate with the herbs and juniper berries, and cover the mold with the lid. Cook in a water bath for about 1 hour, in an oven preheated to 350°. Regulate the oven so that the water temperature reaches no higher than 176°.

A classic game pâté made from venison fillet. The flavor is accentuated by a thick game broth. Truffles and pistachios in the filling enhance both the flavor and the appearance.

A simple terrine with fairly coarse texture, but very spicy and juicy. The same recipe can be used with other game, of your choice.

Checking the cooking time

This is a problem which is by no means restricted to pâtés and pies, because a correct assessment of cooking times is essential to all types of cooking too. But fine pâtés can prove an expensive mistake if anything goes wrong.

Do not rely on manufacturers' recommendations until you have checked your oven for yourself. It is also inadvisable to rely exclusively on the times and temperatures indicated in this book. They are accurate for the oven we use, but may not be so for yours. So you must check the baking times for each pie or terrine you make.

This can be done in several ways. For one, you can look down the funnel at the gravy. If it is completely clear, the pie is cooked. However, this method will not do if you prefer the meat in the pie (for example, breast of chicken) slightly rare.

A more exact method is to test with a skewer. Stick a fairly thin skewer (a trussing needle or similar sized skewer is ideal) into the center of the terrine or pie right down to the bottom. Always leave it in the pie for the same length of time (count from 21 to 30) and then remove it. Draw the skewer slowly across your underlip, where the skin is particularly sensitive to temperature. The needle should be hot at the point, warm in the center and hot toward the top. If it is cold in the center extend the cooking time.

The third method, testing with a meat thermometer, is the safest method providing the thermometer is working properly. It can be used to check all pies, terrines and galantines. Stick the point of the thermometer into the exact center of the pie, but not into the funnel, because this would give a slightly higher reading. Read the thermometer after about 2 minutes. The filling should be at 150–

160°. Pies or terrines which include fillets of meat to be eaten slightly rare should be just over 140°.

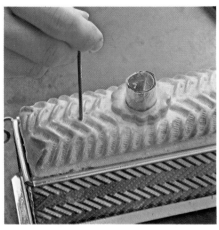

1 **Testing with a skewer is advisable** for all pies, terrines and galantines. Stick a fairly thin skewer (a trussing needle is ideal) through the middle of the pie to the bottom, and remove it after 10 seconds.

2 **The underlip is especially sensitive** to temperature. You can test the temperature exactly by drawing the skewer slowly along the underlip. If the skewer is cold in the center extend the cooking time.

3 **A meat thermometer tells you precisely** when a pie is cooked. It must be inserted into the exact center of the filling, to measure the temperature at the center. But if the bulb of the thermometer is too thick it can leave an unsightly hole in the pie.

Venison Pie

Pâté de chevreuil

¾ lb lean boneless venison
½ lb lean boneless pork
2 teaspoons mixed seasoning for game
forcemeat
1 teaspoon basil
½ teaspoon oregano
10 crushed juniper berries
2 cloves garlic, crushed
grated rind of 1 orange
1½ teaspoons salt
2 tablespoons oil
2 venison fillets (total weight ½ lb)
2 tablespoons butter
2 shallots, finely chopped
2½ tablespoons gin
½ cup jellied game broth
¾ lb fresh pork fatback
1 tablespoon bottled green peppercorns
½ cup diced cooked ham
1½ lb pie pastry
egg yolk and milk or cream for glazing
1½-quart pâté mold
Madeira or port wine aspic
to finish

Cut the venison and pork into fingers. Sprinkle with the seasoning, herbs, 5 juniper berries, 1 garlic clove, orange rind and salt,

cover with foil and leave in the refrigerator.

Heat the oil in a skillet and quickly fry the thoroughly trimmed and salted fillets (the technical term for this is "sealing"). Remove from the pan and pour off the oil. Chill the fillets. Add the butter to the skillet and soften the shallots. Stir in the gin and add the game broth and remaining juniper berries and garlic. Reduce to a thick essence and strain through a sieve.

Grind the chilled meat twice through the finest blade of the grinder. Cut the pork fat into similar strips and grind once. Place the meat over ice in a bowl and work in the fat and the thick essence. Drain the peppercorns thoroughly, coarsely chop and work into the forcemeat with the diced ham.

Cut the chilled, sealed fillets into strips. Line the mold with pastry and add a ½ inch layer of forcemeat. Cover with strips of fillet. Add another layer of forcemeat and press down well. Continue in this way until you have used all the strips of meat and the forcemeat. Cover the pie with pastry and bake. When cool fill up the pie with Madeira or port wine aspic.

Baking time: 55 minutes in all. Begin baking for 10 minutes at 450°, and continue at 400°.

Complement your venison pie with a mixture of whipped cream and cranberry sauce, seasoned with a little salt, sugar and ground ginger.

When broth is included in the list of ingredients, you have three options:

1. Buy the meat on the bone, and use the bones and any trimmings to make a broth before you begin the pie.
2. Use canned broth. There are some good brands available in the stores.
3. The best option of all! Make large quantities of broth to use as required. It freezes well.

Wild Boar Pâté

Pâté de marcassin

An easy way of baking a pâté. The forcemeat and meat are wrapped in pastry and baked on a baking sheet. Fresh ham can be substituted for wild boar in the following recipes.

¾ lb boneless leg of young wild boar
½ lb boneless loin of pork
¾ lb fresh pork fatback
2 teaspoons salt
2 teaspoons mixed seasoning for game
forcemeat
½ teaspoon dried green peppercorns
10 crushed juniper berries
1 teaspoon thyme
1 teaspoon oregano
2 cloves garlic, crushed
grated rind of 1 lemon
2 wild boar fillets (total weight ½ lb)
little salt, pepper and Armagnac
2 tablespoons oil
2 tablespoons butter
¼ cup finely chopped shallots
2½ tablespoons Armagnac
1 cup game broth
⅛ teaspoon cayenne
1¾ lb pie pastry
1 egg yolk and 1 tablespoon cream for
glazing
Madeira aspic to finish

Trim the wild boar and pork thoroughly, carefully cutting away all skin and gristle. This should leave about 14 ounces of lean meat, which should be cut into strips with the pork fat. Mix the salt with the game seasoning, peppercorns, 5 of the juniper berries, half the thyme, the oregano, garlic and half the lemon rind. Sprinkle over the meat and fat. Chill thoroughly!

Trim the boar fillets thoroughly, season with salt and pepper and sprinkle with a little Armagnac. Leave the fillets to marinate for 2 hours and then seal thoroughly in hot oil. Remove from the skillet and pour off the oil. Melt the butter in the pan and soften the shallots. Stir in the Armagnac and add the game broth, remaining lemon rind, juniper berries and thyme and the cayenne. Reduce to a thick essence.

Grind the meat twice and the fat once through the finest blade of the grinder. Transfer the meat to a bowl, place over ice and work a little of the fat at a time into the meat. Finally stir in the cool essence.

Roll out the pastry to 18 × 12 inches. Spread half the forcemeat in a strip (about 3½ × 14 inches) over the lower third of the pastry. Cut both fillets to the same length and place in the center of the forcemeat.

Cover with the remaining forcemeat and shape the top into a semicircle. Press a narrow strip of pastry onto the forcemeat and then roll with the forcemeat, until the end of the pastry is on the underside. Coat the end with the egg yolk and cream mixture and press down firmly. Cut the remaining pastry into leaf shapes to decorate the top and brush the whole pâté with the egg yolk and cream mixture. Cut a funnel opening and fill with a piece of rolled foil.

Baking time: 45 minutes in all. 10 minutes at 450°, then at 400°.

When cool fill the pie with Madeira aspic.

Wild Boar Pâté with Venison Fillet

Pâté de marcassin au filet de chevreuil

A fine game pie based on the above Wild Boar Pie, with the same quantities stuffing and pastry. Replace the boar fillets with 2 venison fillets, use the same seasoning but cover in a pistachio forcemeat. To make this mix $\frac{1}{2}$ cup puréed pistachios into about one-third of the wild boar forcemeat. Spread on slices of pork fat and roll around the venison fillets. Stir $\frac{1}{3}$ cup chopped pistachios and 1 oz truffles into the remaining forcemeat.

Serve with sliced ripe persimmon and freshly whipped cream seasoned with grated orange rind and green peppercorns.

Wild Boar Terrine

Terrine de sanglier

Quite a simple terrine to make, quite coarse in texture, but very moist and tasty.

2 lb boneless loin of wild boar
1 small onion, chopped
1 clove garlic, crushed
2 teaspoons salt
2 teaspoons mixed all-purpose seasoning
½ teaspoon dried green peppercorns
1 teaspoon thyme
⅛ teaspoon ground cloves
1 bay leaf
5 juniper berries
1 cup diced crustless white bread
½ cup red wine (strongly-flavored Rioja)
14 oz fresh pork fatback
1 egg
1 oz truffles, finely chopped
⅓ cup coarsely chopped pistachios
5 oz fresh pork fatback, diced
14 oz fresh pork fatback, thinly sliced
herbs to garnish (bay leaf, thyme)
2-quart pâté mold

Thoroughly trim the meat and cut into strips. Place in a bowl with the onion, garlic, salt, seasoning, peppercorns, thyme, cloves, bay leaf, juniper berries and diced white bread and pour on the wine. Leave to marinate in the refrigerator for 24 hours.

Cut the pork fat into strips and grind with the marinated meat, seasonings and bread (after pouring off the wine) twice through the finest blade of the grinder. Chill thoroughly and beat the egg into the forcemeat. Work in the truffles, pistachios and diced pork fat.

Line the pâté mold with the fat slices and fill with the forcemeat. Fold over the overhanging strips of fat and cover with another slice of fat. Cover the terrine and bake in a water bath.

Cooking time: about 1 hour at 325°. Delicious served with sliced fresh figs and curry cream, lightly salted and seasoned with a little lime juice.

Partridge Pie

Pâté de perdrix

4 partridges
5 tablespoons oil
1 carrot, chopped
1 large onion, sliced
1½ quarts water
bouquet garni (white of 1 leek, 1 piece celery, 3 sprigs parsley, 1 bay leaf)
1 teaspoon salt
21 juniper berries
3 small cloves garlic
6 white peppercorns
¼ lb lean boneless pork
½ lb fresh pork fatback
mixed all-purpose seasoning
white pepper
grated rind of ½ orange
1 tablespoon butter
2 shallots, diced
2 tablespoons brandy
grated rind of ¼ lemon
5 oz goose liver, marinated in port wine
2 oz shelled pistachio nuts
1 oz truffle, diced
¼ cup diced salted tongue
butter for greasing mold
1¼ lb pie pastry
1 egg yolk beaten with 2 tablespoons cream for glazing
1½-quart pâté mold

Bone the partridges, keeping the breasts to one side. The legs should yield about ½ lb meat. Roast the bones, skin and trimmings in a roasting pan in 3 tablespoons hot oil. After 10 minutes add the carrot and onion, and continue roasting, stirring occasionally. Dilute with a little of the water. Transfer to a large saucepan, add the remaining water, bring to a boil, skim and simmer for 2–3 hours. For the final third of the cooking time add the bouquet garni, salt, 8 of the juniper berries, a clove of garlic and the white peppercorns. Strain through cheesecloth and reduce to 1 cup.

Cut the meat from the partridge legs, the pork and fat into strips and sprinkle over mixed all-purpose seasoning, pepper, half the orange rind, a finely chopped clove of garlic, and 8 crushed juniper berries. Chill thoroughly. Grind the meat twice through the finest blade of the grinder, the fat once only. Place the meat in a bowl, over ice, and work in the fat. Finally, pass the forcemeat through a strainer.

Rub the partridge breasts with mixed all-purpose seasoning and pepper. Seal in the remaining hot oil. Remove from the skillet and pour off the oil. Melt the butter in the skillet and soften the diced shallots. Deglaze with the brandy, add ½ cup partridge broth (the rest can be reserved for another use), bring to a boil and skim. Strain this essence over the breasts and leave to cool.

Work the lemon rind, the rest of the orange rind and the juniper berries, the remaining clove of garlic, crushed, the diced goose liver, pistachios, truffles and tongue into the forcemeat. Grease the mold with butter, line with pastry and add one third of the forcemeat. Cut the ends from the partridge breasts and place half of them on the forcemeat. Brush with essence and cover with forcemeat. Add a second layer of partridge breasts and cover with the remaining forcemeat. Bang the mold several times on a damp cloth. Fold the excess pastry over the filling, cover with a sheet of pastry, decorate with any remaining pastry and brush with the egg yolk and cream mixture. Cut an opening in the top and insert a funnel.

Bake in the oven preheated to 425° for 15 minutes, then reduce the heat to 350° and cook for a further 30 minutes.

Fill the cold pie with port wine aspic, and serve, if you wish, with honeydew melon and mint jelly flavored with Armagnac.

Game Terrine with Truffles

Terrine de gibier aux truffes

1 pheasant, weighing about 1¾ lb
5 oz lean boneless venison
5 oz lean boneless pork
½ lb fresh pork fatback
mixed all-purpose seasoning
14 juniper berries, crushed
1 clove garlic, crushed
grated rind of 1½ oranges and ½ lemon
3 tablespoons oil
1 tablespoon butter
2 shallots, diced
1½ tablespoons brandy
1 cup jellied broth
white pepper
⅓ cup coarsely chopped pistachio nuts
2½ oz truffles, diced
about ¾ lb fresh pork fatback, thinly sliced
½ lb goose liver, marinated in sherry
¼ lb truffles
1¼-quart pâté mold
sherry aspic to finish

Remove the legs and breasts from the dressed pheasant and bone them carefully. The two boned breasts weigh about ½ pound, and the legs about the same. Cut the pheasant legs. venison, pork and fat into strips. Add 1 tablespoon poultry seasoning, 8 of the juniper berries, the garlic, and the grated rind of ½ orange and ½ lemon to the meat. Grind the meat twice through the finest blade of the grinder, the fat once only. Over ice, work the fat into the meat and then push through a strainer.

Rub the pheasant breasts with mixed all-purpose seasoning and seal thoroughly in a skillet in hot oil. Remove from the skillet and pour off the oil. Melt the butter in the skillet, soften the shallots, deglaze with brandy and add the jellied broth. Bring to a boil, skim, add the remaining juniper berries and orange rind, season with white pepper and reduce to a thick essence. Strain and leave to cool.

Work the essense into the chilled forcemeat and carefully fold in the pistachios and diced truffles. Line the mold with slices of fat and add one third of the forcemeat. With the palm of the hand press out the goose liver until long and flat and wrap around the whole truffles. Place in the mold and cover with forcemeat. Add the pheasant breasts as a second layer and cover with the remaining forcemeat. Fold over the overhanging fat and cover with a slice of fat. Bang the mold several times on a damp cloth and cover.

Cook in a water bath for 45–50 minutes, in the oven preheated to 350°. Regulate the oven so that the water temperature reaches no higher than 176°.

When cool remove the slice of fat which covers the terrine and glaze the top with sherry aspic.

Add the aspic, but wait until the pâté is quite cool. Meat pâtés should not be ice-cold; on the contrary, the aspic will bind better to the filling at room temperature. Any split in the pastry can be repaired with butter.

Quail Pâté

Pâté de caille

8–10 dressed quails, each weighing about ¼ lb
5 tablespoons oil
1 carrot, sliced
1 large onion, sliced
1½ quarts water
bouquet garni (white of 1 leek, 1 piece celery, 3 parsley sprigs, 1 bay leaf)
1 teaspoon salt
20 juniper berries
1 clove garlic
6 white peppercorns
mixed all-purpose seasoning
1 tablespoon butter
2 shallots, diced
2 tablespoons brandy
5 oz lean boneless pork
½ lb fresh pork fatback
grated rind of ½ orange
white pepper
½ cup coarsely chopped pistachio nuts
1 oz truffles, diced
½ lb goose liver, marinated in dry sherry
butter for greasing mold
1½ lb pie pastry
1 lightly beaten egg for glazing
1¼-quart pâté mold
sherry aspic to finish

Remove the breasts from the dressed quails. Bone the legs and remove the ligaments. Leave the skin on the legs and breasts as it is particularly flavorsome. The boned, trimmed meat and skin of 8–10 quails gives a quantity of about ½ pound for the forcemeat, and the breasts weigh about the same. Roast the bones, ligaments and trimmings in 3 tablespoons of the oil in a

roasting pan. Add the carrot, onion, water, bouquet garni, salt, 8 juniper berries, the garlic and white peppercorns to make a broth. Strain and reduce to a jellifying broth.

Season the quail breasts with mixed all-purpose seasoning, seal in the remaining oil, remove from the skillet and pour off the oil. Melt the butter in the skillet and soften the shallots. Deglaze with brandy and add 1 cup broth. Bring to a boil, skim and add 2 teaspoons all-purpose seasoning and 5 juniper berries, crushed this time. Reduce to a thick essence and push through a strainer over the breasts. Leave to cool.

Cut the quail leg meat, pork and fat into strips. Season with all-purpose seasoning, and add the rest of the juniper berries, crushed, and the orange rind, and white pepper to taste. Grind the meat twice through the finest blade of the grinder, the fat once only. Over ice, gradually work the

fat into the meat, adding a little quail broth. Push through a strainer. Work the coarsely chopped pistachios and diced truffles into the forcemeat. Knead the liver thoroughly with the hands and cut into pieces.

Grease the mold with butter, line with pastry and add some of the forcemeat. Fill the mold with alternate layers of goose liver, quail breasts and the remaining forcemeat. Fold the overhanging pastry over the filling, cover with a sheet of pastry, decorate and brush with egg. Cut openings for the steam and insert funnels.

Bake in the oven preheated to 425° for 15 minutes, then reduce the heat to 350° and bake for a further 30 minutes or so.

When cool fill the pie with sherry aspic.

Hare Pâté

Pâté de lièvre

1 whole dressed hare
1 saddle of hare
1 lb fresh pork fatback
2 carrots, sliced
3 sprigs parsley
1 large onion, coarsely chopped
1 cup red wine (Burgundy if possible)
$1\frac{1}{2}$ quarts water
1 teaspoon salt
1 clove garlic
12 juniper berries
10 black peppercorns
1 clove
1 bay leaf
$\frac{1}{2}$ lb lean boneless pork
4 thin slices white bread,
crusts removed
5 tablespoons cream
1 tablespoon pâté salt
$\frac{1}{2}$ teaspoon dried green peppercorns
1 teaspoon thyme
2 tablespoons oil
5 oz chicken livers
$\frac{1}{2}$ cup coarsely chopped walnuts
$\frac{1}{4}$ cup diced fresh pork fatback
3 tablespoons brandy
2 lb pie pastry
$\frac{3}{4}$ lb fresh pork fatback, thinly sliced
1 lightly beaten egg for glazing
$2\frac{1}{2}$-quart pâté mold
Madeira aspic to finish

Cut up the dressed hare. Remove the meat from the loin. Cut any other large pieces of meat, particularly from the legs and shoulders, off the bone and trim thoroughly. This should give about 1 pound lean meat. Remove the fillets from the saddle of hare. Transfer all the bones and trimmings to a roasting pan. Dice $\frac{1}{4}$ pound of the pork fatback, add it too and roast at $425°$. After 20 minutes add the carrots, parsley sprigs and onion and roast for a further 30–40 minutes, stirring from time to time. Then transfer the contents of the roasting pan to a large saucepan, add the red wine and water and bring to a boil. Skim the scum from the surface of the liquid until it stops forming. Add the salt, garlic, juniper berries, peppercorns, clove and bay leaf and simmer gently for 30 minutes. Strain the broth and slowly reduce it to about $1\frac{1}{2}$ cups.

Cut the pork, hare (not the fillets) and the other $\frac{3}{4}$ pound pork fatback into strips. Moisten the thinly sliced bread with the cream, add to the meat and sprinkle with the pâté salt, crushed green peppercorns and thyme. Leave to stand for 60 minutes in the refrigerator and then grind all the ingredients together twice through the finest blade

of the grinder. Chill again and push the forcemeat through a strainer.

Heat the oil in a skillet and quickly seal the chicken livers. Remove from the skillet and dice. Work into the forcemeat with the walnuts and diced pork fat. In the same oil quickly seal the four hare fillets, then add the brandy. Remove the fillets from the skillet and leave to cool. Add 1 cup hare broth to the skillet, stir well and reduce to about 6 tablespoons.

Line the pâté mold first with pastry, then with the slices of fat. Add half the forcemeat. Wrap the fillets in pork fat slices and place 2 or 3 alongside each other in the mold. Sprinkle with the reduced broth and cover with the remaining forcemeat. Fold over any overhanging pork fat and cover with a pastry lid. Decorate and brush with egg. Cut two openings in the lid, insert funnels and bake in the oven preheated to $425°$ for 15 minutes, then reduce the heat to $375°$ and bake for a further 1 hour and 10–20 minutes until cooked. If you use a mold of the same volume but narrower than that used for the pâté illustrated, reduce the baking time by up to 20 per cent.

When cool fill the pâté with Madeira aspic, poured through the funnels in the top.

Rabbit Terrine

Terrine de lapin

2 dressed rabbits, total weight about $5\frac{1}{2}$ lb
1 lb lean boneless loin of pork
2 teaspoons salt
$\frac{1}{2}$ teaspoon dried green peppercorns
$\frac{1}{2}$ teaspoon ground allspice
1 teaspoon thyme
1 teaspoon fresh chopped lovage
few rosemary leaves
2 bay leaves
1 lb veal bones
3 tablespoons oil
1 onion, sliced
$\frac{1}{4}$ lb carrots, sliced
$\frac{1}{4}$ lb celeriac, chopped
15 white peppercorns
2 tablespoons butter
1 rabbit or chicken liver
$1\frac{1}{2}$ tablespoons brandy
1 clove garlic, crushed
2 shallots, chopped
generous pinch of ground cardamom
2 lb fresh pork fatback
2 eggs
$\frac{1}{2}$ lb cooked ham, diced
$\frac{1}{4}$ lb mushrooms, coarsely chopped
fresh herbs for decoration
2-quart pâté mold

Cut up and bone the rabbits. When trimmed, the back fillets should give about $\frac{1}{2}$ pound meat, and the rest of the rabbit should give about 14 ounces after boning and trimming. Keep the fillets on one side to use whole. Cut the remaining rabbit meat into strips with the pork, place in a bowl and season with the salt, green peppercorns, allspice, thyme, lovage, rosemary and bay leaf. Cover the bowl with foil and leave to marinate in the refrigerator.

Chop the rabbit bones and trimmings and veal bones into small pieces, roast in oil, then add the onion, carrots, celeriac, the remaining bay leaf and 5 white peppercorns. Cover with water to make a broth and then reduce to 1 cup. Strain.

Heat the butter in a skillet and quickly fry the liver and fillets on all sides to seal them. Pour on the brandy, then remove the meat from the pan and leave to cool. Add the

1 **Quickly seal the liver and seasoned hare fillets** in hot butter. The liver will seal better if cut into cubes. The fillets contract slightly when fried, so will keep their shape when cooked in the terrine.

2 **Place the fillets side by side,** but first line the mold with pork fat and cover the bottom with a $\frac{3}{4}$-inch layer of forcemeat. Add the fillets, carefully fill the spaces between them with forcemeat, and press down.

rabbit broth to the juices in the pan and add the crushed garlic, chopped shallots, the remaining 10 peppercorns, crushed, and cardamom. Reduce to about 6 tablespoons, strain through a fine sieve and chill this essence.

Grind the seasoned meat twice through the finest blade of the grinder. Finally grind about half of the fat and work into the forcemeat a little at a time. Then stir in the eggs and the reduced essence. Chill the forcemeat thoroughly once more, then dice the rabbit liver and work it in, with the diced ham and coarsely chopped mushrooms. Line the mold with the remaining fat, cut in thin slices, add half the forcemeat, then top with the two rabbit fillets. Cover with the remaining forcemeat, seal the top with fat and decorate with fresh herbs. Cover the mold and bake, in a water bath, for 1 hour–1 hour 10 minutes. Regulate the oven temperature so that the water does not rise above 176°.

Rabbit Terrine and Syracuse Tomatoes
complement one another admirably. Peeled, diced tomatoes are marinated in olive oil, garlic, scallion, salt and pepper and served decorated with fresh basil leaves.

58

Pheasant Terrine with Goose Liver

Terrine de faisan au foie gras

1 hen pheasant, dressed
½ cup oil
1 carrot, sliced
1 large onion, sliced
2 quarts water
bouquet garni (white of 1 leek, 1 piece celery, 3 parsley sprigs, 1 bay leaf)
1 teaspoon salt
2 cloves garlic
22 juniper berries
8 white peppercorns
¼ lb lean boneless pork
½ lb fresh pork fatback
1½ teaspoons pâté salt
grated rind of 1 orange and 1 lemon
1 tablespoon butter
2 shallots, diced
1½ tablespoons brandy
white pepper
⅓ cup coarsely chopped pistachio nuts
2½ oz truffles, diced
about ½ lb fresh pork fatback, thinly sliced
½ lb goose liver, marinated in port wine and brandy
1-quart pâté mold
port wine aspic to finish

Remove the legs and breasts from the pheasant and trim them carefully. The two breasts should weigh about ½ pound after trimming, and the two legs about the same. Chop the bones, and roast in a meat pan in 5 tablespoons of the oil with any trimmings. Add the carrot, onion, water, bouquet garni, salt, 1 clove of garlic, 8 juniper berries, and the white peppercorns and make a broth. Strain and reduce to about 1 cup jellifying broth.

Cut the meat from the pheasant legs, the pork and fat into strips. Sprinkle the meat with 1 teaspoon of the pâté salt, 8 juniper berries, crushed this time, the second clove of garlic, also crushed, and half the orange and lemon rind. Leave to stand for 60 minutes in the refrigerator, then grind the meat twice and the fat once through the finest blade of the grinder. Place a bowl over ice and work the fat in it into the ground meat, then push through a strainer. Chill.

Season the pheasant breasts with the rest of the pâté salt and in a skillet quickly seal them in the remaining oil. Remove from the skillet and pour off the oil. Melt the butter in the skillet and soften the shallots. Add the brandy and the jellifying broth. Bring to a boil and skim. Add the rest of the juniper berries and grated orange and lemon rind,

and some ground white pepper and reduce to a thick essence, then strain over the breasts and leave to cool.

Carefully work the pistachios and truffles into the thoroughly chilled forcemeat. Line the terrine with the sliced pork fat and add one third of the forcemeat. Add the goose liver, brush with the essence and cover with forcemeat. Add the pheasant breasts as a second layer and cover with the remaining forcemeat. Fold over the overhanging fat and cover with another slice of fat. Leave to stand in a cold place.

Cook for about 42 minutes, in a water bath, regulating the oven so that the temperature of the water does not rise above 176°.

When the terrine is cooked and cooled, remove the top slice of fat and cover it instead with a layer of port wine aspic.

Wild Duck Terrine with Duck Liver

Terrine de canard sauvage au foie de canard

1 wild duck
3 oz lean boneless pork
5 oz fresh pork fatback
grated rind of $\frac{1}{2}$ orange
$\frac{1}{2}$ teaspoon each chopped fresh sage and tarragon
1 teaspoon pâté salt
1 tablespoon oil
1 tablespoon butter
$\frac{1}{4}$ cup diced shallots
$1\frac{1}{2}$ tablespoons orange liqueur
$1\frac{1}{2}$ tablespoons orange juice
$\frac{1}{2}$ cup jellifying game broth
3 juniper berries, crushed
$\frac{1}{2}$ clove garlic, crushed
little fresh sage, tarragon and grated orange rind
$\frac{1}{4}$ lb duck liver, marinated in Madeira and port wine
$\frac{1}{4}$ cup diced cooked ham
1 oz shelled pistachio nuts, halved
1 oz truffles, diced
$\frac{3}{4}$ lb fresh pork fatback, thinly sliced
3-cup pâté mold
port wine aspic to finish

Cut up the duck, remove the breasts from the bone and keep to one side. Remove the remaining meat from the bone and remove all skin and ligaments. Cut the duck (except the breasts), pork and fat into strips and sprinkle with the orange rind, herbs and pâté salt. Cover with foil and leave to marinate in the refrigerator.

Grind the meat twice through the finest blade of the grinder, and the fat once. Over ice, work the fat into the ground meat and push through a fine strainer. As with all forcemeat, chill thoroughly after each stage.

Quickly seal the trimmed breasts by frying them in hot oil. Remove from the skillet and pour off the oil. Melt the butter in the skillet and soften the shallots without allowing them to color. Add the liqueur and orange juice and then the game broth, juniper berries, garlic, herbs and orange rind. Bring to a boil and reduce to a thick essence. Strain the essence over the duck breasts and leave to cool.

Dry the duck's liver on paper towels, cut into pieces and work into the stuffing with the ham, pistachios and truffles.

Line the mold with slices of pork fat and add about half the forcemeat. Add the breasts, brush with essence and cover with the remaining forcemeat. Fold over the excess fat and cover the top with a slice of fat. Cover the mold and bake, in a water bath, for 45 minutes, regulating the oven so that the water temperature does not rise above 176°.

When cool remove the top layer of fat and cover with port wine aspic.

Country-style Terrine

Terrine de campagne

This real country terrine is uncomplicated, hearty and filling. The bacon gives it its spicy flavor.

2 rabbit legs
1 lb lean boneless pork
$\frac{1}{2}$ lb fresh pork fatback
1$\frac{1}{2}$ teaspoons salt
$\frac{1}{2}$ teaspoon ground black pepper
generous pinch of nutmeg
13 juniper berries
4 bay leaves
1 tablespoon dried herbs (marjoram, thyme, sage and savory)
1$\frac{1}{2}$ tablespoons brandy
2 eggs
$\frac{1}{2}$ lb slab bacon
$\frac{3}{4}$ lb fresh pork fatback, thinly sliced
5-cup pâté mold

Bone the rabbit legs and remove skin and ligaments. Dice the rabbit meat, pork and pork fat. Transfer to a bowl, sprinkle with the salt, pepper, nutmeg, 5 of the juniper berries, 1 bay leaf and the herbs, pour on the brandy and mix carefully. Cover with foil and leave overnight to marinate.

Grind the seasoned diced meat and fat a little at a time in a food processor. Chill thoroughly. Work in the eggs and beat the forcemeat vigorously for 5–10 minutes. Cut the bacon into small, equal-sized cubes and work into the forcemeat. Check the seasoning – adding more if necessary. Line the mold with the slices of pork fat, fill with the forcemeat and smooth the top. Garnish with the remaining bay leaves and juniper berries and cover with well-buttered parchment paper. Cover the mold and bake in a water bath for 1 hour. Regulate the oven so that the temperature of the water does not rise above 176°. The terrine will shrink slightly during cooking, so fill any gaps around the edges with lard when the terrine is completely cool. The terrine will then keep in the refrigerator for up to two weeks.

This terrine can also be baked in the oven without a water bath. In that case, cook for 1 hour at 425°. Cooked like this it will lose more of its fat, but that is an advantage in that the fat seals the top of the cooled terrine and keeps it moist.

Pork pâté

Pâté de jambon

A delicious loaf-shaped pâté, with a delicate filling of pork and pork loin with truffles and pistachios. Whole or sliced, it has an appetizing appearance.

$\frac{3}{4}$ lb lean boneless pork
$\frac{1}{2}$ lb fresh pork fatback
1 teaspoon pâté salt
ground white pepper
1 teaspoon each chopped fresh
thyme and marjoram
2 cloves garlic, crushed
6 juniper berries, crushed
5 oz lean boneless pork loin, diced
1$\frac{1}{2}$ oz shelled pistachios, halved
1 oz truffles, diced
butter for greasing mold
1$\frac{1}{2}$ lb pie pastry
1 lb piece lean boneless pork loin
1 lightly beaten egg for glazing
1$\frac{1}{2}$-quart pâté mold
sherry aspic to finish

Cut the pork and pork fat into strips, place on a baking sheet and season with pâté salt, pepper, herbs, garlic and juniper berries. Cover with plastic wrap and chill. Grind the meat twice through the finest blade of the grinder. Grind the fat once only. Over ice, mix the fat thoroughly into the meat a little at a time and push through a strainer. Don't forget to chill the forcemeat thoroughly after each stage.

Mix the diced pork loin, pistachios and truffles into the forcemeat. Grease the mold and line it with pastry. Add about half the forcemeat to the mold, pressing it to the edges of the pastry. Add the piece of pork loin, cover with the remaining forcemeat and fold over the excess pastry. Cover with a pastry lid. Make one or two openings to allow the steam to escape, decorate the pâté, brush with beaten egg and add foil funnels.

Bake in the oven preheated to 425° for the first 15 minutes, then reduce the heat to 350° and bake for a further 35 minutes, or until cooked.

When cool fill the pâté with sherry aspic.

Pâtés and Terrines and Wine

There is no doubt that when we think of pâtés and terrines we cannot help but associate them with French cuisine. But where European wine is concerned France, Italy and Germany spring to mind. For all three countries have extensive wine-producing regions with excellent vineyards. Connoisseurs of wine tend, therefore, not to favor one country more than another, but to value highly the best wines produced by all three. There is international agreement about this. It is also agreed that pâtés and terrines and wine belong together. Neither can be fully appreciated without the other. This is true not only of the best wines of Germany, France or Italy, but also of the wines of the United States, Spain, Austria or Switzerland.

But there is a great difference between the drinking habits of the Romance countries and Germany. A Frenchman would not dream of eating without a glass of wine. Nor would he dream of drinking wine without eating. In France (and other Romance countries) wine is part of the culture of eating. And according to the French it is for this reason that they produce so many dry wines. For only dry wines go really well with fish and meat, poultry and game. This is slowly coming to be recognized elsewhere too.

In Germany, on the other hand, people like a glass of beer in the early evening. Or they enjoy a bottle of wine in the evening, either at home or in a wine bar. It is the rule to drink without eating. In Germany the habit of drinking wine with meals has been slow to catch on. And lately the trend has changed to producing more dry wines whose labels either bear the word *trocken* or the yellow seal (which denotes a dry wine). This is fortunate. For only good wines go well with food. So you will do well to serve a good wine with your pâtés and terrines. But which wine goes with which pâté? Here we can only make recommendations: there are no hard-and-fast rules. In general you can rely on your own taste. Connoisseurs of French pâtés and wines say, for example, that it is entirely a matter of taste

whether you serve white or red wine. The main thing is that the wine should be neither too sour nor too heavy. A few examples will provide a few pointers on the greater enjoyment of pâtés and wine but, with the wide range of wines available today, the list cannot claim to be exhaustive, but it is hoped that it will prove a useful guide.

With all types of pâté with game as the main ingredient you can serve full-bodied red wines. This may be a good French Bordeaux or a Languedoc-Roussillon, a wine from the Ahr, from Baden, or a chianti. A sparkling, medium-dry French white wine or one from north or south Austria could just as well be chosen: a Traminer or Gewürztraminer, for example. With a pork or veal pie or pâté serve light, fresh red wines, a Ruländer from the Ortenau region, or a rosé (maybe a Portuguese rosé).

With poultry you can choose between, say, an Italian Orvieto secco, or a Kaiserstühler Ruländer, and there are also the Frankish wines from the Würzburg region or an Austrian wine which bears the good wine seal. Any fish or shellfish pâté needs a dry white wine, for example an excellent, dry Mosel Riesling or one from Alsace. Dry French wines include Entre-deux-Mers, Chablis or a wine from a sandy Portuguese vineyard. For very special occasions serve a French Champagne or a dry sparkling wine.

Liver pâtés, whether calf's, goose or other poultry liver, go well with a light, but good-quality red from either France or Germany. Wines produced from the Sauvignon grape, as grown in California, go excellently with goose liver pâté. The best of the French wines for foie gras is a Sauternes, providing it is not too sweet. The same is also true of Sauvignon wines from Italy.

With Russian pâtés you might like to try a red wine from the Crimea, or a white Crimean sparkling wine. The red may be too sweet for most palates.

With heavy English pies rosés or reds are your best bet.

Sweetbread Terrine

Terrine de ris de veau

1 lb sweetbreads
salt
little white pepper
2 tablespoons butter
3 tablespoons Armagnac
2 shallots, finely chopped
1 cup veal broth
$\frac{1}{2}$ bay leaf
$\frac{1}{2}$ teaspoon basil
$\frac{1}{4}$ teaspoon allspice
1 piece cinnamon
1 clove
$\frac{3}{4}$ lb veal sirloin (without fat)
$\frac{1}{4}$ lb lean boneless pork
2 teaspoons mixed seasoning for delicate
meat forcemeat
$\frac{1}{2}$ lb fresh pork fatback
1 egg white
$\frac{1}{2}$ cup light cream
$\frac{1}{2}$ cup diced cooked ham
$\frac{3}{4}$ oz truffles, diced
$\frac{3}{4}$ lb fresh pork fatback, thinly sliced
5-cup pâté mold
sherry aspic to finish

Soak the sweetbreads in cold water for 3–4 hours, then blanch for a few moments and carefully remove skin and all veins. Sprinkle the pieces of sweetbread with salt and pepper. Heat the butter in a skillet, seal the sweetbreads, add the Armagnac and remove from the skillet. Lightly soften the finely chopped shallots in the butter, then add the veal broth, herbs and spices (bay leaf, basil, allspice, cinnamon and clove). Reduce the broth to a thick essence, strain over the sweetbreads and leave to cool.

Cut the veal and pork into strips and sprinkle with salt and the mixed seasoning. Cut the pork fat into similar strips. Chill thoroughly, then grind the meat twice through the finest blade of the grinder and the fat once only. Over ice, work the ground fat into the meat a little at a time. Then push through a fine strainer. Over ice, beat the forcemeat until smooth, gradually working in the egg white. Finally beat in the cream a little at a time. Mix the diced ham and sweetbreads into the forcemeat with the essence and diced truffles.

Line the mold with the slices of pork fat. Add the forcemeat a little at a time and press down firmly to prevent any holes. Smooth the top and cover with fat. Cover the mold and bake in a water bath for about 50 minutes in an oven preheated to 350°. Leave to cool slightly, cover with a board and weight the board with a 2-pound can. When the terrine is completely cool unmold and scrape off any fat produced by the forcemeat. Remove the top layer of fat and cut a thin layer from the top of the terrine to give a completely flat surface. Place the terrine back in its mold. Pour a thin layer of lukewarm sherry aspic over the top. Leave to set.

This terrine goes particularly well with a fresh chicory and orange salad, dressed with vinaigrette and a dash of Bénédictine.

Sweetbread Pie

Tourte de ris de veau

This is a pie which can be served either hot or cold. In a fairly flat pie like this the sweetbreads cook quicker and retain all their moisture. A good variation would be to replace the mushrooms with morels.

2 lb veal bones
1½ quarts water
½ leek
1 stalk celery
1 onion
1 bay leaf
2 cloves
5 white peppercorns
1 teaspoon salt
1½ lb sweetbreads
1 cup dry white wine
¾ lb lean pork tenderloin
5 oz fresh pork fatback
½ oz pâté salt (made with mixed seasoning for delicate meat forcemeat)
½ egg white
2 teaspoons finely chopped herbs (parsley, rosemary, sage)
1¾ lb pie pastry
¼ lb mushrooms
1 lightly beaten egg yolk for glazing
10-inch round deep cake pan

Boil the veal bones in the water with the leek, celery, onion, bay leaf, cloves, peppercorns and salt to make a broth, then reduce the volume by half. Soak the sweetbreads, then carefully remove the skin and all blood vessels (to leave at least 1 pound). Add to the broth and simmer very gently for about

10 minutes. Transfer the sweetbreads to a narrow container, cover with broth and leave to cool. Strain the remaining broth through a fine strainer, add the wine and reduce to give a thick essence.

Purée the pork tenderloin a little at a time in a food processor, and then the pork fat. Season with the pâté salt and beat in the egg white until smooth. Season the forcemeat with the finely chopped herbs.

Roll out the pastry evenly and line the pan, pressing the pastry to the sides of the pan and cutting off any excess. Cover the bottom and sides of the pastry case with the forcemeat. Drain the sweetbreads and arrange over the forcemeat. Fill the spaces between the sweetbreads with mushrooms and pour on the thick essence. Fold any excess pastry over the filling and brush with egg yolk. Cover with a pastry lid and press down firmly around the edges. Cut an opening for the funnel in the center. Brush the top of the pie with beaten egg yolk. Cut leaves from the leftover pastry and arrange as petals on the pie. Brush the leaves with egg yolk. Make a funnel with foil or parchment paper and bake for 45–50 minutes in a 425° oven. If the pie is to be eaten cold, make an aspic jelly with the veal broth and sherry and fill the pie.

The most sophisticated Paris creations. You can see and try them at Fauchon's. Among them are a sweetbread terrine with kiwi fruit and a terrine of gourmet vegetables with a variety of meats included. These novel terrines were created by Georges Pralus of Briennon. He describes himself as a "charcutier and inventor." He is continually experimenting with new combinations of flavors and new forcemeats made mainly with new produce: green peppers, exotic fruits and vegetables. Among this wide range of interesting combinations his terrine of rabbit kidney with green peppercorns is notable.

Veal Terrine with Mushrooms

Terrine de veau aux champignons de couche

¾ lb trimmed veal sirloin
½ lb lean boneless pork
1¼ lb fresh pork fatback, thinly sliced
salt
½ teaspoon dried green peppercorns
½ teaspoon basil
½ teaspoon sage
½ teaspoon thyme
3 thin slices white bread,
crusts removed
1 egg white
6 tablespoons cream
¼ cup butter
2 shallots, finely chopped
½ lb calf's liver, diced
1½ tablespoons brandy
1½ tablespoons Cointreau
1 clove garlic, crushed
generous pinch of ginger
generous pinch of cardamom
¾ cup whipped cream

Mushrooms and fresh parsley give quite a dominant flavor, but are particularly good seasonings for veal based terrines.

½ lb mushrooms
2 tablespoons chopped parsley
½ cup diced cooked ham
1-quart pâté mold

Slice the veal sirloin and pork. Spread, with ½ pound of the sliced pork fat, on a baking sheet or place in a large bowl. Sprinkle with 1 teaspoon salt, the peppercorns and herbs and cover with the thinly sliced white bread. Beat the egg white into the cream and pour over the bread. Leave to soak overnight.

Heat half the butter in a skillet, soften the finely chopped shallots in it and seal the diced calf's liver over a high flame. Add the brandy and Cointreau and simmer for a few moments. Remove the skillet from the heat, stir in ½ teaspoon salt, the crushed garlic and spices and leave to cool.

Grind the seasoned meat, fat and bread mixture together with the liver mixture twice through the finest blade of the grinder. Chill thoroughly and then, over ice, beat well, gradually beating in the stiffly whipped cream until the forcemeat is smooth and shiny.

Cut the mushrooms in half and quickly fry in the rest of the butter. Season with salt and parsley. Work this mixture into the forcemeat with the diced ham.

Line the terrine with remaining slices of fat. Add the forcemeat, cover with more fat, cover the mold and bake, in a water bath, for 50 minutes in a 350° oven.

Terrine of the House with Green Beans

Terrine maison aux haricots verts

½ lb boneless breast of chicken
1 lb lean boneless pork loin
2 teaspoons salt
3 tablespoons butter
¾ cup finely diced carrot
¾ cup finely diced celeriac
4 shallots, finely chopped
1 clove garlic, crushed
10 white peppercorns
4 allspice berries
½ teaspoon coriander
1 bay leaf
few rosemary leaves
1 cup Madeira wine
2 cups chicken broth
5 oz calf's liver
¾ lb fresh pork fatback
1 egg white
¼ lb green beans
1 lb fresh pork fatback, thinly sliced
1½-quart pâté mold

Carefully skin the chicken breast and cut into strips with the pork. Sprinkle with salt. To make the marinade, heat the butter in a skillet and fry the carrots, celeriac and shallots. Add the coarsely crushed garlic, peppercorns, spices and herbs. Add the Madeira and chicken broth. Simmer for 15 minutes, then leave to cool. Pour over the chicken and pork and marinate for at least 12 hours.

Drain the meat thoroughly. Strain the marinade through a fine strainer and then simmer gently to reduce to about ½ cup. Cool thoroughly. Carefully skin the liver, cut it into strips and grind with the meat twice through the finest blade of the grinder. Cut the fat into strips and grind once only. Over ice, work the fat into the meat a little at a time. Stir in the egg white and reduced marinade. Check the seasoning and add more if necessary.

Cook the green beans in salted water until half-cooked, plunge into iced water and leave until completely cool. Spread one large or two small slices of fat with a little of

When the terrine is sliced the green beans give it an attractive appearance. Their flavor also goes very well with the delicate taste of the calf's liver.

the forcemeat, cover with beans and roll up. Line the mold with the remaining slices of fat and half fill with forcemeat. Add the bean rolls, cover with the remaining forcemeat and smooth the top. Cover with fat, cover the mold and bake, in a water bath, for 50 minutes in the oven preheated to 350°.

Poultry Pâtés and Terrines

Hot or Cold Chicken Pâté

Pâté de poularde chaud ou froid

This pâté is even better hot than cold. It can be served warm with a Madeira sauce. If served cold, fill the pie with Madeira aspic.

1 fresh roaster chicken, about 3 lb
1 teaspoon salt
1 sprig fresh thyme
$\frac{1}{4}$ cup butter, melted
$\frac{3}{4}$ cup diced shallots
6 oz mushrooms, sliced
1 teaspoon pâté salt (made with mixed
all-purpose seasoning)
1 tablespoon chopped parsley
3–4 fresh basil leaves, chopped
3–4 fresh sage leaves, chopped
3 tablespoons Madeira wine

Broth
1 lb veal bones
3 tablespoons oil
1 onion, sliced
1 carrot, sliced
1 small celeriac, sliced
$1\frac{1}{2}$ quarts water
1 clove garlic
8 white peppercorns
$\frac{1}{2}$ bay leaf
2 juniper berries
$\frac{1}{2}$ teaspoon salt

Forcemeat
$\frac{1}{2}$ lb lean boneless veal
$\frac{1}{2}$ lb lean boneless pork
$\frac{1}{2}$ lb fresh pork fatback
1–2 teaspoons salt
ground white pepper
generous pinch allspice
generous pinch ground ginger
generous pinch mace
generous pinch rosemary
$\frac{1}{2}$ teaspoon thyme
$\frac{1}{2}$ teaspoon basil
$\frac{3}{4}$ cup heavy cream, lightly whipped

Pastry
4 cups flour
2 (.6 oz) cakes compressed yeast
$\frac{3}{4}$ cup milk
6 tablespoons butter
1 egg
1 teaspoon salt
generous pinch of nutmeg

butter for greasing pan
1 egg yolk, mixed with 1 tablespoon cream
and a generous pinch of sugar
10-inch round deep cake pan

Rub the inside of the chicken with salt and place the sprig of thyme inside. Brush with melted butter and roast in a preheated 475° oven for 12–15 minutes until golden. Leave to cool, then remove the legs. Thinly slice the breast and leg meat and transfer to a bowl. Save the carcass to use for the broth. Lightly soften the shallots in the cooking juices from the chicken, add the sliced mushrooms, season with pâté salt and simmer for 4–5 minutes. Pour all the contents of the pan over the chicken in the bowl, sprinkle with the chopped herbs and add the Madeira. Cover with foil and leave to stand for 24 hours in the refrigerator.

Cut up the chicken carcass with the skin and any remaining meats and chop the veal bones. Brown lightly in the oil, add the vegetables and soften, then add the remaining broth ingredients. Simmer to make a broth, then strain and reduce to $\frac{3}{4}$ cup. While still warm, pour over the chicken and mushrooms, so that the flavor is absorbed by the meat.

Make a forcemeat from the veal, pork, fat and seasonings and, over ice, beat in the lightly whipped cream.

Use the pastry ingredients to make a yeast pastry, following the instructions in the section "Piecrusts." When risen, chill in the refrigerator. Roll out two thirds of the pastry into a 13-inch diameter circle, and use to line the lightly greased pan. Press firmly to the sides. Add half the forcemeat, covering the sides and bottom of the pan. Thoroughly mix the seasoned chicken and mushrooms in the bowl and transfer to the pan. The pan should now be three-quarters full. Add the rest of the forcemeat and brush the pastry around the sides of the pie with egg yolk. Roll out the remaining pastry as thinly as possible and cover the filling. Press the pastry lid firmly to the sides of the pie with your thumbs. Cut off any excess pastry evenly with a pastry wheel or knife. Work the leftover pastry into a ball, roll out again and cut into small leaf shapes. Brush the top of the pie with egg yolk and arrange the leaves on the top in a flower pattern, working from the outside to the center and overlapping the leaves slightly. In the center cut an opening for steam, insert a funnel and brush the top of the pâté once more with the egg yolk mixture. Cover the pâté with a cloth and leave to stand for 20–25 minutes at room temperature, then bake for about 50–55 minutes in a preheated 425° oven. If the pâté browns too quickly, cover the top with foil.

Chicken Terrine with Liver

Terrine de poulet au foie de volaille

1 lb boneless chicken breasts
2 teaspoons pâté salt (made from mixed seasoning for delicate forcemeat)
5 white peppercorns, crushed
$\frac{1}{2}$ bay leaf
4 thin slices white bread, crusts removed
2 tablespoons butter
1 cup diced shallot
$\frac{3}{4}$ cup white wine
1 egg white
1 cup cream
$\frac{1}{2}$ lb chicken livers
3 tablespoons oil
1 tablespoon Calvados
$\frac{3}{4}$ cup chicken or veal broth
$\frac{1}{2}$ teaspoon chopped basil
1 teaspoon chopped parsley
$\frac{1}{2}$ teaspoon salt
ground white pepper
$\frac{3}{4}$ cup light red wine
butter for greasing pan
$\frac{1}{4}$ lb fresh spinach
$\frac{1}{4}$ lb fresh pork fatback, thinly sliced
1 hard-cooked egg, sliced
1-quart pâté mold

Skin the chicken breasts, cut into strips and sprinkle with the pâté salt, peppercorns and bay leaf. Arrange the sliced bread over the chicken. Heat the butter in a skillet and lightly soften half the diced shallot. Dilute with the white wine, reduce to about 3 tablespoons and leave to cool. Beat the egg white into $\frac{1}{4}$ cup of the cream and pour over the bread and chicken. Cover with foil and

leave to stand in the refrigerator, preferably overnight.

Remove any skin or blood vessels from the chicken livers. Heat the oil in a skillet and seal the livers on all sides. Add the Calvados and cook for 2–3 minutes over a low heat. Remove the livers from the skillet and add the rest of the shallots. After a few moments add the chicken or veal broth and simmer for a few minutes. Add the herbs, salt and pepper, then the red wine and reduce to a thick liquid. When cool dice the livers, cover with the liquid and leave to stand, preferably overnight.

Grind the marinated chicken and bread twice through the finest blade of the grinder, chill and then press through a fine strainer. Over ice, beat the forcemeat until smooth and gradually work in the remaining cream until the forcemeat shines. Add more seasoning if necessary. Grease the mold sparingly with butter and add two-thirds of the forcemeat, bringing it up the sides of the mold. Cover with half the lightly cooked, thoroughly drained spinach. Add the diced liver mixture and cover with the remaining forcemeat. Cover the top with slices of pork fat. Cover the mold and bake, in a water bath. Regulate the oven so that the water temperature does not rise above 176°. When cool remove the slices of fat, cover with the remaining spinach and garnish with the egg slices. Cover with a chicken broth aspic.

Poultry Pâté with Goose Liver

Pâté de volaille au foie gras

1 piece turkey, weighing about 2½ lb
little pâté salt (made from mixed seasoning
for delicate forcemeat)
1 duck, weighing about 3¾ lb
½ lb lean boneless pork
1 teaspoon salt
2 teaspoons thyme
½ teaspoon hyssop
15 white peppercorns
¼ teaspoon allspice
½ bay leaf
2 juniper berries, crushed
1 onion, sliced
1 carrot, sliced
1 piece of celeriac, chopped
1½ quarts bone broth or water
½ teaspoon basil
2 teaspoons sweet paprika
½ clove garlic
¾ cup red wine
½ lb goose liver
¾ cup port wine
¼ lb truffles, in pieces
5 tablespoons oil
½ cup finely chopped shallots
½ lb fresh pork fatback
butter for greasing mold
1½ lb pie pastry
1 egg yolk
1½-quart pâté mold
port wine aspic to finish

Remove the breast from the turkey, trim thoroughly, sprinkle with a little pâté salt and keep to one side to be used whole. For the forcemeat remove the meat from the remaining turkey and from the duck, mainly from the breasts and legs. Remove the bones and all skin or gristle. Cut the lean poultry meat (you should be left with about 1 pound) and pork into strips, sprinkle with salt, 1 teaspoon thyme, the hyssop, 10 crushed peppercorns, the allspice, bay leaf and juniper berries, and leave to stand in the refrigerator for 1–2 hours.

Chop the carcasses of the turkey and duck with the skin and any trimmings and simmer with the onion, carrot, celeriac, broth or water, basil, paprika, garlic, wine and remaining thyme and peppercorns to make a broth, then reduce by half.

Skin the goose liver and remove all blood vessels. Knead gently, sprinkle with pâté salt and pour on the port wine. Cover with foil and place in the refrigerator. When the liver has soaked thoroughly drain and wrap it around the pieces of truffle.

Heat the oil in a skillet, seal the turkey breasts and remove from the skillet. In the same oil soften the shallots and add the broth. Over a low heat reduce to a thick essence and press through a fine strainer over the turkey breasts. Leave to cool.

To make the forcemeat grind the seasoned meat twice through the finest blade of the grinder. Cut the fat into strips, grind once and then, over ice, work into the meat in small portions. Push the forcemeat through a strainer and beat firmly for 5–10 minutes until light and airy.

Line the lightly buttered mold with pastry and add half the forcemeat. Add the turkey breasts, halved if preferred, the essence, and the liver and truffles to the pie. Cover with the remaining forcemeat and smooth the top. Fold any overhanging pastry over the filling and brush with egg yolk. Add a pastry lid and seal the edges firmly. Decorate with pastry flowers, cut an opening and insert a funnel. Bake for 10 minutes in the oven preheated to 425°, then reduce the temperature to 400° and bake for a further 40–45 minutes until cooked.

When cool fill the pie with port wine aspic.

Goose Giblet Terrine

Terrine d'abatis d'oie

giblets of 2 geese (heart, gizzard, neck, head and wings)
2 goose livers (not force-fed)
1¾ lb double pork loin center rib roast
1 carrot, coarsely chopped
1 small onion, coarsely chopped
1 piece celeriac, coarsely chopped
1½ quarts bone broth or water
10 white peppercorns
1½ teaspoons marjoram
1 teaspoon basil
1 clove garlic
2–3 teaspoons salt
½ teaspoon dried green peppercorns
1 teaspoon mild paprika
1 teaspoon thyme
1 bay leaf
5 allspice berries
3 slices white bread
¾ cup cream
1 egg
2 tablespoons oil
4 shallots, diced
¼ cup port wine
1 tablespoon cranberry sauce
½ cup diced cooked ham
⅓ cup coarsely chopped pistachios
¾ lb fresh pork fatback, thinly sliced
1½-quart pâté mold

Remove the flesh of the gizzards from the tough skin. Remove the arteries from the hearts and the blood vessels from the livers. Bone the pork and trim the meat thoroughly. Chop the bones. Roast the bones in a meat pan for 10 minutes with the chopped necks and heads and the giblet trimmings. Add the carrot, onion and celeriac and after a further 20 minutes transfer all the ingredients in the meat pan to a saucepan. Add the bone broth and bring to a boil. Skim and add the white peppercorns, 1 teaspoon marjoram, the basil and garlic. Simmer gently over a low heat for 30 minutes, strain and if necessary remove fat, then reduce to one-eighth the quantity.

Cut the giblets and pork into strips, sprinkle with the salt, green peppercorns, paprika, thyme, bay leaf, allspice and remaining marjoram and chill. Place the sliced bread in a large bowl and pour on the cream and beaten egg.

Heat the oil in a skillet and thoroughly seal the livers. Remove from the skillet and chill. Soften the diced shallots in the skillet, add the port wine and after 2–3 minutes add the reduced broth and cranberry sauce. Cook the sauce over a very low heat until syrupy, strain and cool.

Grind the seasoned meat with the bread (with the cream and egg) twice through the finest blade of the grinder. Add the sauce and beat in until evenly incorporated into the forcemeat. Dice the ham and livers and stir into the forcemeat with the chopped pistachios.

Line the mold with the fat slices and add the forcemeat a little at a time, pressing down well to make sure there are no gaps. Cover with pork fat. Decorate with sprigs of herbs, cover the mold and bake, in a water bath, in the oven preheated to 300° for about 1 hour and 10 minutes.

Polish white cabbage salad. Shred ½ lb white cabbage and blanch for a few moments. Cut a fairly tart apple into thin sticks. Mix with ⅓ cup chopped pecans or walnuts and dress with a sharp sauce made from cream, a pinch of pepper, salt, a little lemon juice and a dash of Calvados.

A non-fattening, lean terrine containing no fat (in the forcemeat) but very juicy and highly flavored. The interest is provided by the highly seasoned giblets. Excellent with a white cabbage salad.

Duck Terrine

Terrine de canard

1 duck, dressed weight 3¾ lb, with liver
1½ quarts water
¾ cup red wine
bouquet garni
10 peppercorns
3 tablespoons brandy
2 tablespoons orange juice
2 tablespoons oil
1 small onion, diced
1 clove garlic, crushed
¾ lb lean boneless pork
¾ lb fresh pork fatback
2–3 teaspoons salt
2 teaspoons mixed seasoning mixture for
country-style forcemeat
1 teaspoon thyme
1 teaspoon grated orange rind
1 egg
¾ lb fresh pork fatback, thinly sliced
1½-quart pâté mold

Bone the duck. Remove the breasts and carefully remove skin and ligaments from the remaining meat. Chop the trimmings and bring to a boil with the water, red wine, bouquet garni and peppercorns over a low heat until reduced to ¾ cup, skimming to remove scum and fat from time to time.

Place the duck breasts and liver in a narrow container, pour on the brandy and orange juice and marinate for 3 hours. Heat the oil, seal the breasts and liver on all sides and remove from the skillet. Soften the onion and garlic and add the marinade and reduced broth. Over a low heat reduce again to about 1 cup and strain. Cut the duck meat (excluding the breasts), pork and two-thirds of the pork fat into strips. Season with salt, mixed seasoning, thyme and orange rind. Grind through the fine blade of the grinder and work in the egg and cooled sauce to make a smooth forcemeat. Finely dice the sealed liver and the remaining fat and mix into the forcemeat. Line the mold with the slices of pork fat and add half the forcemeat. Wrap the duck breasts in fat and place one behind the other in the mold. Cover with the remaining forcemeat and finally with the remaining fat. Garnish with herbs and a slice of orange. Cook for about 1 hour 20 minutes in a 300° oven.

Duck Terrine with Truffled Breast of Duck

Terrine de canard au poitrine de canard truffée

½ lb trimmed duck meat
¼ lb lean boneless pork
½ lb fresh pork fatback
pâté salt
grated rind of 1 orange
½ teaspoon chopped fresh sage
2 breasts of duck, total weight
about 10 oz
1 tablespoon oil
¼ lb truffles
3 tablespoons port wine
¼ cup jellifying chicken broth
5 oz foie gras, marinated in
brandy and port wine
¾ oz shelled pistachios
¼ cup diced cooked ham
¼ cup diced smoked beef tongue
about ½ lb fresh pork fatback, thinly sliced
5-cup pâté mold

Cut the trimmed duck, pork and pork fat into strips, sprinkle with pâté salt, orange rind and sage and chill. Grind the meat twice through the finest blade of the grinder, then grind the fat once only. Work the fat thoroughly into the meat, push through a fine strainer, then beat over ice until the forcemeat is smooth and silky. Chill after each stage.

Season the breasts of duck with pâté salt, seal in hot oil, remove from the skillet and cool thoroughly. With a sharp pointed knife, cut a slit along the center of the breasts. Cut three-quarters of the truffle, preferably one large one, into ⅛-inch slices, dip in port wine and carefully insert in the slit in the breasts. Pour the chicken broth over the breasts. Finely dice the rest of the truffles and the foie gras, halve the pistachios and stir into the forcemeat with the ham, tongue and half the broth. Line the mold with the slices of fat and add about half the forcemeat, bringing it up the sides of the dish slightly. Cut the ends of the breasts straight so that they fit closely together in the mold, place in it and sprinkle with the remaining broth. Cover with the remaining forcemeat and smooth the top. Bang the mold several times on a damp cloth to settle the contents. Fold the overhanging fat over the filling and press down. Top with a whole slice of fat and cover the mold. Cook for about 45 minutes, in a water bath; regulate the oven so the water temperature does not rise above 176°.

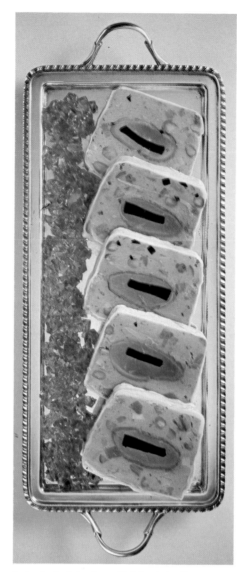

A classic duck terrine, which lends itself to interesting variations. One unusual variation is to replace the truffles inside the breasts with cooked morels soaked in port wine.

Truffled Turkey Terrine

Terrine de dindon truffée

1 lb lean boneless breast of turkey
½ lb lean boneless pork
1 teaspoon salt
14 white peppercorns, crushed
⅛ teaspoon ground ginger
⅛ teaspoon cardamom
⅛ teaspoon mace
2 sage leaves
½ bay leaf
4 thin slices white bread, crusts removed
3 tablespoons butter
1 cup diced shallots
¼ cup cream sherry
1 egg white
½ lb turkey or chicken liver
2 tablespoons oil
1½ tablespoons Grand Marnier
1 clove garlic, crushed
1 cup jellying chicken broth
⅛ teaspoon allspice
⅛ teaspoon ground cloves
1 teaspoon grated orange rind
1 teaspoon basil
1½ oz truffles, diced
½ lb fresh pork fatback, cut in strips
1 cup light cream
¾ lb fresh pork fatback, thinly sliced
1½-quart pâté mold

Cut the turkey and pork into strips, place in a bowl and sprinkle with 1 teaspoon salt, 8 crushed peppercorns, the ginger, cardamon, mace, sage and bay leaf. Arrange the sliced bread over the meat. Heat the butter in a

skillet and soften half the shallots. Leave to cool slightly and add the sherry and egg white. Pour this mixture over the bread and meat so that it moistens all the bread. Cover with foil and leave to stand in the refrigerator.

Remove any skin and blood vessels from the turkey liver. Heat the oil in a skillet and seal the liver all over, over a high flame. Add the Grand Marnier. Turn the liver a few times in the skillet and then remove. Soften the rest of the shallots and the crushed garlic in the skillet and add the chicken broth, allspice, cloves, orange rind, basil, salt and remaining peppercorns. Simmer for about 5 minutes, push through a fine strainer and reduce to a thick essence. Dice the liver and pour the essence over. Add the truffles, cover with foil and leave to stand in the refrigerator.

Grind the marinated meat with the other ingredients in the bowl twice through the finest blade of the grinder. Then grind the strips of pork fat once only. Over ice stir the fat a little at a time into the meat. Then gradually add the cream and beat until the forcemeat is smooth and silky. Cook a test ball of forcemeat and increase the seasoning if necessary. Stir the diced liver and truffles into the forcemeat with all the essence. Line the mold with the slices of fat and add the forcemeat. Cover with a slice of fat, cover the mold and cook, in a water bath, for about 50–55 minutes, regulating the oven so that the water temperature does not rise above 176°.

The terrine can be served in the usual way with its covering of fat, or can be covered with a layer of chaudfroid sauce, as illustrated. When cold, unmold the terrine, remove the pork fat and wipe the terrine thoroughly dry with paper towels. Line the mold with a layer of chaudfroid sauce made with chicken broth, so that a thin layer adheres to the sides. Return the terrine to the mold and fill any gaps at the side with sauce. Cover the top with a layer of chicken broth aspic.

Squab Terrine with Basil

Terrine de pigeon au basilic

4 squabs
salt
ground white pepper
¾ lb veal bones
½ onion
½ carrot
1 piece celeriac
½ teaspoon thyme
½ teaspoon powdered sage
½ teaspoon paprika
½ bay leaf
3 tablespoons butter
1½ tablespoons brandy
1½ tablespoons Bénédictine
1 shallot, diced
¾ cup red wine
¾ oz dried mushrooms
⅛ teaspoon ground ginger
⅛ teaspoon allspice
¼ teaspoon mace
½ lb lean veal
¼ lb fresh pork fatback
1 tablespoon egg white
1 tablespoon cracker crumbs
¾ cup light cream
1 tablespoon chopped fresh basil
butter for greasing mold
2 oz fresh pork fatback, thinly sliced
2-cup pâté mold

Cut up the dressed squabs; i.e. remove the breasts and meat from the legs, and trim.

Dice the lean meat (you should have about ½ lb) and place it in a bowl. Sprinkle with ½ teaspoon salt and pepper to taste, cover with foil and chill.

Make a broth with the squab carcasses, trimmings, veal bones, onion, carrot, celeriac, thyme, sage, paprika and bay leaf. Strain and reduce to ¾ cup. Heat half the butter in a skillet and quickly seal the diced meat, stirring continuously. Add the brandy and Bénédictine, stir again and transfer to a bowl. Melt the remaining butter in the skillet, soften the shallot and add the squab broth. Add the wine with the dried mushrooms, ginger, allspice and half the mace. Over a very low heat reduce slowly to a thick essence and strain over the diced squab meat. Cover with foil and leave to stand in the refrigerator, preferably overnight.

To make the forcemeat, dice the veal and fat. The small quantities involved are best puréed in a food processor. Over ice first stir in the remaining mace, ½ teaspoon salt and pepper to taste, then the egg white and cracker crumbs and finally add the cream a little at a time. The forcemeat should be smooth and silky. Stir the diced squab meat into the forcemeat with the essence and chopped basil. Grease the mold with butter and fill with the forcemeat. Cover the top of the forcemeat with pork fat slices, cover the mold and bake for 35–40 minutes in the oven, in a water bath. Regulate the oven temperature so that the temperature of the water does not rise above 176°.

Remove the slice of fat from the top of the terrine. It can then be covered with a layer of chicken broth aspic or, as illustrated, with a layer of chaudfroid sauce and decorated with a truffle flower and blanched celery leaves.

Guinea Fowl Terrine

Terrine de pintadeaux

2 guinea fowl, weighing 2 lb each,
with livers
5 oz lean pork tenderloin
1 tablespoon pâté salt (made with mixed
all-purpose seasoning)
3 thin slices white bread,
crusts removed
1 egg
$\frac{1}{4}$ cup cream
2 teaspoons sweet paprika
$\frac{1}{2}$ teaspoon allspice
1 bay leaf
1 lb veal bones
1 onion
1 carrot
1 piece celeriac
1 teaspoon salt
2 sprigs parsley
8 white peppercorns, crushed
3 tablespoons oil
3 tablespoons Armagnac
$\frac{1}{2}$ cup diced shallots
1 clove garlic, crushed
1 cup red wine
$\frac{1}{8}$ teaspoon mace
$\frac{1}{8}$ teaspoon cardamom
grated rind of $\frac{1}{2}$ orange
$1\frac{1}{2}$ cups heavy cream
1 oz truffles, diced
$\frac{3}{4}$ lb fresh pork fatback,
thinly sliced
5-cup pâté mold
Madeira wine aspic to finish

Bone the guinea fowls and trim the breasts thoroughly. Keep the breasts to one side to use whole. Remove any ligaments from the other large pieces of meat to give about $\frac{3}{4}$ lb meat.

Cut this meat and the lean pork tenderloin into strips and sprinkle with 2 teaspoons pâté salt. Arrange the sliced bread over the meat. Beat the egg and cream with the paprika, allspice, and $\frac{1}{2}$ bay leaf and pour this mixture over the bread. Cover with foil and leave to stand in the refrigerator.

Make a broth from the guinea fowl carcasses, skin and trimmings, the veal bones, onion, carrot, celeriac, salt, parsley, peppercorns, and remaining $\frac{1}{2}$ bay leaf. Strain the broth and boil it until it has reduced to 2 cups.

Remove the skin and blood vessels from the guinea fowl livers and seal in hot oil with the lightly salted breasts. Add the Armagnac and simmer for 1–2 minutes. Remove the meat from the skillet. Add the shallots and garlic to the juices in the skillet, add $\frac{3}{4}$ cup guinea fowl broth and simmer for 5

minutes, then add the remaining broth and the wine. Add the rest of the pâté salt, the mace, cardamom and orange rind and simmer over a low heat to reduce to a thick essence. While hot strain over the breasts and liver and leave to marinate for at least 2–3 hours.

Cut up the liver and add to the bread and meat mixture with the essence. Grind all the ingredients together twice through the finest blade of the grinder. Chill the mixture well and sieve it until smooth. Then beat the forcemeat vigorously until really smooth and silky. Lightly whip the cream and stir into the forcemeat mixture a little at a time. Finally add the diced truffles.

Line the mold with slices of fat and add a thin layer of forcemeat. Place the breasts in the mold, either one on top of the other or side by side depending on the shape of the mold. Cover with forcemeat and press down well to prevent gaps. Cover with fat, cover the mold and bake, in a water bath, for 45–50 minutes. Regulate the oven so that the water temperature does not rise above 176°.

Leave the terrine until it is completely cold, then remove the fat from the top and cut evenly around the sides of the mold. Wipe any remaining fat from the top of the terrine with absorbent paper towels and cover the terrine with an even layer of Madeira wine aspic.

Guinea Fowl Terrine with Sweetbreads and Morels

*Terrine de pintade au ris de
veau et morilles*

This is a good example of a terrine with no fat covering. Instead the dish is liberally greased with butter. To unmold the terrine, stand in hot water when cold. If the dish is lined with roasting film, it will be easier to unmold.

1 lb veal bones
$1\frac{1}{2}$ quarts water
bouquet garni (white of 1 leek, small
piece celery, $\frac{1}{2}$ small onion, $\frac{1}{2}$ small bay
leaf)
1 teaspoon salt
5 white peppercorns, crushed
$\frac{3}{4}$ lb lean guinea fowl meat
6 thin slices white bread, crusts removed
1 egg white, lightly beaten
6 tablespoons light cream
$\frac{1}{4}$ oz pâté salt
little sage, rosemary, and ground white
pepper
$1\frac{1}{2}$ cups whipped cream
1 lb sweetbreads
$1\frac{1}{2}$ oz dried morels
1 tablespoon chopped parsley
butter for greasing mold
1-quart pâté mold

Boil the veal bones with the water, bouquet garni, salt and peppercorns to make a broth and strain.

Cut the guinea fowl into strips and place on a baking sheet. Arrange the sliced bread over the meat, moisten with the egg white and cream and sprinkle with the pâté salt, sage, rosemary and pepper. Cover with foil and chill. Grind the meat and all the ingredients in the bowl twice through the finest blade of the grinder, sieve and, over ice, work in the whipped cream a little at a time.

Soak the sweetbreads and carefully remove all skin and blood vessels to give about $\frac{1}{2}$ lb meat. Blanch. Transfer to a saucepan, add half the cooled broth and bring to a boil. Simmer for 10 minutes, then leave to cool in the broth. Remove the sweetbreads from the pan and cut into pieces. Reduce the veal broth to a thick

essence. Dip the sweetbreads in the essence and chill. Rinse the morels, thoroughly wash away the sand and soak several times in fresh water until they have completely swollen up. Boil the morels in the remaining veal broth for about 25 minutes, then remove from the pan. Reduce the broth to a thick essence and leave the morels to cool in the essence. Mix the sweetbread and morels into the force-meat with the parsley. Grease the mold with butter, line with roasting film and fill with the forcemeat. Smooth the top and bang the mold several times on a damp cloth. Fold over any excess film, cover the mold and cook, in a water bath, for about 40 minutes. Regulate the oven so that the water temperature does not exceed 176°.

This terrine is excellent with a grape sauce. Stew peeled grapes in butter, season with lime juice, sugar and a little freshly ground pepper and add a dash of sloe gin.

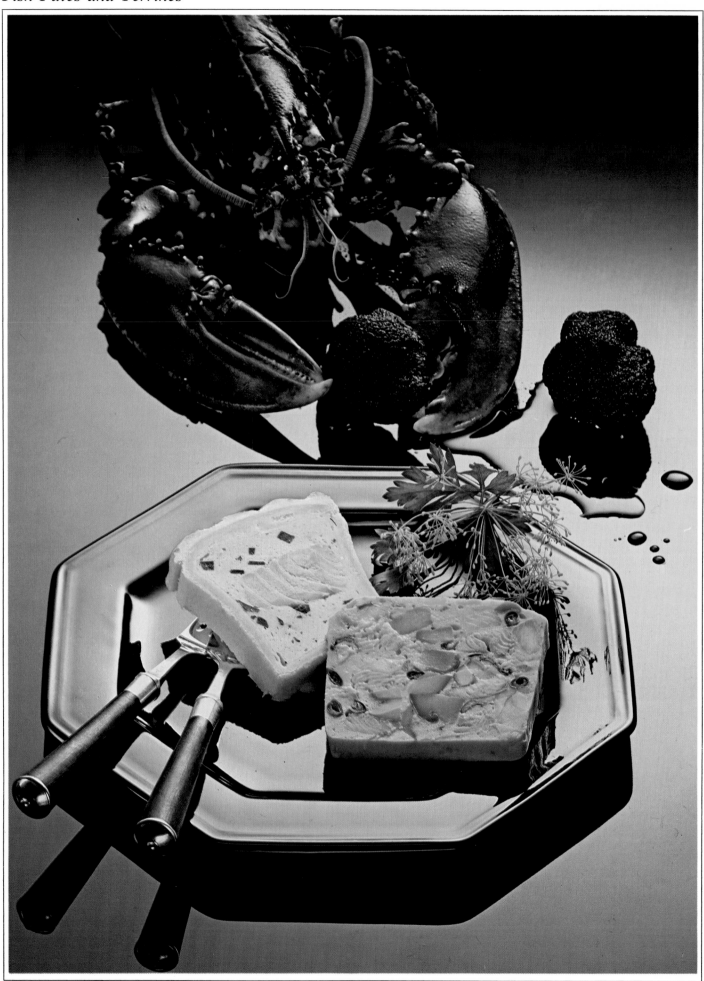

Fish Pies and Pâtés

These are the newest and, with a few exceptions, also the lightest of the pâtés and terrines.

Fish or shellfish pâtés or terrines have no long tradition behind them and, with a few exceptions, have in the past been much less popular than those made with pork or game. Their low fat content meant that they did not keep well and, in addition, fish was usually eaten fresh. Fish pâtés and terrines first came into fashion at the turn of the century, made by great French chefs for a gastronomic élite. Nowadays *charcutiers* offer a wide selection of fish pies and pâtés, dishes which at one time would never have been included in the stock of a "pork butcher."

The reason for the increase in popularity is obviously their slimming aspect, although this is somewhat deceptive, for a good fish pâté includes a lot of calories in the shape of cream and bread or flour panada, which are used as lightening agents. Even so these light, airy stuffings are less rich than those made with meat. Fish mixes excellently with a variety of vegetables and can be served with a wide range of sauces and salads. For these reasons fish pâtés have become popular in the *nouvelle cuisine*, a branch of cooking which relies heavily upon the freshness and quality of its ingredients.

With fish, freshness is of prime importance. With modern methods of transportation this has ceased to be a problem, but you must buy carefully and confine your pâté making to those days when freshly caught fish are available. If you are not sure about the freshness of the fish, it is better to choose a freshwater fish, which fish merchants can keep live in tanks.

Not every fish is equally suitable for use in pâtés and terrines. Of the freshwater fish, pike, with its dense flesh, is especially good, or salmon, and also eel, perch and trout. Whether you choose freshwater or sea fish, the expensive varieties are usually best for a particularly fine dish. Compared with other luxury foodstuffs, truffles for example, even the best fish is not overly-expensive. Nevertheless you can make an excellent pâté with inexpensive varieties and combined with vegetables you can use it for a fine, light terrine.

Salmon Pâté

Pâté de saumon

1½ lb salmon fillet
¼ lb (about 6–8 slices) fresh white bread
2 egg whites
2 cups cream
1 teaspoon butter
½ cup sliced onion
salt
ground white pepper
⅛ teaspoon each of nutmeg and English mustard powder
1 oz diced truffle
butter for greasing mold
1½ lb pie pastry
1 egg yolk and 2 tablespoons cream for glazing
1¾-quart pâté mold
white wine aspic to finish

Remove any bones from ¾ lb of the salmon and cut it into strips. Remove the crust from the bread, slice thinly and pour over the egg whites and ½ cup of the cream. Melt the butter, soften the onion without allowing it to color and then leave to cool. Place the salmon, bread and onion on a baking sheet and sprinkle with 1 teaspoon salt, pepper to taste, nutmeg and mustard. Grind twice through the finest blade of the grinder. As with any forcemeat, chill well after each stage. Push the forcemeat through a strainer and gradually work in the rest of the cream.

Remove any bones from the rest of the salmon fillet and season with salt and pepper. Work the truffles into the forcemeat. Grease the mold with butter and line with pastry. Place half the forcemeat in, lay the salmon fillet along the center and cover with the remaining forcemeat. Fold over the overhanging pastry and cover the top with a sheet of pastry. Decorate the pâté, make an opening in the lid and insert a funnel. Brush the top of the pâté with the egg yolk and cream mixture.

Bake for 40 minutes in all, 15 minutes in the oven preheated to 475° then lower the temperature to 425° and bake for a further 25 minutes. When cool fill the pâté with white wine aspic.

Chef's Fish Terrine

Terrine de poisson du chef

1 teaspoon butter
1 shallot, sliced
6 oz fish fillet, e.g. sole or sea bass
salt
ground white pepper
⅛ teaspoon each of nutmeg and English mustard powder
1 egg white, lightly beaten
¼ cup flour panada
¾ cup whipped cream
¼ lb flat mushrooms, diced
½ lb sea trout fillet, diced
½ lb sea bass fillet, diced
¼ lb lobster claw meat, diced
¼ cup diced green beans
⅓ cup diced carrots
16–20 leaves fresh lemon balm
butter for greasing mold
1-quart pâté mold

Melt the butter, soften the shallot in it without allowing it to color and leave to cool. Cut the fish fillet into strips and sprinkle with ½ teaspoon salt, pepper to taste, the nutmeg, mustard and shallot. Grind the fish twice through the finest blade of the grinder. Over ice beat in the egg white a little at a time. Sieve the flour panada a little at a time into the forcemeat and work in. Push the forcemeat through a strainer and beat until smooth and silky. Work in the whipped cream a spoonful at a time. Chill the forcemeat after each stage.

Blanch the mushrooms, drain and leave to cool. Season the sea trout, bass and lobster with salt and pepper and fold with the diced vegetables and lemon balm into the forcemeat. Grease the mold with butter, line with roasting film and fill with the forcemeat. Bang the mold several times on a damp cloth and seal.

Cook for about 45 minutes, in a water bath. Regulate the oven so that the water temperature does not exceed 176°.

Eel Terrine

Terrine d'anguille

1 teaspoon butter
1 shallot, sliced
4 thin slices white bread, crusts removed
½ egg white, lightly beaten
2 tablespoons light cream
5 oz pike fillet
salt, ground white pepper, nutmeg and
English mustard powder
¾ cup whipped cream
¼ cup chopped dill
1 lb fresh eel, boned and skinned
½ lb smoked eel fillet
butter for greasing mold
1-quart pâté mold
chopped dill and white wine aspic to finish

Melt the butter, soften the shallot in it and leave to cool. Moisten the bread with the egg white and light cream. Remove any bones from the pike fillet, cut into strips and place on a baking sheet with the moistened bread and shallot. Sprinkle with salt, pepper, nutmeg and mustard. Grind twice through the finest blade of the grinder. Push through a strainer and beat until smooth and silky. Gradually beat in the whipped cream and finally add half of the dill.

Fillet the skinned fresh eel and carefully flatten with the back of a meat pounder; ie pound flat without damaging the fish. Cut into equal pieces to fit the size of the mold and sprinkle with salt, pepper, nutmeg, mustard and the remaining dill. Cut the smoked eel into strips the same length as the mold. Grease the mold and line it with roasting film. Place the fresh eel in the mold, skin side outermost, leaving no gaps. Cover with about one-third of the forcemeat, bringing it up the sides of the mold. Fill the mold with layers of smoked eel and forcemeat, finishing with a thin layer of forcemeat. Bang the mold several times on a damp cloth, fold the overhanging film over the top and seal the mold.

Cook for about 40 minutes, in a water bath, regulating the oven so that the water temperature does not exceed 176°.

When cool unmold the terrine, sprinkle with chopped dill, coat with several layers of white wine aspic and sprinkle again with some more chopped dill.

Line the mold with eel fillets. Cut the fillets to the same length and sprinkle with dill. Line the mold with film and lay the fillets side by side to leave no gaps. Then fill the mold with the pike forcemeat and smoked eel fillets.

Fish Pâté in Brioche Pastry

Poisson en brioche

1 teaspoon butter
1 shallot, sliced
½ lb fish fillet, e.g. sole
salt
ground white pepper
⅛ teaspoon each of nutmeg and
English mustard powder
1 medium egg white, lightly beaten
⅓ cup flour panada
1 cup whipped cream
1 teaspoon each chopped dill and tarragon
4 cups flour
2 (.6 oz) cakes compressed yeast
1½ tablespoons milk
1 egg
5 tablespoons melted butter
¾ lb salmon fillet
1 beaten egg for glazing

Melt the butter and soften the shallot in it without allowing it to color. Leave to cool. Cut the sole into strips and sprinkle with ½ teaspoon salt, pepper to taste, the nutmeg, mustard and shallot. Grind the fish twice through the finest blade of the grinder. Over ice beat the egg white a very little at a time into the fish. Sieve the panada into the fish a little at a time and beat in thoroughly. Sieve the forcemeat through a fine strainer and beat until smooth and silky. Beat in the cream a spoonful at a time. Finally add the herbs.

Sift the flour into a bowl and make a well in the center. Stir the yeast into the lukewarm milk, pour into the well and mix with a little of the flour. Leave to rise for 15 minutes at room temperature. Stir the egg, ½ teaspoon salt and a pinch of nutmeg into the melted butter and work into the yeast mixture and remaining flour in the bowl. Beat until you have a light dough and leave to rise for another 15 minutes. Cover with a damp cloth and leave to stand in the refrigerator for a further 15 minutes, so that the dough will be chilled before coming into contact with the heat-sensitive filling. Roll out the dough to ¼ inch thick and use a cutter to cut 2 fish shapes, or cut around a cardboard pattern.

Cover one piece of dough with half the forcemeat, leaving ¾ inch clear around the edge. Place the salmon fillet in the center of the forcemeat, cover with the remaining forcemeat and smooth the top to seal the salmon fillet completely. Brush the edges of the dough with egg. Lay the second sheet of dough carefully over the forcemeat and press the edges firmly together, making sure

to leave no air gaps between dough and filling. Cut the remaining dough to make a mouth and fins, brush with egg and press onto the fish. Leave to rise at room temperature for 15 minutes, then decorate as required. Cut out the eye, insert a funnel and brush the dough all over with egg.

Bake in a preheated 425° oven for 10 minutes, then reduce the heat to 400° and bake for a further 35–40 minutes or until cooked.

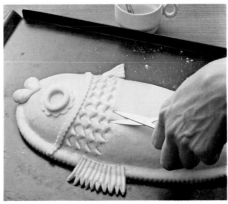

Use scissors to cut scales. This is a simple way of decorating the fish. Leave the dough to rise at room temperature for 15 minutes, then cut with a small pair of scissors to make scales. Be careful not to hold the scissors too straight to avoid cutting right through the dough. Finally brush with egg following the direction of the scales, so that only the tips of the scales brown during baking.

Rainbow and Sea Trout Terrine

Terrine de truites arc-en-ciel et truites saumonées

½ tablespoon butter
⅓ cup sliced shallots
6 thin slices white bread, crusts removed
1 egg white, lightly beaten
¼ cup light cream
½ lb sea trout fillets, skinned and boned
(from about a 1-lb sea trout)
a little salt, ground white pepper and
nutmeg
1 cup whipped cream
2 tablespoons chopped dill
4 trout, each weighing about ¾ lb
butter for greasing mold
½ lb smoked trout fillet
1-quart pâté mold

Melt the butter, soften the shallots in it and leave to cool. Moisten the bread with the egg white and cream. Cut the sea trout into strips and arrange on a baking sheet with the moistened bread and shallots and season with salt, pepper and nutmeg. Grind twice through the finest blade of the grinder. Push through a strainer and beat until smooth. Gradually add the whipped cream, working in thoroughly. Finally fold in half the dill.

Before you use the trout they should be left to stand in the refrigerator for at least 12 hours because fillets of fresh-caught trout contract too much when cooked. Fillet the trout and season the fillets. Grease the mold with butter and line with roasting film and then with the fillets, placing them skin side outermost and leaving no gaps between. Sprinkle with the remaining dill. Cut the smoked trout into pieces, fold into the forcemeat and fill the mold. Bang it several times on a damp cloth. Fold the excess film over the filling and seal the mold.

Cook for about 40 minutes, in a water bath, regulating the oven so that the water temperatures does not exceed 176°.

Sole Terrine with Lobster Filling

Terrine de sole au homard

1 tablespoon butter
⅓ cup diced shallots
5 oz shrimp in shell
¼ lb fresh lobster meat
4 thin slices white bread, crusts removed
1 egg white
¼ cup light cream
a little salt, ground white pepper and
nutmeg
1 oz fresh lobster roe
1½ cups whipped cream
1 oz truffles, diced
½ cup diced mushrooms
1 lb sole fillets, skinned
5 oz cooked lobster meat
butter for greasing mold
1-quart pâté mold

Heat the butter, soften the shallots in it and leave to cool. Shell and devein the shrimp and place on a baking sheet with the lobster. Cover with the shallots and white bread. Beat the egg white with the cream, season with salt, pepper and nutmeg and pour over the bread. Chill, then grind with the shrimp and lobster mixture twice through the finest blade of the grinder. Sieve the lobster roe into the forcemeat and mix in, then sieve the forcemeat. Beat thoroughly and add the whipped cream a little at a time. Fold in the truffles and mushrooms. Chill thoroughly after each stage.

Flatten the sole fillets and season with a little salt. Grease the mold with butter and line with roasting film. Line the mold with the sole fillets, placing the skin side outermost and leaving no gaps between them. Add some of the lobster forcemeat, bringing it up the sides of the mold. Then add the lobster meat. Cover with the remaining forcemeat and bang the mold several times on a damp cloth. Fold over the overhanging sole fillets and cover with the film. Seal the mold and cook, in a water bath, for about 40 minutes, regulating the oven so that the water temperature does not rise above 176°.

Garnish with blanched celery leaves and flowers made from cooked carrot and truffle. Cover with a fish broth aspic.

Sole Terrine with Goose Liver

Terrine de sole au foie gras

This is an unusual combination which gives a very good flavor. The recipe is a variation of the preceding Sole Terrine with Lobster Filling recipe, with the lobster and shrimp in the forcemeat replaced by fresh sea trout, skinned and boned. The cooked lobster is replaced by 5 oz fresh goose liver, with all skin and ducts removed, kneaded with a little pâté salt and shaped into a roll, the same length as the mold. The roll of liver is placed in the middle of the terrine embedded in the forcemeat. When completely cool cover the terrine with fish aspic to seal in the flavor.

The cooking time is about 40 minutes, in a water bath regulated at 176°.

This terrine goes well with a celery salad. Cut the celery into very thin sticks and braise in highly seasoned veal bone broth – the celery should still have a "bite." When cool flavor with a little brandy and dress with vinaigrette sauce.

Sea Trout Terrine with Oyster Paste

Terrine de truites saumonées au parfait d'huitres

Sea trout forcemeat
5 oz sea trout fillet
2 thin slices white bread, crusts removed
1 small egg white
3 tablespoons light cream
¼ cup sliced onion, softened in butter
½ teaspoon salt
ground white pepper and English mustard powder
about ¾ cup whipped cream
Oyster forcemeat
1½ oz shucked oysters
1½ oz sea bass fillet
1 slice white bread, crusts removed
1 small egg white
2 tablespoons light cream
salt, ground white pepper and cayenne
about ½ cup whipped cream

butter for greasing mold
1 teaspoon chopped dill
1 carrot, in julienne strips
1 oz green beans
2-cup pâté mold

Prepare the two forcemeats separately.

Grease the mold with butter and line with roasting film. Transfer about three-quarters of the sea trout forcemeat to a pastry bag fitted with a plain tube. Pipe into the mold and smooth up along the sides with a spatula. Sprinkle with the dill and then fill the mold with layers of oyster forcemeat and carrot fingers and beans, cooked until crisp-tender. Cover with the remaining sea trout forcemeat. Seal the mold and bake, in a water bath, for about 25–30 minutes, regulating the oven so that the water temperature does not exceed 176°.

Salmon Terrine

Terrine de saumon

Salmon forcemeat
½ lb salmon fillet
3 slices white bread, crusts removed
1 egg white
5 tablespoons light cream
¼ cup sliced onion
½ teaspoon butter
1 teaspoon salt
freshly ground white pepper
little cayenne
about 1 cup whipped cream

1¼ lb salmon fillet
little salt and freshly ground white pepper
¾ oz truffle, finely diced
1-quart pâté mold

Prepare the salmon forcemeat and chill it.

Spread about half the forcemeat onto a piece of roasting film, covering an area about the same size as the mold. Cut ¾ lb of the salmon fillet to exactly the same size and lay it over the forcemeat, skin side uppermost. Season it with salt and pepper. Keep a little forcemeat to one side and stir the truffle into the remainder. Spread over the salmon. Season the remaining salmon fillet and place along the center of the forcemeat. Place in the mold with the film, bang several times, and cover with the remaining forcemeat. Fold over the overhanging film, bang again, seal and cook, in a water bath, for about 42 minutes, regulating the oven so that the water temperature does not exceed 176°.

Garnish the salmon terrine with whirls of whipped cream and caviar and serve on top of finely diced fish aspic.

Sea Bass Terrine with Fresh Basil

Terrine de turbot au basilic frais

Sea bass forcemeat
½ lb sea bass fillet
8 slices white bread, crusts removed
1 egg white
6 tablespoons cream
1 teaspoon butter
2 shallots, sliced
1 teaspoon salt
ground white pepper
a pinch each of nutmeg and English mustard powder
1 cup whipped cream
Sea bass and spinach filling
3 oz fresh bulk spinach
about 10 fresh basil leaves
¾ lb sea bass fillet
salt and ground white pepper
¾ oz truffle, diced
butter for greasing mold
1-quart pâté mold
white chaudfroid sauce to finish

Remove any bones still in the bass fillet and cut into strips. Moisten the bread with the egg white and cream. Melt the butter and soften the shallots in it without allowing them to color. Leave to cool. Place the bass strips, bread and shallots on a baking sheet and season with salt, pepper, nutmeg and mustard. Grind twice through the finest blade of the grinder. Push the forcemeat through a fine strainer and beat until it becomes silky. Over ice beat in the cream a spoonful at a time.

Quickly blanch the spinach and basil separately, place immediately in iced water and leave until completely cool. Drain the spinach and place on roasting film. Drain and finely chop the basil leaves. Season the

sea bass fillet to be used whole with salt and pepper, lay over the spinach and, using the film to help you, wrap the spinach around the fish. Stir the diced truffle and basil into the forcemeat. Grease the mold with butter and line with roasting film. Add half the forcemeat and in the center place the bass fillet wrapped in spinach. Cover with the remaining forcemeat. Bang the mold several times on a damp cloth and seal.

Cook for about 35–40 minutes, in a water bath, regulating the oven so that the water temperature does not exceed 176°.

When cool unmold the terrine and cover with a white chaudfroid sauce made with fish broth. Decorate as desired, for example with carrot hearts and pieces of truffle.

Salmon Mold

Tourte de saumon

Pike forcemeat
$\frac{3}{4}$ lb pike fillet
$\frac{1}{2}$ teaspoon butter
$\frac{1}{4}$ cup sliced shallots
1 teaspoon salt
freshly ground white pepper
little nutmeg and English mustard powder
1 large egg white
10 tablespoons flour panada
1$\frac{1}{2}$ cups whipped cream
Salmon forcemeat
5 oz salmon fillet
$\frac{1}{2}$ teaspoon butter
1 thick slice onion
$\frac{1}{2}$ teaspoon salt
freshly ground white pepper
a little nutmeg and English
mustard powder
1 medium egg white
$\frac{1}{4}$ cup flour panada
$\frac{3}{4}$ cup whipped cream
Salmon rolls
$\frac{3}{4}$ lb salmon fillet
salt and freshly ground white pepper

butter for greasing mold
1-quart dome-shaped mold

Prepare the two forcemeats separately.

For the salmon rolls, cut ½ lb of the salmon fillet lengthwise into sheets ¼-inch thick. Place, touching each other, on roasting film, sprinkle with salt and pepper and spread thinly with some of the pike forcemeat. Use the film to help you roll the salmon, tie securely in place and poach for about 10 minutes in the oven in well-seasoned fish broth at 176 . Leave to cool in the broth and chill.

Grease the mold with butter and line with roasting film. Cut the salmon roll into thin slices and line the mold. Add about half the remaining pike forcemeat, cover with the remaining salmon fillet and cover with the rest of the pike forcemeat. Then cover with salmon forcemeat. Bang the mold several times on a damp cloth, seal and cook, in a water bath, for about 60–65 minutes, regulating the oven so that the water temperature does not exceed 176°.

Unmold the salmon mold, cover with a thin layer of light fish aspic and garnish with whirls of cream and pieces of truffle.

Lobster Terrine with Vegetables

Terrine de langouste aux légumes

½ lb lobster meat
1 teaspoon salt
ground white pepper
⅛ teaspoon cayenne
1 egg white, lightly beaten
½ cup flour panada
½ cup light cream
1 cup whipped cream
1 lobster tail, weighing about 12–14 oz
lemon juice
½ cup each cooked and diced celery and carrots
½ cup green peas
butter for greasing mold
1-quart pâté mold

Cut up the lobster meat and sprinkle with salt, pepper and cayenne. Grind twice through the finest blade of the grinder. Over ice beat in the egg white a little at a time. Then sieve the flour panada a little at a time into the forcemeat and mix in. Push the forcemeat through a strainer and work in first the light cream, then the whipped cream a spoonful at a time.

Place the lobster tail on a small wooden board and tie it so that it lies straight. Boil for 5 minutes in water with a little salt, pepper and few drops lemon juice and then leave to stand in the water for 15 minutes. Transfer to the wooden board and leave to

An effective decoration – made from very simple ingredients. Arrange blanched celery leaves and chives over a coating of chaudfroid sauce and cover the whole with fish aspic.

cool, then remove the shell. Fold the diced celery and carrot and the peas into the forcemeat. Grease the mold with butter and line with roasting film. Add half the forcemeat, top with the lobster tail and cover with the remaining forcemeat. Seal the mold.

Cook for about 40 minutes, in a water bath, regulating the oven so that the water temperature does not exceed 176°.

When cool cover the terrine with a white chaudfroid sauce made with fish broth and cream and garnish with celery leaves and chives.

Individual Salmon and Rainbow Trout Terrines

Petites terrines de saumon et truites arc-en-ciel

½ lb salmon fillet, skinned
a little salt, freshly ground white pepper, cayenne and English mustard powder
2 medium egg whites, lightly beaten
⅓ cup flour panada, sieved
1 cup whipped cream
1 tablespoon chopped dill
¾ lb trout fillet, skinned
butter for greasing cups
4 custard cups or small molds, each about 6-oz capacity

Cut the salmon fillet into strips, season with salt, pepper, cayenne and mustard and chill. Grind twice through the finest blade of the grinder, and, over ice, gradually work in the egg whites and flour panada. Push the forcemeat through a strainer and beat in the whipped cream a little at a time. Finally stir

A good gift suggestion. Cook the individual terrines in cups and then garnish decoratively. Add a saucer and side plate to make a most attractive gift.

in the dill. Chill once more.

Sprinkle the trout fillet with salt, and cut to fit the custard cups. Grease the cups well and line with the trout fillets, placing them skin side outermost and leaving no gaps between them. Fill any small gaps with little pieces of fillet. Add the forcemeat and smooth the top. Cook, in a water bath, for 15–18 minutes, regulating the oven so that the water temperature does not exceed 176°.

When cool cover the terrines with a white chaudfroid sauce made with fish broth and garnish with pieces of truffle and slices of carrot.

Snail Pâté

Pâté d'escargots

1 teaspoon butter
⅓ cup sliced shallots
3 slices white bread, crusts removed
½ egg white, lightly beaten
1 tablespoon light cream
¼ lb lean boneless veal
a little salt and ground white pepper
½ cup whipped cream
½ lb canned snails
1 tablespoon each Pernod and brandy
½ cup jellifying veal broth
2 small cloves garlic, crushed
1 teaspoon each chopped fresh thyme
and marjoram
butter for greasing mold
¾ lb pie pastry
1 egg mixed with 2 tablespoons cream
3-cup pâté mold

Melt the butter, soften the shallots in it and leave to cool. Moisten the bread with the egg white and light cream. Cut the veal into strips and place on a baking sheet with the moistened bread and half the softened shallots, and season. Grind twice through the finest blade of the grinder. Push the forcemeat through a fine strainer and beat until smooth and silky. Gradually beat in the whipped cream, chilling well after each stage.

Drain the snails and cut each in half, keeping the liquid to one side. Add the Pernod and brandy to the rest of the shallots, and dilute with the veal broth and snail liquid. Add salt and pepper, the garlic and half the herbs. Reduce to a thick essence, strain, add the snails and leave to cool. Work into the forcemeat with the remaining thyme and marjoram. Grease the mold and line it with pastry. Fill with the snail forcemeat. Fold over the overhanging pastry and top with a sheet of pastry. Cut an opening for the steam, decorate the pâté, brush with egg and cream mixture and insert a funnel.

Bake for about 30 minutes in all, first in a preheated 475° oven for 15 minutes, then lower the temperature to 350°.

Artichoke Pâté

Pâté d'artichauts

5 oz fresh pork fatback
½ lb boneless veal, trimmed
½ lb boneless pork, trimmed
2 tablespoons oil
½ cup diced onion
1¼ cups cream
2 egg whites
salt
1 teaspoon mixed seasoning for
delicate meat forcemeats
1 teaspoon basil
12 canned artichoke hearts
freshly ground white pepper
a little ground ginger
1 cup dry white wine
1½ tablespoons good brandy
½ cup coarsely chopped pistachios
⅔ cup diced cooked tongue
butter for greasing mold
yeast dough made with 4 cups flour
1 beaten egg yolk for glazing
5-cup pâté mold
Madeira or sherry wine aspic to finish

Finely dice and freeze the pork fat. Dice the veal and pork. Heat the oil in a skillet, soften the onion and spread over the meat. Beat ¼ cup of the cream with the egg whites, 1 teaspoon salt, the mixed seasoning and basil and pour over the meat. Cover with foil and leave to stand for a few hours in the refrigerator.

Thoroughly drain the artichoke hearts (you can, of course, use fresh artichokes if preferred), place in a narrow container, sprinkle with salt, pepper and ginger and add the wine and brandy. Marinate for 2–3 hours.

Purée the marinated meat with its other ingredients in a food processor. Use the frozen fat to cool the meat, adding a few cubes to each portion you purée. Beat the forcemeat with a wooden spoon until smooth and silky. Then gradually beat in the remaining cream and increase the seasoning if necessary. Finally fold in the coarsely chopped pistachios and diced tongue.

Grease the mold with butter (an oval mold is best). Roll out about two-thirds of the pastry to about ¼-inch thick and line the mold. Leave ¾ inch overhanging pastry around the edges. Add two-thirds of the forcemeat. Drain the artichokes very well and press them base down into the forcemeat. Cover with the remaining forcemeat. Brush the inside of the pastry rim with egg yolk, roll out the remaining pastry to make a lid, place over the filling and press the edges firmly together. Cut off any excess

Deliciously wrapped in brioche pastry, and decorated with cut-outs the exact shape of the 'leaves' of a globe artichoke, this must be one of the most beautiful and satisfying of vegetable-based pâtés. It would make an elegant centrepiece to a fine but informal buffet table.

pastry and reroll the trimmings. Cut into leaves which look like artichoke leaves, brush the top of the pâté with egg yolk and arrange the leaves over the top to overlap. Cut an opening in the center for the steam, insert a funnel and brush the top of the pâté with egg yolk. Bake in a preheated 425° oven for 55–60 minutes.

When cold fill the pâté with Madeira or sherry wine aspic.

Vegetable Terrine with Goose Liver

Terrine de légumes au foie gras

¾ lb skinless, boneless chicken breast
2 tablespoons butter
½ cup diced shallots
½ cup diced celeriac
4 slices white bread, crusts removed
2 egg whites
1¾ cups cream
salt and freshly ground white pepper
grated rind of ½ lemon
⅛ teaspoon allspice
½ lb fresh artichoke hearts (about
6–10 artichokes)
3 large carrots
5 oz green beans
¾ lb fresh goose liver
¾ cup port wine
2½ oz truffles
¾ lb fresh pork fatback, thinly sliced
1½-quart pâté mold

Dice the chicken breast and place it in a bowl. Heat the butter and soften the diced shallots and celeriac. Spread over the chicken. Cut the bread into small pieces and add to the bowl. Beat the egg whites with ¼ cup of the cream, 1 teaspoon salt, pepper to taste, the lemon rind and allspice and pour over the bread. Cover with foil and leave to stand overnight.

Wash the artichoke hearts thoroughly. Trim the carrots and beans, then blanch the vegetables one after the other in salted water and transfer to iced water.

Season the goose liver (after removing all blood vessels), cover with the port wine and leave to marinate, preferably overnight. Then knead a few times in the marinade. On a large piece of foil place the pieces of liver side by side in a row. Cut the truffle into slices (saving trimmings to go in the forcemeat) and place between the pieces of liver. Shape the liver into a compact roll. Chill thoroughly.

Purée the seasoned chicken with the bread, egg white and cream in a food processor. Over ice, beat the forcemeat until light and fluffy and gradually beat in the

A **vegetable terrine** made of a delicious blend of flavors, but which you can easily vary; for example, replace the vegetables (artichoke hearts, carrots and beans) with various kinds of mushroom: ½ lb open mushrooms, 5 oz chanterelles and 5 oz wild mushrooms. The mushrooms are cut into pieces, braised in butter and sprinkled generously with chopped parsley and a little basil. Cool thoroughly before folding into the forcemeat. This mushroom terrine can be served with a cold chive sauce and a green salad.

remaining cream. Dice the artichoke hearts and truffle trimmings and fold into the forcemeat. Line the mold with the slices of pork fat and add about one-third of the forcemeat. Intersperse the beans and carrot (cut into fingers). Place the goose liver roll along the center of the mold and fill it with the remaining beans, carrots and forcemeat. Cover with fat, seal and cook, in a water bath, for 50–55 minutes, regulating the oven so that the water temperature does not exceed 176°.

Broccoli Terrine

Terrine de brocoli

Broccoli forcemeat
1 lb broccoli, cleaned
2 egg whites
1 teaspoon salt
freshly ground white pepper,
nutmeg and ground ginger
½ cup lightly whipped cream
Celeriac forcemeat
1 lb celeriac, cleaned
2 egg whites
1 teaspoon salt
freshly ground white pepper
⅛ teaspoon garlic salt
½ cup lightly whipped cream

butter for greasing mold
1 cup light chaudfroid sauce
6 oz (about 1½ cups) broccoli florets
aspic to finish

Simmer the broccoli in salted water for 10–12 minutes. Leave to cool and drain thoroughly. Purée in a food processor. Beat the egg whites a little at a time into the purée. Add salt, pepper, nutmeg and ginger and then, over ice, beat in the lightly whipped cream a little at a time.

Quarter the celeriac and cook in salted water until soft. Prepare a celeriac forcemeat as for the broccoli.

Grease the terrine with butter and fill the mold with two alternate layers of broccoli and celeriac forcemeat. Seal the mold.

Cook for about 45 minutes, in a water bath, regulating the oven so that the water temperature does not exceed 176°.

When cool cover the top of the terrine with a layer of chaudfroid sauce. Top with steamed broccoli florets and cover with a light aspic.

Mushroom Terrine à la Maison

Terrine de champignons à la maison

2 tablespoons butter
1 cup sliced shallots
½ lb lean veal sirloin, diced
2 slices white bread, crusts removed

1 egg white
1 cup cream
salt
ground white pepper
⅛ teaspoon each of ground ginger, allspice and mace
1¾ lb mixed mushrooms (flat, field, button, chanterelles), cleaned
3 tablespoons oil

½ clove garlic, finely chopped
1 cup jellifying chicken broth
1 teaspoon dried basil
½ teaspoon dried thyme
½ teaspoon dried sage
½ teaspoon crushed caraway seeds
¼ lb truffles
butter for greasing mold
1-quart pâté mold

Heat 1 tablespoon of the butter, soften half of the sliced shallots in it and spread them over the veal. Cut the bread into small pieces and add to the veal. Beat the egg white into 3 tablespoons of the cream, add ½ teaspoon salt, pepper to taste and the spices and pour over the bread. Cover with foil and leave to stand, preferably overnight.

Cut the larger mushrooms into fairly large pieces and leave small ones whole. Heat the oil in a skillet and add all the mushrooms. Braise the mushrooms for a few minutes, continually shaking the pan, and transfer to a strainer. Keep the mushroom juice to one side. Melt the remaining butter in the skillet, soften the remaining shallots and the garlic, then add the mushroom juice and chicken broth. Add the herbs, caraway and salt and, over a moderate heat, reduce slowly to a thick essence. Strain over the mushrooms through a conical strainer and stir in well. Cover and leave to stand overnight.

Purée the veal, bread, egg white and cream mixture a little at a time in a food processor. Chill thoroughly, then beat until light and fluffy. Gradually beat in the rest of the cream until the forcemeat is smooth and silky. Fold the marinated mushroom mixture and chopped truffles into the forcemeat. Grease the mold with butter and fill with the forcemeat. Shake the mold to make sure there are no air gaps in the forcemeat. Seal the mold and cook, in a water bath, for 45–50 minutes, regulating the oven so that the water temperature does not exceed 176°.

A vegetable terrine, very light in consistency, which when cooked is just firm enough to cut. It can also be served hot (without the chaudfroid sauce of course) with parsley or chive sauce.

Individual Mushroom Terrines

Petites terrines de champignons de couche

A veal forcemeat, as given in the recipe for Mushroom Terrine à la Maison goes particularly well with the flavor of mushrooms. Or you can use the same quantity of a fine chicken forcemeat.

2 tablespoons butter
$\frac{1}{2}$ cup finely diced shallots
$\frac{3}{4}$ lb mushrooms, diced
about $\frac{1}{2}$ teaspoon salt
freshly ground white pepper
$\frac{1}{8}$ teaspoon mace
$\frac{1}{8}$ teaspoon ground ginger
2 tablespoons chopped fresh herbs (parsley, basil, rosemary)
1 lb veal or chicken forcemeat
butter for greasing molds
6–8 $\frac{2}{3}$–$\frac{3}{4}$ cup molds
chaudfroid sauce to finish

The strongly flavored chaudfroid sauce with which the terrine is covered provides a contrast in flavor with the delicately flavored stuffing. The decoration is made with cut-outs of hard-cooked egg and braised carrot. The stems are thin sprigs of chives.

Heat the butter in a skillet, soften the shallots in it and add the mushrooms. Sauté the mushrooms for 3–4 minutes, shaking the pan continuously. Sprinkle with salt, pepper, spices and herbs, stir in and leave to cool. Mix into the forcemeat. Grease the molds lightly with butter, fill with forcemeat and smooth the tops. Cook, in a water bath, for 18–20 minutes, regulating the oven so that the water temperature does not exceed 176°.

Unmold the cold terrines onto a wire rack and cover with white or green chaudfroid sauce.

Chanterelle Terrine

Terrine de chanterelles

1 tablespoon butter
2 shallots, sliced
3 thin slices white bread, crusts removed
½ egg white, lightly beaten
2 tablespoons light cream
5 oz lean boneless veal
little salt and ground white pepper
¾ cup whipped cream
1½ lb fresh, whole, small chanterelles
3 tablespoons oil
⅓ cup diced shallots
¾ cup jellifying veal broth
1 teaspoon chopped caraway seeds
2 tablespoons chopped parsley
butter for greasing mold
1-quart pâté mold
port wine aspic to finish

Melt 2 teaspoons of the butter, glaze the sliced shallots in it and leave to cool. Moisten the bread with the egg white and cream. Cut the veal into strips and place on a baking sheet with the moistened bread and shallots. Season with salt and pepper. Grind twice through the finest blade of the grinder. Push the forcemeat through a fine strainer and beat until smooth and silky. Gradually add the whipped cream and beat in thoroughly. Chill thoroughly after each stage.

Braise the chanterelles in the oil and drain well. Soften the diced shallots in the remaining butter and add the veal broth. Add the caraway and reduce to a thick essence. Push through a strainer, add the drained chanterelles and simmer for a few moments. Leave to cool and then stir into the forcemeat with the parsley. Grease the mold with butter, add the forcemeat and bang several times on a damp cloth. Seal and cook, in a water bath, for about 35 minutes, regulating the oven so that the water temperatures does not exceed 176°.

When cool cover the terrine with an aspic made with port wine and finely chopped parsley.

Mushroom Terrine

Terrine de cèpes

1 tablespoon butter
⅓ cup sliced shallots
3 slices white bread, crusts removed
½ egg white, lightly beaten
1 tablespoon light cream
¼ lb lean boneless veal
little salt and ground white pepper
½ cup whipped cream
1 lb fresh flat mushrooms, sliced
2 tablespoons oil
⅓ cup diced shallots
¾ cup jellifying veal broth
1 teaspoon crushed caraway seeds
1 clove garlic, crushed
1 tablespoon finely chopped chives
butter for greasing mold
3-cup pâté mold
Madeira wine aspic to finish

Melt 1 teaspoon of the butter, soften the sliced shallots and leave to cool. Moisten the bread with the egg white and cream. Cut the veal into strips and place on a baking sheet with the moistened bread and shallots. Season with salt and pepper. Cover with foil and chill. Grind twice through the finest blade of the grinder. Push through a strainer and beat until smooth and silky. Gradually beat in the whipped cream.

Braise the mushrooms in the oil and drain well. Soften the diced shallots in the remaining butter, add the jellifying veal broth, caraway and garlic and reduce to a thick liquid. Push through a strainer. Add the mushrooms and simmer for a few minutes. Leave to cool then fold into the forcemeat with the chives. Grease the mold with butter, fill with the mushroom forcemeat, bang the mold several times on a damp cloth and seal.

Cook for about 30 minutes, in a water bath, regulating the oven so that the water temperature does not exceed 176°.

When cold cover the terrine with Madeira wine aspic.

Aspic Jellies and Sauces

Many galantines, terrines or other types of cold pies and pâtés would be unthinkable without aspic jellies or chaudfroid sauces. These may be the crystal-clear cubes of aspic, served on the plate with a slice of pâté, or a fine ivory-colored coating of chaudfroid sauce on a duck galantine. Both increase the enjoyment of the dish tremendously. They improve the taste by bringing out the flavor of the pâté and visually they set off a real culinary masterpiece. They also have a very practical effect. Aspic jellies and sauce coverings help the pâté keep, preserving its freshness longer.

Whether your aim is decoration or freshness, you should pay a lot of attention to your aspics and sauces. They can complement a pâté or terrine admirably and their flavor will bring out the flavor of the pâté, even though they may be rather time-consuming to make. The bones or carcass of the meat used for the pâté are boiled to make a broth, thus you will use a game broth with a venison pie or chicken broth for a poultry galantine. This well-seasoned broth forms the basis of an aspic or chaudfroid sauce. There should be no foreign taste to disturb the unity of the pâté when you fill up a pie with aspic or cover a galantine.

Crystal-clear perfection

How long aspic jellies have been used in pâté-making cannot be ascertained with any certainty. But aspic as a separate dish was not unknown to the Romans. Their aspic must have been rather cloudy for the method of clarifying aspic with egg white was not discovered until La Varenne came along. At least it was he who published the method for the first time in his book *Le Cuisinier françois*. An auspicious time for the art of cookery, at least for cold cooking. Of course a cloudy aspic of unclarified broth tastes just as good, but just imagine an aspic pâté with its brightly colored vegetables without its clear, shining coating. Not to mention the various aspic jellies which are served in cubes with pâté and melt tenderly on the tongue.

In the old days considerable time was spent making a form of gelatin from gristle and bones, particularly calf's feet which had to be boiled for hours on end. One highly flavored type of aspic, known in Bavaria as *Knöcherlsulz*, is still made in this way. But now this long process can be eliminated for good quality gelatin is available in powder form and has a completely neutral taste. It is a natural product, consisting of soluble proteins, animal proteins, treated in a certain way. But other modern aids, in the shape of canned broths, create more problems. High quality instant gelatins or aspic powders are very practical and can be used quite well with a simple, strongly-flavored country-style terrine. But if you are making a gourmet game terrine with truffles, with its expensive ingredients and time-consuming preparation, you cannot risk spoiling it by using anything other than a homemade aspic, preferably made with the original broth.

Chaudfroid – first warm, then cold

Louis Alexandre Berthier, Marshall of France, was eating a chicken fricassée, but was called away from the table for a considerable length of time. He returned to find the fricassée cold and congealed. Louis was angry, but continued his meal – and discovered how good the food tasted cold. From that time on this dish, which the Marshall named *Chaudfroid* was never missing from his banquet table. In English the term means something like "First hot, then cold."

The term has come to be used in cooking for any dish which is prepared hot but intended to be eaten cold. With terrines and galantines we have the chaudfroid sauces, covering sauces. They are not transparent like aspics and completely mask the beautiful terrine or galantine, so a variety of colors have been introduced for these coatings. A chaudfroid sauce made from a light broth and white sauce, or as made more frequently today from light broth and reduced cream, is white in color. This gives a particularly beautiful cream-colored sauce. It can, however, be made shades of green, pink or red by adding spinach, lobster roe or tomato paste. To make a brown chaudfroid sauce, for demiglaces, jellifying beef broth is used. This concentrated broth also guarantees a concentrated flavor. So a good chaudfroid sauce should not be considered merely as a decorative element which helps preserve freshness, to be left on the side of the plate like a sausage skin. Its flavor should not compete with that of the terrine, but its flavor and seasoning should complement that of the terrine. They should be related in taste. If you make a broth specially for the sauce this is no problem, a fish broth for a fish terrine, a poultry broth for a duck terrine, for example. But as with aspic jellies, these sauces can also be flavored with wine or spirits to give highly satisfactory results.

Chaudfroid sauces and aspics are often used together to decorate a terrine or galantine, as, for example, with a terrine covered in white chaudfroid sauce: this forms an excellent base for a decoration of herbs, truffles or vegetables. The decoration is then covered with a layer of crystal-clear aspic. This prevents it from drying out, preserves its color and prevents it being disturbed when the terrine is sliced.

93

Aspic jelly, a shimmering complement to pâtés and terrines

The basis is always a meat or fish broth, preferably made with the carcass or bones from the meat used in the pâté. Veal bones can be added to the broth for they contain a lot of natural gelatin which has a relatively neutral taste. This broth is then clarified before gelatin is added to make an aspic.

It is always clarified with egg white. Egg white is used in the following recipe and in the alternative method on the next page. Beef is also used in this recipe as a clarifying agent which gives a good flavor without detracting from the natural flavor of the broth.

Aspic jelly, clarified with egg white

This is a basic recipe which provides for a wide range of variations. You can alter the seasoning to suit the recipe. Or the wine. Use Madeira and port, for example, for meat or poultry broth, a sparkling, dry Riesling, Chablis or Champagne for a fine fish broth. But only good quality ingredients should be used. This is particularly true of the gelatin. Only good quality aspic powder or, better still, powdered gelatin will be neutral in flavor.

½ cup egg white,
beaten until soft peaks form
½ cup finely diced onion
½ cup finely diced leeks
½ cup finely diced celeriac
few stems of parsley
1 teaspoon salt
8 white peppercorns
1 piece bay leaf
1 quart light broth (meat, poultry or fish, depending on the type of pâté)
½ cup white wine or 3 tablespoons wine vinegar
3 envelopes aspic powder or unflavored gelatin

1 **Tip the finely diced vegetables** and seasonings into the egg white. The egg white should have been beaten until soft peaks formed. Work the ingredients in with your hand or a wooden spoon.

2 **Tip the egg white and vegetable mixture into the broth.** The broth should be cold at this stage. Place over the highest possible heat and whisk continuously with a wire whisk.

3 **Beat firmly with the whisk,** scraping around the bottom of the pan to prevent the egg white solidifying. It is easier if you use a spatula for this. Bring to a boil and reduce the heat.

4 **The egg white separates** and floats on the surface. Add the white wine or vinegar. Simmer the broth very gently for 40–50 minutes without allowing it to boil. This gives the broth time to absorb all the flavor from the vegetables and seasonings.

6 **Add the gelatin to the clarified broth.** If the broth has become too cool during filtering, reheat to allow the gelatin to be completely dissolved.

5 **The broth is clarified.** You can see from looking at the pan that the egg white has absorbed even the tiniest impurities, leaving the broth completely clear. Line a conical strainer with filter paper and strain the hot broth. An alternative method is shown on the next page. A sheet of cheesecloth is attached to the legs of an upturned kitchen stool.

7 **A crystal-clear aspic of exactly the right consistency,** firm enough to cut but still tender. Three envelopes aspic powder or gelatin to 1 quart broth is about the average requirement. This quantity will keep the aspic firm at normal room temperature.

Aspic jelly clarified with egg white and beef

A method of preparation which gives a particularly fine result, a real "gourmet" aspic. The addition of beef to the vegetables, together with egg white, guarantees superb quality. Shank of beef is particularly good as it contains a lot of gelatin. But it must be absolutely free from fat. It is ground through the largest blade of the grinder or finely chopped. It is important to beat the meat vigorously into the egg white and vegetables. Use a strong wooden spoon, or better still, work it in thoroughly by hand.

5 oz clarifying meat (fat-free shank of beef)
¼ cup diced carrots
¼ cup diced leeks
¼ cup diced celeriac
¼ cup diced onion
1 or 2 small tomatoes
1 clove garlic
10 white peppercorns
1 teaspoon salt
1 small piece bay leaf
3 large egg whites
1 quart light broth
(game, poultry or meat)
½ cup white wine
3 envelopes aspic powder or unflavored gelatin

The broth must be completely free from fat. If you allow the broth to become cold the fat will solidify and is easy to remove. Remove any tiny particles from the surface with a piece of filter paper.

1 **Prepare the ingredients.** Grind the beef through the largest blade of the grinder. Dice the vegetables and peel the tomatoes. Crush the garlic and lightly crush the peppercorns.

2 **Mix the meat and vegetables together** and add the salt, bay leaf and egg whites. Work the ingredients thoroughly together with a wooden spoon or, better still, by hand, so that all the ingredients bind as well as possible.

3 **Add the broth.** Place the pan on the heat and add the broth, from which you have carefully removed all fat. Turn up the heat to the highest setting and boil for a few minutes.

4 **Stir the broth.** A spatula is best for this for its flat shape makes for extra contact with the bottom of the pan and prevents the egg white sticking before it separates. Then simmer gently for 40 minutes without allowing to boil.

5 **The egg white has separated** and has taken even the smallest impurities out of the broth. Add the white wine and stir in very gently.

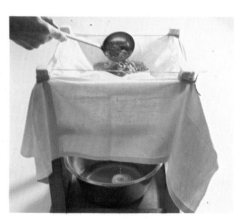

6 **Filter the broth through a sheet of cheesecloth.** Attach the cheesecloth to the feet of a stool. Line with filter paper, place a bowl under the cloth and pour all the contents of the pan into the cloth. Warm the broth and dissolve the gelatin in it.

Coating with warm aspic, which the experts call "glazing." A thin layer of suitably flavored aspic jelly makes slices of pie or pâté look as if they have been prepared individually, giving an appetizing shine and bringing out the color. Brush on the aspic gently with a wide brush. To glaze delicate decorations sprinkle on the aspic with the brush.

Flavoring with wine

By far the most popular are the Southern wines Madeira and port. But sherry, tokay and full-bodied white wines, such as a Muscatel, give a good flavor.

1 cup Madeira to 1 quart broth is about the average requirement, but you should always adjust the amount of wine to suit the type of pâté you are making. It is advisable to test by adding a small amount first, for many wines can make the broth cloudy.

Aspic temperature
Regardless of whether you are filling a pie or covering a galantine, the correct temperature of the aspic jelly is always important. It should be used just before it reaches setting point, while still slightly fluid, but allowing it to set as quickly as possible once used. There is a very simple and reliable method of checking the temperature.

Pour a little liquid aspic into a bowl and keep the remaining warm aspic to hand. Place the bowl in iced water and stir gently with a small slotted spoon or pastry brush. Vigorous stirring would cause bubbles which would not look very good when poured over a terrine. Before setting you can see clearly that the aspic becomes slightly thick. Remove from the water at once and use. This ideal temperature period is quite short. If the aspic in the bowl begins to set, add a little of the warm aspic and if necessary cool again until you have the right consistency.

Chaudfroid, a coating sauce for cold dishes

Unlike a transparent aspic, this aspic-based sauce is an opaque covering for terrines and galantines. It encloses the pâté, protecting it from the air and keeping it fresh, as well as setting off its flavor. Last but by no means least it is an effective form of decoration, whose color can be easily varied.

Light chaudfroid sauce was once, and still is today to a lesser extent, made with a velouté, i.e. a white *roux*-based sauce. This can taste very good but tends to be rather sticky. A more modern method is to bind with gelatin, which, when used with reduced cream, is light and airy. A good compromise is to use an aspic sauce with a very little starch for binding and some gelatin. This

combines the advantages of aspic with the smoothness of a flour-based sauce.

The basic recipe for the light sauce allows an almost limitless color variation. Spinach, tomato paste, saffron or lobster roe can be used for coloring, but bear in mind that the flavor of the coloring agent must harmonize with the flavor of the dish. As with aspic, always use a suitably flavored broth.

For the brown chaudfroid no cream is used. Here the fat-free, brown, jellifying chicken, game or veal essence provides the color. The sauce is thus semi-transparent, but particularly strong in flavor. It is generally used with strongly flavored terrines or to contrast with a particularly delicately flavored pâté. Thus a brown chaudfroid sauce can give the final touch to a delicately flavored veal terrine.

Stir the chaudfroid sauce until cold. Place half the sauce in a bowl in iced water and stir very gently with a ladle to avoid bubbles. If it becomes too firm it can be diluted with a little of the warm sauce – but only as long as it has no lumps. In that case the sauce must be completely melted again.

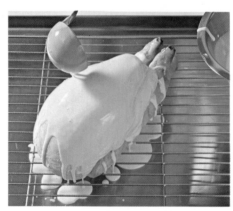

The exact temperature is important. The sauce should begin to set (begin to thicken), then it is ready to use. With galantines in particular make sure that the sauce is completely fat-free, otherwise the sauce will separate. Wipe the skin of the galantine dry with paper towels.

Natural Chaudfroid

1½ quarts fat-free light veal,
poultry or fish broth
2½ cups light cream
5 tablespoons cornstarch
1 tablespoon dry white wine
2 envelopes unflavored gelatin
salt and freshly ground white pepper

These ingredients give 1 quart chaudfroid
sauce

Reduce the broth over a moderate heat to about 2½ cups. Reduce the cream by half (1¼ cups) and pass through a fine strainer into the broth. Dissolve the cornstarch in the white wine and use to bind the sauce. Bring to a boil once, remove from the heat and stir in the gelatin until dissolved. Put the sauce once more through a fine strainer or, better still, through cheesecloth and season. The seasoning will depend on the type of galantine or terrine to be covered.

The basic flavor of the chaudfroid can be varied by using a reduced mushroom, asparagus or other suitable broth.

Chaudfroid sauce and aspic jelly combined for a duck terrine. The dish is lined with hot chaudfroid. The pâté is returned to the dish after removing the fat layer and covered with chaudfroid. This coating is decorated and covered with a light aspic jelly.

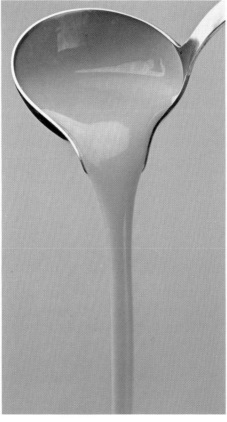

Red Chaudfroid

1½ quarts fat-free light veal,
poultry or fish broth
3½ tablespoons cornstarch
1 tablespoon water
½ teaspoon sweet paprika
1 tablespoon light broth
½ cup tomato paste
2½ cups light cream
2 envelopes unflavored gelatin
salt, sugar, white pepper and cayenne

These ingredients make 1 quart sauce

Reduce the broth over a moderate heat to
about 3 cups. Dissolve the cornstarch in the
water and use to bind the broth. Stir the
paprika into 1 tablespoon broth and stir
thoroughly into the sauce with the tomato
paste. Boil through once. Reduce the cream
to 1¼ cups and sieve into the broth through a
hair strainer. Bring back to a boil, remove
from the heat and stir in the gelatin until
dissolved. Sieve again and season.

Green Chaudfroid

¾ lb fresh bulk spinach
1½ quarts fat-free light veal,
poultry or fish broth
2½ cups light cream
5 tablespoons cornstarch
1 tablespoon water
3 envelopes unflavored gelatin
salt and white pepper

These ingredients make 1 quart sauce

Mince the spinach leaves, squeeze in a cloth
and catch the juice in a bowl. Heat the juice
slowly in a saucepan, stirring continuously.
Any bits of leaf which rise to the surface
should be removed with a small fine
strainer. Then strain through a hair strainer.
Reduce the broth over a moderate heat to
about 3 cups. Reduce the cream by half and
strain into the broth. Dissolve the cornstarch in the water and bind the sauce. Bring
to a boil once, remove from the heat and stir
in the gelatin until dissolved. Stir in the
spinach juice, sieve the sauce again and
season.

Brown Chaudfroid

1½ quarts fat-free, highly jellifying veal,
game or poultry broth
1½ tablespoons cornstarch
3 tablespoons sherry or Madeira wine
2 envelopes unflavored gelatin
salt and white pepper

These ingredients make 1 quart sauce

Reduce the broth over a moderate heat to 1
quart, skimming the top continuously and
pass through a hair strainer. Dissolve the
cornstarch in the sherry or Madeira and
bind the broth. Bring to a boil once, remove
from the heat and stir in the gelatin until
dissolved. Strain again and season.

The brown chaudfroid contains no cream
and remains semi-transparent.

Liver Pâtés and Terrines

Liver pâtés are a culinary delicacy, but goose liver pie or goose liver terrine, blasphemously called pâté, is the jewel of these delicacies. As the following chapter deals with liver pâtés in general, with special attention obviously given to goose liver pâtés, we must first look at the history of liver pâté in general. First of all we discover that at all periods of history man has been in the habit of fattening animals which were intended for eating purposes. This was equally true of poultry, pigs or other domestic animals. This was not so much intended to produce better meat, as to produce bigger, tenderer, juicier liver. A favorite animal, and possibly the first domestic animal, was the goose, which was domesticated in ancient times. "The birds of Arabia, anointed with myrrh, flying over Egypt like clouds." Migratory birds in fact. Geese were cooked on glowing embers, and it was not long before they were beginning to be fattened. Sculptured reliefs like the one in the illustration offer a striking example of this. Geese were portrayed on frescoes, and also on grave paintings, usually in scenes where they were being force-fed.

Our illustration shows a reproduction from the grave paintings of a high Egyptian official called Ti, who is remembered as Pharoah's only friend. It is from a period 2,500 years before Christ and clearly shows that force-feeding of geese was by no means a French invention and could certainly not have been discovered by the French several centuries later.

The ancient Romans later perfected the art of feeding pigs on huge quantities of figs to increase the size of the liver which was eaten roasted, but also used to make pâtés. When man finally discovered that cranes, pheasants, storks and peacocks were quite good to eat, they were also force-fed. They were kept in so-called *ornithos*. They were fed principally on noodles, barley bread and masticated wheat bread, but geese were specially fed on figs. As early as Cato's time (234–149 BC) his *De agri cultura* contains advice on force-feeding geese. The drive for increased sensual satisfaction has been present in every age.

Then, in the second half of the eighteenth century, pâté de foie gras was discovered in a most spectacular way. It is thought to have been discovered in 1762 (but many historians give other dates) by Jean-Pierre Clause, cook to the governor of Alsace, Marshall de Contades. Anyone who knows anything of the customs of the time will not be surprised that the cook dedicated the dish to his master, calling it initially Pâté à la Contades. It is an established fact that this was a pâté encased in pastry, without truffles. Thus it was similar to goose liver pâté cooked in brioche or pie pastry, and which is one of the noblest dishes known to us. For this pâté, whose popularity naturally spread at lightning speed, tradition demanded that you use the livers of geese fattened in Alsace. One of the most select delights of the art of cooking had been born.

One may regret it or not, but for the normal consumer, or to put it better, for the gourmet with a small budget, a goose liver will not be beyond his means, but is nevertheless a considerable investment.

But liver pâtés don't necessarily have to be goose liver pâtés: you can make excellent pâtés with the liver of other birds. A fattened duck's liver is second in taste only to goose liver, but due to increased demand they have become almost as expensive. But turkey or chicken liver, mixed with a good quantity of pork or poultry, make excellent forcemeats. And livers of this kind, in direct contrast with fattened livers, are not exactly variety meat products but are extremely inexpensive. They can never replace the fattened liver for they have not received the same special treatment and their naturally much stronger flavor makes them unsuitable for pure liver stuffings, but as a flavoring ingredient in a forcemeat, well-seasoned and maybe marinated, they are certainly worthy of inclusion and produce their full aroma.

Amid the prestige attributed to foie gras, the best of the pâtés, those made with pork or veal liver have gone almost unnoticed. These are the most popular types of pâté and they include wonderful, melting forcemeats, delicately seasoned and marinated, with truffles or other fine ingredients. A calf's liver pâté made with high quality, fresh ingredients can impress even the most spoiled gourmet.

Goose liver, homemade or bought?

This is a question you never need ask, not in this book at least. Inevitably, bought products can never have the same flavor as something freshly made, and this is especially true of a gourmet dish such as goose liver. Anyone who has made a terrine with a good liver and has tasted the uncooked liver after it has marinated for 24 hours, must have asked themselves why on earth it has to be cooked, for they taste excellent even uncooked. A goose liver terrine is merely poached very gently at 176° and remains a delicacy of the first rank. But the problem is that the consumer seldom has the chance to compare. For the average man goose liver means bought goose liver, either semi or fully preserved in earthenware dishes or cans which line the shelves of our gourmet shops. Unlike France, goose liver terrines are seldom sold here in the piece for slicing. So a good tip, if you want goose liver, is to make sure you buy it fresh or, better still, make it yourself.

It is certainly not difficult to make goose liver pâté. The method of preparation presents no problems at all. But where in this country can you find a market stall, as you can in France, which simply sells goose livers, as ours sell vegetables. And even if you could find somewhere to buy it who

Even for French housewives goose livers, like these in Périgueux market, are not cheap. So you must check very carefully for quality and look for a liver of the right color and the required consistency.

Best quality geese are a must for Monsieur Grimand, but they are not difficult to come by with the quantities available in Gascony. He makes huge quantities of goose liver terrines. One of his best products is his pâté de foie gras *en brioche.*

Bought or freshly made goose liver pâté? For beginners it is not easy to tell the difference, for both homemade and bought blocks of liver pâté can be the same shape. It is only when you taste it that you can tell the difference. One sure way to success for the gourmet: buy a fresh goose liver and make your own pâté.

would be capable of judging its quality? This needs a lot of experience which here only top chefs possess (and they also know how to get hold of fresh goose liver). There are several different opinions concerning goose liver. There are experts who will not buy extremely large, light-colored liver – the less fat the liver contains the lighter it is in color. They prefer a yellow to amber color. But you can't go on color alone for you never know what the goose may have been fed on. And the color of the food affects the color of the liver. Other signs which experienced pâté chefs look for are: the liver should give slightly under thumb pressure and the depression remain visible. The two sides should also separate easily, they should be firm and should not spring back together like rubber. Fattened geese weigh 13–18 pounds with livers weighing $1\frac{1}{2}$–$2\frac{1}{4}$ pounds.

In Gascony and Périgord it is mainly gray Gascony geese which are used for goose liver. In Alsace they use white geese, and also in Poland and Hungary. It is only in Gascony that goose liver pâté makers are self-sufficient and use their own products. Périgord and Alsace import a lot of liver from the Eastern Bloc and Israel. It is interesting to note that long ago Marx Rumpolt was using liver from Bohemia. In his cookbook of 1587 he writes, "I had a goose liver, fattened by Bohemian Jews, which weighed just over three pounds. This can also be made into a purée."

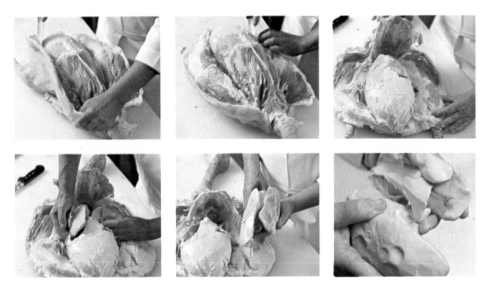

To remove a goose liver requires great care in cutting open the goose. Cut from the neck along the breast and cut the breast meat off the rib cage. Lift off the carcass to leave the liver exposed, embedded in fat. Lift out carefully. It separates very easily from the fat and can then be tested for quality. Thumb pressure should leave a lasting depression and the two sections of the liver should be firm and pull apart easily without springing back together like rubber.

Confit, when the goose is merely a by-product

Confit, a specialty of southwest France, is often served in this area where geese are reared for their livers. Confit is a traditional dish found throughout France. It can also be made with turkey or duck, but is best when made with goose as this is particularly rich in fat which is an essential part of *Confit d'oie*. So as to use all the goose, as well as the liver, goose liver manufacturers also make *Confit*.

Pieces of goose simmer in a generous amount of goose fat over a low heat until cooked and juicy.

Confit d'oie

Cut up the goose. Add $2\frac{1}{2}$ tablespoons salt per 2 pounds meat. Cover and leave to stand for 24 hours in the refrigerator. Rub the pieces of goose. Warm a generous quantity of goose fat until lukewarm, but not completely melted. Add the pieces of goose so that they are covered by fat. Simmer over a low heat. Add 1 unpeeled garlic clove, 5 cloves and 5 peppercorns for each 2 pounds goose fat. Cook for up to 3 hours, stirring frequently. Prick the meat with a trussing needle. If it is soft and gives off clear juice, lift out of the fat with a slotted spoon. Remove bones if desired. Line an earthenware pot with fat, fill with the pieces of goose and cover with goose fat. Leave to stand in a cool place for 2 days. Fill the pot with hot goose fat. Leave to set. Then add a layer of lard. Cover with parchment paper and press down. Seal with parchment paper. Serve cold or rewarmed.

Home-made confit. French housewives always store it in earthenware pots. Shops sell it in glass bottles.

Goose liver terrine

Terrine de foie gras

It is interesting to note that foie gras, as it is called in the French-speaking countries, means fattened goose liver. (Fattened duck's liver is called foie gras de canard.) And it has been traditional to fatten geese for at least 150 years in France. Even before farmers in Gascony and Périgord began doing it, fattening of geese was an organized industry in Strasburg. Later they began fattening ducks too to produce fattened duck's liver. At one time this was because of

A foie gras specialist par excellence! M. Jean Legrand is a master chef in the classic tradition. For him, the quality of the goose liver he meticulously chooses to make his masterpiece is of paramount importance. Crucial, too, is the temperature of the water bath in which he cooks the terrine – it must not exceed 176°.

their lower price. But today they cost almost as much as goose livers, although experts claim they are of inferior quality. And they are certainly right in that goose liver has the better flavor.

One is quite justified in describing pâté de foie gras as the most luxurious of all pâtés, providing the ingredients are of top quality. This is what basically guarantees the ideal ratio of protein to fat in the liver, a ratio which can only be achieved by force-feeding. It is surprising how easy it is to make such an expensive, luxury pâté. The series of photographs below illustrate the traditional method. Here the terrine is cooked in the oven, in a water bath. But many of these methods have now disappeared. Not only in industry, but famous chefs, too, cook goose liver pâté by the quick method, wrapped in foil. Or they are cooked in steamers which work like pressure cookers. There is disagreement about the resulting flavor, but we believe that traditional methods give better results. No matter how much one likes exact recipes, no precise quantities can be given for terrine de foie gras, the reason being that quantities depend on the weight of the goose liver and it is not possible to buy these by the ounce. A liver of about 1¾ pounds – a medium-sized liver – is just right for a mold which holds 1 quart. In the following recipe there are no seasonings or alcohol – except for the pepper, salt, port wine and dash of brandy used in the marinade. You are free to decide what additional seasoning you prefer. For every 1 pound liver you can add ½ teaspoon of the mixed seasoning for delicate meat forcemeat (page 22). Or add a little allspice. You can also add extra flavor to the marinade with Armagnac. But the alcohol content should not be too high or it can give the liver a strong flavor.

1 fattened goose liver, weighing about 1¾ lb
1 teaspoon salt
freshly ground white pepper
1 cup port wine
dash of brandy
1-quart pâté mold
port wine aspic to finish

This terrine can also include truffles. For this about ¼ lb boiled black truffles are placed in a row in the center of the mold, so that they come in the center of each slice when the pâté is cut.

Cooking time is 35–40 minutes, in a water bath, with water at 176°. As with any terrine, you will have to check the water temperature because – despite the claims made by manufacturers – oven temperatures often vary.

Alternatively you can use duck liver for this recipe and for any recipe which uses goose liver.

1 **Break up the goose liver.** Break each section into several pieces and where necessary carefully remove any skin or blood vessels. Work carefully, avoiding damaging the liver more than necessary.

2 **Knead the carefully trimmed liver until soft.** Opinions on whether or not you should knead the liver differ considerably. Many people only knead the firm ends where the liver comes to a point. But our chef kneads the whole liver until soft.

3 **Season the liver with salt and pepper.** If you want to add additional seasonings you can do so. But a good goose liver has so much natural flavor that salt and freshly ground pepper are sufficient.

4 **Marinate the liver.** Transfer the liver to a bowl and add the port wine. A dash of brandy will add extra flavor. Old Armagnac is used for this in Gascony.

5 **Knead in the marinade.** Work the liver gently with your fingers to prevent breaking it up more than necessary. Cover with foil and leave in a cool place to marinate for 24 hours.

6 **Fill the terrine.** Arrange the pieces in the mold one at a time. Press down lightly to ensure that there are as few air gaps as possible between them. This will give a homogenous terrine when cooked.

7 **Flatten the top,** i.e. even out the surface with your hands to get rid of any gaps. You can gently press down the liver again with your hands.

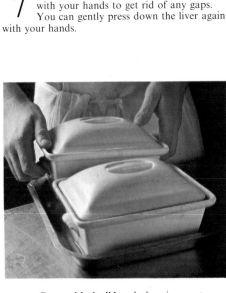

8 **Cover with the lid** and place in a water bath in the preheated oven. The water temperature should be exactly 176° (about 275° oven temperature). Check with a thermometer where possible.

9 **Leave the cooked liver terrine to stand for at least a day** before unmolding. If any fat has come out of the terrine during cooking it can be removed when you unmold it. Then return the pâté de foie gras to the mold and cover with a thin layer of port wine aspic. This is primarily a protective layer which prevents the terrine drying out, but it also adds to the flavor, providing of course the flavor of the aspic goes with the flavor of the terrine.

Goose Liver in Brioche Pastry

Foie gras en brioche

Illustrated on page 100
1 goose liver (weighing about 1¾ lb)
¼ oz pâté salt (made with mixed seasoning
for delicate forcemeat)
½ teaspoon ground white pepper
1 cup port wine
1½ tablespoons Armagnac
10 × 5 inch loaf pan
port wine aspic to finish

Brioche pastry
4 cups flour
2 (.6 oz) cakes compressed yeast
¾ cup milk
10 tablespoons butter
2 eggs · 1 teaspoon salt
½ teaspoon sugar
beaten egg yolk for glazing

Carefully remove all skin and ducts from
the goose liver. Season the liver and any
pieces which have come away when cleaning
the liver with the pâté salt and pepper. Place
in a bowl and add the port wine and
Armagnac. Cover with foil and leave to

marinate in the refrigerator for 24 hours.
The liver is shaped to give it a good, solid
shape in the brioche. The best way to do this
is to use a loaf pan slightly smaller (to allow
for the thickness of the pastry) than the pan
you use to cook the brioche. Remove the
liver from the marinade and place in a
strainer. Boil the marinade, reduce to about
2–3 tablespoons and leave to cool. Press half
the liver into the pan, add the reduced
marinade and then the remaining liver.
Unmold from the pan when ready to place
in the brioche.

Sift the flour into a bowl. Stir the yeast
into the lukewarm milk until it dissolves.
Melt the butter, leave to cool and stir in the
eggs, salt and sugar. Add the dissolved yeast
and butter mixture to the flour and work in
to give a smooth, dry dough. If it is too firm
add a little more milk. Leave the dough to
rise for 30 minutes at room temperature.
Roll out to a sheet about 24 × 16 inches.
Place in the loaf pan so that it overhangs the
pan evenly all around. Add the pre-shaped
goose liver, brush the pastry edges with egg
yolk, fold the dough over the filling and
press down firmly to enclose the liver
completely. Cut a cross in the top with a
sharp knife. Make two openings and insert
two funnels. With yeast dough you should

not use foil or parchment paper, for yeast
dough expands during baking and could
easily squash funnels of this type; two small
round metal cutters are ideal. Leave the pâté
to rise for a further 20–30 minutes at room
temperature (on no account should it be
allowed to become warmer than room
temperature). It should almost double in
volume. Then brush the top with egg yolk
and bake for 45–55 minutes in the oven
preheated to 400°. When completely cool
(leave to cool overnight if possible) fill the
brioche with port wine aspic.

Chicken Liver Terrine

Terrine de foies de volaille

This recipe is suitable not only for chicken
liver, but also for turkey liver or unfattened
duck or goose liver. The terrine is equally
good in a pasta shell. It can include various
pieces of meat, e.g. chicken breasts sealed in
oil, or can be varied by adding diced truffles,
pistachios, mushrooms or calf's liver marinated in Armagnac.

½ lb chicken livers
5 oz pork liver
¾ lb piece lean boneless pork
¾ lb piece fresh pork fatback
grated rind of ½ orange
2 teaspoons sweet paprika
½ teaspoon bottled green peppercorns,
crushed
⅛ teaspoon each ginger and allspice
1 teaspoon basil
½ teaspoon thyme
½ teaspoon rosemary
1 bay leaf
1½ tablespoons Armagnac
3 thin slices white bread, crusts removed
½ cup diced shallots
1 clove garlic, crushed
1 egg white
¼ cup light cream
2 teaspoons salt
¾ lb fresh pork fatback, thinly sliced
5-cup pâté mold

Remove any skin and blood vessels from the
livers. This should leave about ¾ pound
liver. Cut the liver, pork and pork fat into
strips. Arrange in layers in a shallow dish
and sprinkle on the orange rind, paprika,
peppercorns, ginger, allspice, herbs and
Armagnac. Arrange the white bread over
the meat. Sprinkle the shallots and garlic
over the bread. Beat the egg white and
cream together and pour over the ingredients in the bowl. Cover with foil and leave
to stand in the refrigerator for at least 3–4
hours, but preferably overnight.

Chicken liver forcemeat, a blending of simple
ingredients flavored with Armagnac. If you do
have them to hand, other, more exotic poultry
livers can be used equally successfully instead. In
that case you might also consider letting your
imagination have freer rein with the other
ingredients – truffles, pistachios and wild
mushrooms, for example.

Grind all these ingredients (liver, meat, fat, seasonings, bread and liquid) twice through the finest blade of the grinder, or purée a little at a time in a food processor. Over ice, beat with a wooden spoon until smooth and silky and work in the salt. Line the mold with slices of fat, fill with the forcemeat and cover with more fat. Decorate the top with herbs. Cover the mold and bake in the oven, in a water bath, regulating the oven so that the water temperature does not exceed 176°.

The terrine will have a more unusual flavor if baked without the water bath. With this method the terrine loses more of its fat but this has the advantage of acting as a seal when cool, keeping the terrine very moist. In this case, bake for 45–50 minutes in a preheated 400° oven.

Individual Liver Pâtés in Brioche Pastry

Petits pâtés de foie en brioche

No one can explain why it should be so, but liver pâtés are particularly delicious baked in brioche dough. It is not only goose liver which goes well with this slightly sour dough; any kind of liver goes with it equally well.

You can make these individual pies using the pastry for Goose Liver in Brioche Pastry (recipe opposite) and the filling for the Chicken Liver Terrine. You will need 8–12 small brioche pans, round or oval. Line the pans with dough rolled out to $\frac{1}{4}$-inch thick and fill with the forcemeat. Brush the edges of the dough with egg yolk, add a pastry lid of the same thickness, and press the edges carefully together to seal. Cut off any excess dough. Cut small openings in the top for the steam to escape. Decorate the pies and brush with egg yolk. Insert the funnels and leave the pies to rise at room temperature. Bake in a preheated 425° oven for 20–25 minutes. After baking leave the brioches until completely cool and fill with port wine aspic.

Truffled Liver Pâté

Pâté de foie truffé

$\frac{3}{4}$ lb calf's liver
2 tablespoons oil
2 teaspoons sweet paprika
$\frac{1}{4}$ lb pork liver
$\frac{3}{4}$ lb piece lean boneless pork
$\frac{1}{2}$ cup sliced shallots
2 teaspoons butter · $\frac{1}{2}$ cup port wine
$1\frac{1}{2}$ tablespoons Armagnac
2 slices white bread, crusts removed
1 egg white
$1\frac{1}{2}$ teaspoons salt
$\frac{1}{2}$ clove garlic, crushed
$\frac{1}{2}$ teaspoon dried green peppercorns
$\frac{1}{2}$ teaspoon basil
1 teaspoon mixed seasoning for delicate meat forcemeat
$\frac{1}{2}$ lb fresh pork fatback
$\frac{1}{2}$ cup diced cooked ham
2 lb pie pastry · $1\frac{1}{2}$ oz black truffles
1 beaten egg for glazing
$1\frac{3}{4}$-quart pâté mold

Dice the trimmed calf's liver. Heat the oil in a skillet and quickly seal the liver, shaking the skillet continuously. Sprinkle with the paprika and keep one third to one side to use whole. Put the remaining two-thirds in a bowl. Cut the carefully trimmed pork liver and pork into strips and add to the bowl. Soften the shallots in the hot butter, add the port wine and Armagnac and slowly reduce to about half the quantity. Arrange the bread over the meat and liver mixture. Add the egg white and sprinkle with the salt, garlic, peppercorns, basil and mixed seasoning. Finally pour on the cooled shallot and port mixture and leave to stand.

Cut the pork fat into strips and grind with the seasoned meat and liver mixture twice through the finest blade of the grinder. Over ice, beat the forcemeat until smooth and light. Fold the diced fried liver and diced ham into the forcemeat. Line the mold with pastry and add half the forcemeat. Place the pieces of truffle in a row along the center and cover with the remaining forcemeat. Cover with a pastry lid and decorate with overlapping pastry leaves. Cut an opening in the center, insert a funnel and brush the top of the pie with egg.

Bake for about 55 minutes in all, first for 15 minutes at 420°, then reduce the temperature to 375° and continue until cooked.

Calf's Liver Terrine

Terrine de foie de veau

This is a particularly fine and moist liver terrine. The ingredients and method of preparation are the same as the recipe for Truffled Liver Pâté, with the pork liver replaced by pork. The truffles are not used whole, but chopped and folded into the forcemeat. The diced ham is omitted. Line a $1\frac{3}{4}$-quart pâté mold with $\frac{3}{4}$ lb fresh sliced pork fatback or grease the mold with butter. Cook, in a water bath, for 50–55 minutes, regulating the oven so that the water temperature does not exceed 176°.

This terrine goes very well with a fine orange sauce. To make this reduce freshly squeezed, strained orange juice with sugar and fine strips of orange rind. When it has reduced to a thick liquid leave to cool and season with a little cayenne, Cointreau and brandy.

Black Truffles and Goose Liver

"When you say truffle you are referring to something great," according to Jean-Anthelme de Brillat-Savarin, writer and authority on the pleasures of the table (1755–1826). In his book *La Physiologie du Goût* (*The Philosopher in the Kitchen*) he described the truffle as "the black diamond" of cooking and did not overlook a warning on its erotic effect on both sexes. This effect was confirmed by George Sand (1804–1876) when she wrote "the truffle is the black magic apple of love." This famous campaigner for women's right to free love ought to have known what she was talking about. But we know nothing about the amount of truffles she actually ate. Many famous writers have mentioned truffles, among them Alexandre Dumas (1824–

1895). The creator of the "Lady of the Camelias" called the truffle "the holy of holies." Truffle is a word which centuries of gourmets have been unable to utter without heaping praises upon it. There is no doubt that the mere mention of the word sets gourmets reeling. Gourmets of centuries gone by and of the first decades of the present century were able to eat their fill of truffles, for then they were inexpensive and widely available. Things have changed a great deal in the last few years. Today you need a full purse or a checkbook when you go to buy truffles. For in the shops 2 pounds can cost up to $450. It has always been expensive to have a refined palate! This is equally true of the incomparably tender and flavorsome fattened goose liver. This now costs between $50 and $60 for 2 pounds. Both these are exclusive ingredients for exquisite dishes, but the most exquisite of all are the black Périgord truffles. This is their botanical name rather than a description of their place of origin, referring to winter truffles. They can just as easily come from Provence or Spain. Truffles have become an essential feature of haute cuisine, and so has the foie gras from which the most delicious terrines are made. Doubt it or not, it is nevertheless a fact that only force-fed geese produce large livers. The animals

are reared for the first 5–6 months on free-range methods, like Bresse chickens, so that natural feeding can give flavor to the meat and liver. Then they are force-fed for 21 days: four times a day each goose is force-fed 1 pound corn, usually with an electric feeder. A spindle in the feeder chops the feed and delivers it to the feed-pipe. If the goose were left to its own devices it would eat 1 pound of feed per day at most. To make the corn more digestible and easier to dispense it is poached with a little salt and fat. Farmers from Gascony, Alsace and Périgord specialize in rearing geese.

Whether one agrees or disagrees with these methods, foie gras is indeed a delicacy and when prepared properly and combined with truffles has a flavor impossible to equal. Of course the one can be eaten without the other, for example, natural goose liver terrine, which consists entirely of marinated, seasoned liver and has a pure liver flavor. Or truffles, poached for 5 minutes in port wine, Madeira or Champagne, and eaten with nothing more than bread, salt and butter. But a foie gras pâté with truffles is for many gourmets a dish which must have been invented in heaven. Usually a dish of this kind takes pride of place in top restaurants, being the high point of the menu, coming at the start of the meal and setting the tone for what is to follow. For a terrine is always an hors d'oeuvre: whether plain or truffled they caress the palate in an indescribable way, and have brought sighs of pleasure to the lips of many. The skill of a professional chef in the restaurant kitchen is required to produce this enjoyment. It takes an expert in his field who has his own recipes at his fingertips, and years of experience in handling basic ingredients to make a perfect terrine. Their handling of the expensive ingredients must be faultless.

below the ground. Where there are truffles no grass will grow. Farmers in Perigord sày "the earth burns". In fact the presence of truffles beneath an oak destroys any other vegetation. This is a reliable sign that truffles can be found here, but one still cannot predict with any accuracy where they grow. Man's sense of smell is not keen enough for him to be able to detect them, so pigs and dogs are used to smell out the truffles. There is also a small fly which lays its eggs where truffles are to be found, and this can often point the way.

In Périgord Madame rears gray geese with "golden livers." Continually increasing demand sends the price of this delicacy ever higher and higher.

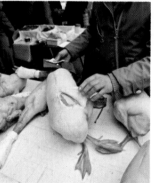

Like all foods truffles also have their own history. Long ago Marcus Gavius Apicius, the much-quoted author of the oldest existing Roman cookbook, appreciated the value of truffles. Natural, undamaged and, above all, dry truffles were layered in jars with sawdust, sealed with gypsum and then stored in a cool place. In the first volume of his four-volume work he also describes a sauce to accompany truffles. We are not surprised to read that it is made with honey, oil, pepper, lovage and coriander. But the fact that it also contained fish brine, a favorite sauce of the time, might make us shudder slightly. To bring out the full flavor of the truffle he recommended braising in a mixture of oil, wine, honey, mint, rue and pepper.

In the course of the centuries other truffle recipes were developed; today, perhaps surprisingly, more so than ever before. Despite their high price great chefs in France, and gradually in other countries too, are beginning to use this supreme delicacy more generously. Its price seems to present no problem. But, from the botanical viewpoint, truffles still present problems. They are symbiotic, found mainly with oak trees. A network of fungus threads, the mycel, spreads 4–12 inches

"Diamond trading" in the street. Every Wednesday – from November to March – ordinary people can buy truffles in Perigueux market. Although truffles are not exactly cheap even here, not to mention the price of goose liver, it is quite common for people to make their own foie gras. And no one buys the liver in the goose like a pig in a poke. The seller will willingly cut a window at the right point on the bird.

Pigs are still the best truffle hunters. They have only one disadvantage: they like eating truffles too. The truffle farmer has to act quickly and divert the pig with a little corn if he is to harvest his valuable fungus untouched by the pig. Dogs are less self-centered. They enjoy hunting for their masters and gladly give up their prey, but they have to be given the scent of the special truffle smell. There is also a type of fly which is a reliable guide to the whereabouts of the black diamonds. When the sun is low in the sky the truffle hunter walks slowly over the bare ground: anywhere he sees the fly taking to the air, he can be sure to find truffles.

Danish Liver Terrine

Leverpostej

This simple country-style terrine is a kind of culinary common property shared by all Danes. There is scarcely anybody who does not like it, scarcely a housewife who doesn't know how to make it. It is usually made with pork liver but for special occasions this is mixed with calf's liver.

In Denmark *Leverpostej* is usually found as part of a cold buffet, providing all the ingredients for guests to make up their own *Smørrebrøds*. But in this country Danish liver pâté can be served as an hors d'oeuvre for a simple menu or as a supper dish.

Delicious: cranberries to go with it and bring out the flavor. A cream sauce is used as the panada (technical term for the lightening agent).

$1\frac{1}{4}$ lb pork liver
$\frac{3}{4}$ lb fresh pork fatback
1 onion
2 eggs
2 anchovy fillets
salt
$\frac{1}{2}$ teaspoon dried green peppercorns
$\frac{1}{2}$ teaspoon allspice
$\frac{1}{4}$ teaspoon ground cloves
$\frac{1}{4}$ teaspoon ground ginger
2 tablespoons butter
2 tablespoons flour
1 cup cream
$\frac{3}{4}$ cup meat broth
$\frac{3}{4}$ lb fresh pork fatback, thinly sliced

1 **Trim the liver thoroughly,** i.e. remove blood vessels and skin. The sharper the knife the less liver you will lose. Coarsely dice the liver and the pork fat. Peel and chop the onion.

2 **Liver and bacon** are ground twice through the grinder. Grind the onion with the last of the meat. Cover the bowl and leave in a cool place (but not in the refrigerator) until you are ready to continue with the mixture. Meanwhile prepare the other ingredients and make and cool the cream sauce.

3 Beat the eggs, puréed anchovy fillets, $\frac{1}{2}$–1 teaspoon salt, the peppercorns and spices in a bowl until thoroughly mixed. Heat the butter in a saucepan, stir in the flour and cook 1 minute. Beat in the cream and broth. Simmer, stirring, until thickened. Add 1 teaspoon salt.

4 Leave the cream sauce (panada) to cool. Then beat in the egg mixture until smooth. Finally add the liver, fat and onion mixture. Beat carefully and thoroughly until smooth and elastic.

5 Line the bottom and sides of a $1\frac{3}{4}$-quart pâté mold with slices of fat, so that they overlap the sides generously. Add the forcemeat in an even layer, using a pastry scraper. Smooth the top of the forcemeat.

6 Cover the forcemeat with the overhanging slices of fat. Fold over a long side first, then a short side, then other long side and finally the remaining short side. The forcemeat should be completely covered by fat, to prevent it drying out during cooking.

7 Cover the pâté mold with foil, securing the edges firmly. Bake in a water bath in an oven preheated to 350° for $1\frac{1}{2}$ hours. Remove from the oven. Remove the foil and leave to cool, then cover again and store in a cool place.

Although not authentically Danish the following variation on liver pâté is very tasty. The ingredients for the above recipe remain unchanged. In addition $\frac{1}{2}$ lb calf's liver is carefully skinned and cut into small cubes, about $\frac{1}{4}$ inch square. Place the liver in a bowl with 1 tablespoon orange juice and $\frac{1}{4}$ cup port wine. Season with a little freshly ground pepper and allspice. Marinate for 2–3 hours, add salt and then fold into the prepared forcemeat.

Galantines

GAME AND POULTRY LUXURIES

This is most *galant* of the pâtés, for without doubt the term galantine is of French origin from the word *"galant,"* meaning elegant or gentlemanly. It is an accepted fact that galantines were already being eaten in the days of the knights. It is also a fact that pâtés in pastry, made to resemble the animal in question as nearly as possible, formed the high point at banquets throughout the civilized world. With pheasant pâtés, for example, the bird was recreated with great exactitude; feathers were cut out of thin sheets of pastry, shaped and attached to the body one at a time. For magnificent swan pies a wire framework had to be made to hold these enormous confections together. These were real works of art, using a lot of pastry and little filling, certain to win the approval of the guests. Another favorite method was to stick the plucked feathers back into the cooked pastry to give the natural effect expected by the guests. This method does not sound particularly appetizing, but it did allow the recreated bird to appear in all its glory to form a magnificent centerpiece for the grandest banquets.

But whenever too much emphasis is placed upon the appearance of the food, whether in pâté making or in cooking in general, it usually follows that the flavor suffers. Architectural cooking has only one aim – appearance – and those who cared more about flavor had to seek another means of expression. And they found it by sticking to the fundamental principles of pâté making, as presented by Habs and Kasner in their *Appetitlexika* published in 1894. "The more beautiful the drapery of the clothes, the more beautiful must be what they contain." In other words, the pâté should be appetizing in appearance, and the filling of the highest quality. This is an aim which can be achieved with carefully prepared galantines. In French dictionaries they were prosaically described as "meat aspics," which was technically incorrect and in no way typical of the usually flowery language of French cuisine. Galantines are more, much more than this. They are a culinary delicacy.

Duck pâté roll, the galantine rationalized. Free from elaborate decoration and reduced to its essential elements, its appearance bears little relationship to the classic galantine of cooking history. The basic criterion of cooking a stuffing in boned meat has, however, been followed and, correctly prepared the galantine is one of the most luxurious members of the pâté family.

On the one hand there are the classic examples, where the filling is served in the boned meat or just in its skin: in the case of chickens, for example, or pheasant, duck or separate cuts such as shoulder of lamb, breast of veal or even pig's feet – the Italian specialty known as *Zampone*. Boning can be a time-consuming job, for you have to keep the shape of the animal or the cut. This can be achieved, for example, by leaving the feet and wings intact. Making the stuffing and filling the animal is then the easiest part of the process. Prepared in this way the animal can retain its original shape even after cooking.

But modern tastes have had an effect on the techniques used by professional chefs. For some time now this kind of time-consuming galantine has been replaced by a more modern variation, by a rolled pâté. These usually come undecorated like a simple sausage. Neither is rolled pâté a particularly inspiring description of them, but luckily their appearance is in direct contrast to their wonderful flavor. Pâté rolls can be made with boned poultry, fish fillets or even seaweed (see our recipe for Galantine of Scallops). In every case galantines are poached in a suitable broth, but can be baked in the oven or smoked at a later stage. Nouvelle cuisine – for example – has become famous primarily through such creations as fish galantine.

Whether we are speaking of a true galantine or a pâté roll, their fillings are always excellent. For festive occasions master chefs will, even today, make a chicken or pheasant galantine, for example, in its original shape or even stuff a wild boar's head in the traditional way. This is entirely for the sake of appearance.

Any garnish used should take into account that one is dealing with a real luxury pâté. Thus any ingredients from simple carrots and leeks on the one hand to expensive truffles on the other can be used here. And classic French cuisine has created true works of art without sacrificing anything of the flavor.

There are also the ballotines, little sisters to the galantines. These take the form of stuffed chicken pieces, for example legs or breasts, whose shape should remain recognizable after stuffing. They can be made in exactly the same way as galantines.

Boning poultry or duck for a galantine

As with many other pâtés and terrines, a galantine is a delicious filling in an edible case. In this instance the case is not made of pastry but from the flesh and skin of the animal in question – in this case a duck. And there is one other important difference: galantines are not baked, but poached in broth, that is, cooked in liquid. The original galantine took the form of a stuffed animal, retaining its original shape as closely as possible and boned only in so far as this would facilitate carving. Typical examples of this method are stuffed chicken with feet and wings, or Italian *Zampone*, stuffed pig's feet. The main drawback with galantines of this kind is that when carving a chicken, for example, the first few slices take all the breast, leaving only the filling.

The galantine rationalized

The fact that cooks are not only artists but can also think scientifically is demonstrated by the invention of the rolled galantine. Here the meat, poultry, breast of lamb or game is completely boned, covered with the stuffing, possibly topped with other ingredients, before being rolled. This galantine, which has now become a pâté roll, is cooked in foil or wrapped in a cloth. Meat and filling is thus distributed more or less evenly in every slice.

1 **Trim the bird.** Place the plucked, dressed, washed and singed duck breast side up on a board. Using a sharp knife or poultry shears chop off both wings at the joint.

For a galantine only the best is good enough

Domestic poultry, at least the smaller varieties such as duck, chicken, guinea fowl and squab are, together with game birds, the perfect basis for a galantine. But even with these you should look for the best possible quality. Best quality poultry will be more tender and, in addition, boned poultry provides the perfect casing for a galantine.

It should go without saying that fresh meat must be used, never frozen. But the poultry industry has created a situation where for the consumer, chicken and deep-freezing seem made for one another.

This is not true in France where 80 percent of poultry is bought fresh. In other countries, however, buying fresh birds may cause some problems, for they are not available in every market

and they may often be expensive, sometimes much more expensive. Recently the increasing demand for quality has caused more fresh birds to become available in the markets, and naturally reared chickens or ducks are available on the market at moderate prices. But there is a kind of quality guarantee with poultry, for which you will have to dig rather deeper into your pocket. Even here quality has its price. With ducks the best are the fleshy migratory ducks from the Loire Valley (known as Barbary ducks in France), which contain almost no fat and at $3\frac{1}{4}$–$4\frac{1}{2}$ pounds are the ideal weight for galantines. With fresh chickens or hens France also offers quality controlled poultry in the form of Breton chickens (gourmets swear by them) or Bresse chickens. There certain rules of poultry raising have become legal requirements such as, for example, the ruling of 10 square meters of ground per bird. Only those farmers who adhere strictly to the regulations are entitled to label their chickens "Poulet de Bresse," and the consumer can, through the labeling, trace the chicken back to the original farmer. This is made possible by a ring bearing the production number which is attached to the leg of every chicken.

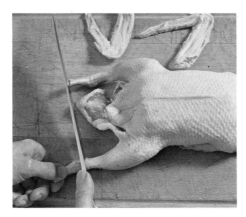

2 **Remove the feet from the legs.** Cut off both lower legs at the knee joint. It is necessary to remove the tips of the wings and legs at this stage to facilitate further boning.

3 **Cut the duck open.** Turn the duck over onto the breast. Working from the neck (previously removed) to the tail (pope's nose) cut the skin along both sides of the backbone.

4 **Loosen the wings at the shoulder.** Locate the joint with your fingers and cut through the fulcrum with a sharp knife, holding the wing bone in your left hand and turning it slightly in the joint.

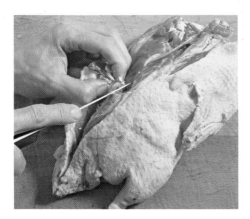

5 **Loosen the legs at the thigh joint.** Treat the legs as you did the wings. Again locate the joint with your fingers and loosen the legs from the thigh joint.

6 **Loosen the carcass.** Hold the duck firmly in the left hand. With a sharp knife cut along the rib cage to remove the meat. Cut with the blade of the knife toward the carcass not the meat.

7 **Remove the breast bone.** Here special care is needed for the breastbone joins directly onto the skin. The skin must not be damaged during this stage so hold the breast bone up well away from the skin while you cut.

8 **Cut around the wing bone.** Cut through the ligaments around the knuckle of the bone. Scrape the meat off the bone with a small knife. Pull the bone through holding the meat firmly in place.

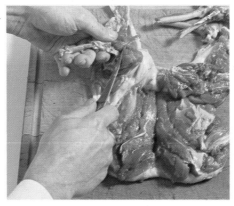

9 **Remove the ligaments.** Deal with the leg bones in the same way as the wings. Remove the wing and leg ligaments, using pliers where necessary.

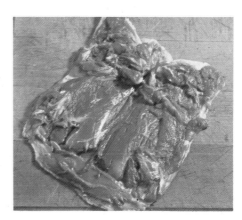

10 **Even out the duck meat.** Cut off the pope's nose. Cut off the strips of skin at the base of the breasts which have no meat on them, so that all the skin is now covered with meat.

1 **Stuff the duck.** Spread evenly with about half the forcemeat. Cut the ends of the sealed breasts to straighten them, place along the center of the forcemeat, brush with the cooled essence and cover with the remaining forcemeat.

2 **Seal the duck.** First fold the tail end over the forcemeat and then fold over the neck end. Press down to seal all the joins, so no forcemeat can escape. Shape to an even, thick roll.

3 **Wrap the galantine.** For this use either heat-resistant film, e.g. roasting film, or a dish towel. Place the galantine on the film and wrap firmly but not too tightly.

Duck Galantine

Galantine de canard

2 ducks, each weighing 3¼–4¼ lb
3 bouquets garni
¼ lb lean boneless pork
½ lb fresh pork fatback
pâté salt
grated rind of 1 orange
3 fresh sage leaves, chopped
¼ cup diced cooked ham
⅓ cup chopped pistachios
¾ oz truffles, diced
2 tablespoons oil
chaudfroid sauce to finish

Carefully bone the ducks. Set one duck aside to be used whole. Boil half the bones with one bouquet garni to make a broth in which the galantine will be cooked.

Finely chop the remaining bones and simmer with vegetables, second bouquet garni and seasoning to make a broth. Strain, add further seasoning and reduce to a thick essence.

Set the duck breasts aside to be used whole. Remove all skin and ligaments from the remaining duck meat (there should be about ½ pound) and cut into strips with the pork and fat. Sprinkle with pâté salt, the orange rind and sage. Chill. Grind the meat twice through the finest blade of the grinder, the fat once only. Chill again. Work the fat into the meat a little at a time, finally add 2 tablespoons of the duck essence and then sieve through a fine strainer. Fold in the ham, pistachios and truffles.

Season the duck breasts with pâté salt, quickly seal in hot oil, remove from the skillet, drain and pour on the remaining duck essence.

Trim the reserved whole boned duck and spread with about half the forcemeat. Top with the breasts, brush with about 2 tablespoons duck essence and cover with the remaining forcemeat. Roll the duck from the tail to the neck, wrap in roasting film and tie into place with string. Poach gently in sufficient duck broth to cover, with the third bouquet garni, for 40 minutes to every 2 pounds weight. Do not exceed the cooking time. Test with a needle to check when cooked. Leave the galantine to cool in the broth. Weight with a board and a 2–4 pound can and leave in a cool place for 24 hours. Then remove from the broth, remove the film, thoroughly wash off all fat under warm running water and wipe dry. The galantine is now ready for covering with a light chaudfroid sauce.

Duck galantine, alternative method

(Illustrated on page 114)

Prepare the forcemeat as in the recipe alongside, changing only the additional ingredients. Fold ¼ lb marinated foie gras of goose or duck, sieved through a strainer, ½ cup quartered almonds, ½ cup diced smoked tongue and 1½ oz diced truffles into the forcemeat. Omit the duck breasts. Spread the forcemeat along the center of the duck from neck to tail and fold the two sides over the forcemeat, carefully sealing the joins. In this way the stuffed galantine follows the natural shape of the duck. It is also wrapped in roasting film or a dish towel and bound with string.

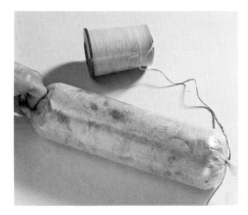

4 **Bind the galantine.** Seal both ends of the film with string and knot firmly into place. The galantine should not be wrapped too tightly for it expands during cooking and could cause the film to split.

5 **Tie up the galantine.** Tie with string at about 1-inch intervals. Take the string through the cross pieces and secure each with a running knot. Finally, knot firmly.

6 **The galantine made by method 1.** A cross-section of the galantine rolled from tail to neck, showing that by this method the rolled breast and leg meat is evenly distributed.

Poaching the galantine. Make a broth with duck bones, bouquet garni and seasoning. Strain and simmer the galantine in the broth with a bouquet garni. Make sure that the liquid temperature remains at a constant 176° from the time you put the galantine into the broth until it is cooked. Check the temperature repeatedly with a thermometer. The cooking time for a galantine depends on its weight. It needs 40 minutes for every 2 pounds. Leave the galantine to cool in the broth, weight with a board and a 2–4 pound can and leave to stand for 24 hours in a cool place. Then remove from the broth, take off the wrapping, carefully wash off any fat under warm running water, wipe dry and cover with a light aspic or chaudfroid sauce.

Wild Duck Galantine

Galantine de canard sauvage

1 wild duck
pâté salt
dried sage and basil
5 oz fattened duck's liver
a little salt and ground white pepper
$\frac{1}{2}$ cup port wine
5 oz wild duck breast meat, trimmed (or breast of domestic duck)
$\frac{1}{4}$ lb lean boneless pork
2–3 juniper berries, crushed
grated rind of $\frac{1}{2}$ orange
$\frac{1}{2}$ clove garlic, crushed
5 oz fresh pork fatback
$\frac{1}{2}$ cup diced smoked tongue
$\frac{1}{2}$ cup diced cooked ham
$\frac{1}{4}$ cup chopped pistachios
$\frac{3}{4}$ oz truffles, diced

Bone the wild duck as shown in the photographs on pages 116–117. Trim to shape, so that the meat is evenly distributed over the whole skin. Sprinkle with 1 teaspoon pâté salt and a little finely rubbed dried sage and basil. Boil the carcass, ligaments and trimmed skin to make a broth. Strain.

Remove the skin from the fattened duck's liver together with any blood vessels. Add salt and pepper and marinate in the port wine.

Dice the duck breast meat and pork. Sprinkle with 1 teaspoon pâté salt, the juniper berries, orange rind, garlic and a little sage and basil and chill. Dice the pork fat and deep-freeze. In a food processor purée small amounts of seasoned meat and frozen fat. Chill thoroughly once more. Sieve the marinated duck's liver through a fine strainer and work into the forcemeat. Chill again and then sieve the forcemeat. Fold the tongue, ham, pistachios and truffles into the forcemeat. Lay the boned duck out on a board and spread with the forcemeat. Roll up, bind in roasting film or a dish towel and leave to stand in a cool place.

Poach the galantine in the broth for 45–50 minutes.

A particularly fine variation of this recipe is Wild Duck Terrine with Truffled Liver. For this the duck is boned in the same way as the Chicken Galantine on page 124. The stuffing is made up omitting the duck liver and diced truffles. $\frac{1}{2}$ pound fattened duck liver is marinated in port wine and a dash of brandy. 3 oz truffles in large pieces are wrapped in the liver and embedded in the center of the forcemeat. Sew up the duck to return as closely as possible to its original shape and poach in broth.

Galantine of Lake Trout

Galantine de truites de torrent

1 tablespoon butter
2 thin slices onion
$\frac{1}{4}$ lb sea trout fillet, skinned
2 thin slices white bread, crusts removed
$\frac{1}{2}$ small egg white
1–2 tablespoons light cream
a little salt, ground white pepper, nutmeg
and English mustard powder
$\frac{1}{2}$ cup whipped cream
1 heaping teaspoon chopped dill
7 lake trout fillets, skinned,
weighing about 3 oz each

Melt the butter, soften the sliced onion without allowing it to color and leave to cool. Cut the sea trout fillet into strips and arrange on a flat dish. Cover with the onion and thinly sliced white bread. Moisten with the egg white and cream, sprinkle with salt, pepper, nutmeg and mustard, cover with plastic wrap and chill. Grind all these ingredients twice through the finest blade of the grinder, then sieve through a strainer. Beat well and, over ice, gradually beat in the whipped cream. Finally stir in the dill.

Flatten the lake trout fillets with a meat pounder, season with salt, cut to shape where necessary and place touching side by side, skin side uppermost, on a large piece of roasting film. Fill any gaps between the fillets with small pieces of fish. Transfer the forcemeat to a pastry bag and pipe onto the fillets to cover completely. Use the foil to help roll the galantine and tie into position. Poach in fish broth or salted water for about 30 minutes, with water at $176°$.

Scallop Galantine

Galantine de coquilles Saint-Jacques

3 lb fish trimmings (head, bones,
skin etc.)
2 quarts water
juice of $\frac{1}{2}$ lemon
1 cup dry white wine
bouquet garni (white of 2 leeks, 1 small
sprig parsley, 1 small sprig thyme, $\frac{1}{2}$ small
bay leaf)
$\frac{1}{2}$ small onion
$\frac{1}{2}$ small clove garlic
3 white peppercorns, crushed
1 clove
salt
1 teaspoon butter
$\frac{1}{4}$ cup sliced shallots
$\frac{1}{2}$ lb scallops
4 thin slices white bread, crusts removed
1 egg white
3 tablespoons light cream
ground white pepper and nutmeg
$\frac{3}{4}$ cup whipped cream
$\frac{1}{2}$ lb seaweed (available from
oriental grocery)

Wash the fish trimmings, place in the cold water and bring to a boil with the lemon juice and wine. Skim thoroughly, add the bouquet garni, onion, garlic, peppercorns, clove and 1 teaspoon salt and simmer for 30 minutes. Strain through cheesecloth.

Heat the butter, soften the sliced shallots and leave to cool. Wipe the scallops dry, cut into strips, arrange on a flat dish and cover with the shallots and thinly sliced white bread. Moisten with egg white and cream and sprinkle with a little salt, pepper and nutmeg. Chill. Grind the scallops, shallots and bread twice through the finest blade of the grinder, stir well and sieve through a strainer. Over ice, beat the forcemeat until smooth and silky. Then beat in the whipped cream a little at a time. Chill repeatedly after each stage.

Wash the seaweed, blanch for about 10 minutes and transfer immediately to lightly salted iced water. Leave until completely cool. Drain the seaweed thoroughly and spread over a large sheet of roasting film to cover an area 7×8 inches. Put the chilled forcemeat into a pastry bag and pipe over the seaweed without moving the seaweed from position. Using the film to help you, roll the galantine lengthwise. Bind and poach in the fish broth for about 30 minutes with the liquid at $176°$.

Classic Galantines

When too much attention is paid to the appearance of the food (at least in pâté making) it follows logically that the flavor of the dish suffers as a consequence. The galantine was the way out of the dilemma for those who were concerned about flavor. It was made with the best meat and finest fillings and the shape of the animal was preserved into the bargain. More recently this type of galantine has been largely replaced by the rationalized pâté roll, but the traditional galantine has not disappeared completely. For festive occasions in Europe a hen or boar's head is still stuffed in the old way, although this method of preparation is used mainly for poultry. Skillful boning which retains the bones which give the bird its shape (feet and wings), stuffing and trussing creates a new bird which retains the shape of the original.

The extra ingredients included should be ideally suited to the luxury of the pâté. So, various ingredients such as carrots and leeks on the one hand, and delicious truffles on the other, give ample opportunity to let your imagination take flight; the essential thing is that they should look good.

Chicken Galantine

Galantine de poulet

1 chicken weighing, without neck and
giblets, about 2–2½ lb, weight without
carcass: about 1¼–1½ lb (the weight of the
stuffing should be about the same as the
bones)
pâté salt
carcass, neck and giblets
(without liver), made up to 1 lb
with chicken bones if necessary
2½ quarts water
2 teaspoons salt
3 oz leeks (white only)
3 oz celeriac
½ bay leaf
5 white peppercorns, crushed
½ onion
5 oz fattened (or prepared) goose liver
1 cup milk
1 tablespoon port wine
1 tablespoon Armagnac

Season the boned chicken with 1 teaspoon pâté salt and chill. Chop and wash the chicken bones. Finely chop the carcass, neck and giblets. Add to a pan of cold water with the chicken bones and bring to a boil. Pour off the water. Bring the bones back to a boil in the measured water, add the salt and skim. Simmer for 1 hour, repeatedly

Boning a chicken for a galantine made in its original shape

In contrast to the rolled galantine, this chicken galantine is only partially boned. It is essential to use a fresh chicken with the skin completely undamaged. Use a chicken which still has its feet for these are cut off short of the joint, to prevent the skin receding. With the carcass, the bones in the body cavity are removed completely, but the leg and wing bones are left in the chicken to help preserve its original shape. Further preparation is as for the rolled galantine.

1 Cut off the neck and feet. Push back the skin and chop off the neck as close to the base as possible. Chop off the feet short of the joint to prevent the skin receding during cooking.

2 Cut through the skin along the backbone. Starting from the tail – which should be left intact – make a sharp cut along the backbone to the neck. Remove the glands and any fat.

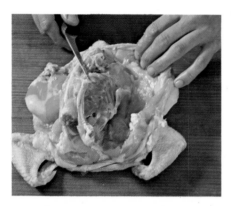

3 Remove the carcass. Working to left and right along the backbone separate the meat from the carcass and fold open. Hold the rib cage with the left hand and carefully separate the breast bone from the skin.

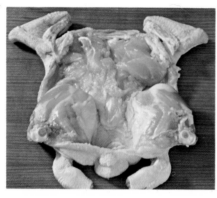

4 The boned chicken. Carefully lift out the carcass, taking care not to damage the skin. Leg and wing bones remain in the chicken. Lay out flat on a board and sprinkle with pâté salt.

5 Fill the chicken with forcemeat. The quantity should roughly correspond to the volume of the carcass. Arrange the forcemeat from neck to tail along the center of the chicken. Do not overfill.

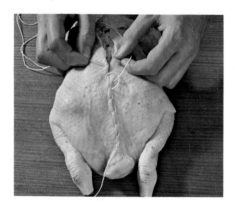

6 Sew up the chicken. Pull the skin together from each side. With a trussing needle sew up from tail to neck. Tie off the ends of the thread and sew up the tail.

7 Truss with string. Take the string under the chicken and cross under the thighs. Wrap the string inward over the thighs and tie firmly to bring the legs close together.

8 Tie the base of the chicken. Bring the ends of the string forward under the wings, take them back around the legs and knot to secure legs and wings firmly to the body.

skimming off the foam as it forms. Tie together the leeks, celeriac and bay leaf to make a bouquet garni, add to the broth with the crushed peppercorns and onion and simmer gently for a further 30 minutes. Again, skim off any fat and scum and strain through cheesecloth.

Carefully remove the skin and blood vessels from the goose liver and place in the milk. This "washes out" any remaining blood. After 1 hour remove the liver and wipe dry on paper towels. Mix the port wine and Armagnac. Season the liver with pâté salt, place in a small bowl and cover with the port and Armagnac mixture. Marinate for several hours.

Forcemeat and filling

$\frac{1}{4}$ lb trimmed chicken meat
$\frac{1}{4}$ lb lean boneless pork
5 oz fresh pork fatback
pâté salt
freshly ground white pepper
1 teaspoon chopped rosemary
1 teaspoon chopped sage (2 leaves)
$\frac{1}{2}$ cup diced cooked ham
1 oz truffles, diced

Cut the trimmed chicken, pork and fat into strips, sprinkle with pâté salt, pepper and the finely chopped herbs and chill. Grind the meat through the finest blade of the grinder, chill again and repeat. Finally grind the fat and chill both meat and fat. Then mix the fat into the meat, increase the seasoning if necessary and chill well. With a metal scraper to help you sieve the forcemeat through a strainer and chill again.

Break the marinated liver into small pieces and mix carefully into the forcemeat with the ham and truffles. Spread the forcemeat over the boned chicken and sew together. With your hands re-form the chicken to its original shape as closely as possible and truss with string to help keep its shape. Wrap in roasting film which should fully enclose the galantine without being too tight. Tie up both ends. Heat the chicken broth to 176° and cook, allowing 40 minutes to each 2 pounds weight. You will have to calculate the time yourself. During cooking keep the liquid temperature at exactly 176°. Leave the chicken galantine to cool in the broth and then weight with a 2-pound can. Place in the refrigerator for 24 hours before removing the wrapping.

If the galantine is to be covered with aspic or chaudfroid sauce, you will have to wash off any fat under warm running water before drying with paper towels.

Chicken galantine with a light chaudfroid sauce. The sauce should suit the flavor of the galantine. In this instance chicken broth is used in the sauce. The forcemeat is made from the recipe alongside, but without the added goose liver.

Stuffed Goose Neck

Cou d'oie farci

giblets of 2 geese (neck and head, crop,
heart and unfattened liver)
1 teaspoon salt
a little ground white pepper, mace,
allspice, sweet paprika and marjoram
½ clove garlic, crushed
3 tablespoons butter
5 oz lean boneless pork
2 tablespoons white bread crumbs
1 tablespoon oil
2 tablespoons diced onion
2 tablespoons port wine
6 tablespoons veal broth
a little fresh thyme, hyssop and lovage
½ cup frozen diced fresh pork fatback
¼ cup diced cooked ham
½ cup coarsely chopped pistachios
1 quart chicken broth

Cut around the skin on both necks below
the head and pull off the skin. Remove the
tough skin from the meaty part of the crops.
Remove the blood vessels from the hearts
and livers. Transfer the giblets to a bowl and
sprinkle with salt, pepper, mace, allspice,
paprika, marjoram and garlic. Heat the
butter in a skillet and quickly seal the
giblets, continuously shaking the skillet,

and then chill. Dice the pork and add to the
giblets. Sprinkle with the bread crumbs.

Heat the oil in a skillet and soften the
diced onion. Add the port and veal broth,
then the herbs, and reduce to a thick
essence. Strain over the giblets and pork.
Leave to marinate.

Purée the thoroughly chilled mixture of
giblets, pork and reduced essence with the
frozen diced fat in a food processor. Fold
the diced ham and coarsely chopped
pistachios into the forcemeat.

Sew the neck skins together along one
side and fill with the forcemeat, making sure
you leave no air gaps. Sew up the stuffed
neck. Cook for about 20 minutes, in the
chicken broth, keeping the temperature of
the liquid at 176°. Leave to cool in the broth.

Stuffed Pig's Feet

Zampone

2 pig's feet, each weighing about 1¾–2 lb
1 lb lean boneless pork
¾ lb fresh pork fatback
about ½ oz pâté salt
freshly ground white pepper
fresh thyme and marjoram
12 juniper berries, crushed
3 cloves garlic, crushed
1 cup diced smoked tongue
1 lb pork tenderloin, diced
¾ cup shelled pistachios
beef broth for cooking

Scald the feet and scrape off any bristles
with a sharp knife, taking care not to
damage the skin. Remove the inside of the
feet as far as the toes, so that the skins are
completely free from meat. Soak for 24
hours.

Cut the pork and fat into strips, sprinkle
with pâté salt, pepper, herbs, juniper berries
and garlic and chill. Grind the pork twice
through the finest blade of the grinder.
Grind the fat once only, work into the meat
and sieve the forcemeat through a strainer.
Finally fold in the tongue, pork tenderloin
and pistachios. Dry the feet and stuff with
the forcemeat, leaving no air gaps, but not
overfilling. Sew up the ends with strong
thread. (It will be easier to sew the thick skin
if you make the holes in advance.) Prick the
stuffed feet several times with a thin trussing
needle, to allow air to escape during
cooking. Wrap with strips of linen about 2-
inches wide and secure with thread. This
will help the feet keep their shape during
cooking and prevent the skin splitting.
Cook in beef broth for about 3½ hours,
maintaining the temperature of the liquid at
176°, and leave to cool in the broth.

Even better smoked. Both neck of goose and
Zampone are suitable for smoking. You can get
your butcher to smoke them or, better still,
smoke them yourself. Smoking gives both a
particularly spicy flavor and will help them to
keep longer.

Stuffed Breast of Veal

Punta di vitello ripieno

2 lb boned, trimmed breast of veal
salt
a little ground white pepper
1 lb lean boneless veal
¾ lb lean boneless pork
½ lb fresh pork fatback
2 teaspoons mixed all-purpose seasoning
1 teaspoon thyme
1 teaspoon basil
1 bay leaf
1½ tablespoons butter
1 small onion, cut into rings
1 clove garlic, crushed
1½ tablespoons Grappa or marc
2 slices bread, crusts removed
1 egg
3 tablespoons light cream
½ cup diced cooked ham
1 cup braised mushrooms
1 tablespoon chopped parsley
1 oz truffles, chopped
veal broth for cooking

Cut a slit in the breast of veal and rub the inside with salt and pepper. Leave to stand in the refrigerator. Cut the veal, pork and pork fat into strips, place in a bowl and sprinkle with 1 teaspoon salt, the mixed seasoning and herbs. Heat the butter in a skillet, soften the onion and crushed garlic and add the Grappa. Allow to cool slightly and pour over the meat. Crumble the bread over the meat. Beat the egg into the cream and pour over the bread. Cover the bowl with plastic wrap and leave to stand in the refrigerator for 3–4 hours.

Grind the meat and all the other ingredients in the bowl twice through the finest blade of the grinder. Over ice, beat the forcemeat until smooth and silky, then fold in the ham, mushrooms, parsley and truffles. Stuff the breast of veal and sew up with thread. Cook in highly seasoned veal broth for 1 hour or so, maintaining the temperature of the liquid at 176°, and allow to cool in the broth.

Stuffed Wild Boar's Head

Hure de sanglier farcie

The original idea of stuffing a wild boar's head was probably suggested by its elongated shape which seems made for stuffing. But probably many hunters also wanted to impress their guests with its frightening, yet beautiful, appearance. It is a classic French preparation and included more for historical than culinary interest.

1 small young boar's head, weighing about 9–10 lb
pâté salt
ground white pepper
chopped fresh marjoram
chopped fresh thyme
2 tablespoons chopped parsley
1 cup diced onion, softened in butter
3 cloves garlic, crushed
1 lb lean wild boar meat
½ lb lean boneless pork
1 lb fat (use wild boar fat if possible)
juniper berries
grated lemon rind
¼ cup diced onion
1 tablespoon butter
½ lb wild boar fillet, diced
2 tablespoons oil
3 tablespoons brandy
½ cup wild boar essence
½ lb pork tenderloin, diced
¾ cup pistachios
1½ oz truffles, diced
½ lb foie gras, seasoned with pâté salt and marinated in port wine and brandy

The truffled trophy

To describe this procedure in great detail might be said to be akin to "taking coals to Newcastle," for anyone who is willing to try this recipe must either be a very expert or a very brave cook. Nevertheless it is quite an experience to make this, the king of the galantines. And, without doubt, young boar's meat served in the

boar's head with truffles makes a really attractive dish. Beginners are advised to use a young boar, for they are smaller and easier to handle.

The head should be cut from the body with as much of the neck as possible. Bristles are removed by scalding the head. It is best to begin with the water at 113° and to increase the temperature slowly to about 140° maximum. Shave off the bristles with a sharp knife (or razor blade), taking care not to damage the rind. Then soak the boar's head for at least 12 hours.

Rub the head with pickling salt, place in an earthenware jar, cover with prickling brine, cover and leave to stand in the refrigerator for about 24 hours. Rinse several times before proceeding.

The inside of the boar's head is removed from the lower jaw side. Cut the skin between the bones of the lower jaw and cut the skin free of the cranial bone at each side. Cut out the ear muscles but leave the ears in place on the head. This leaves only the skin with the flesh attached to it. In the meantime make the stuffing to go in the head and prepare the other ingredients to be included in the stuffing.

After soaking, dry the head thoroughly. Place on a board. Carefully sew up the eye, ear and snout opening to prevent the stuffing escaping. Turn the head upside down and season the inside with salt and pepper. Mix together 1 tablespoon each

marjoram and thyme, the parsley, softened onion and one crushed garlic clove and spread evenly over the inside of the head.

Cut the wild boar meat, pork and fat into strips, season with pâté salt, pepper, marjoram, thyme, crushed juniper berries, lemon rind and another crushed garlic clove, and chill. Soften the onion in the butter and cool. Grind the seasoned meat and onion twice through the finest blade of the grinder, the fat once only. Over ice, beat the fat into the meat mixture. Chill well.

Seal the diced wild boar fillet in oil, then remove from the skillet. Deglaze the skillet with brandy, then add the wild boar essence (made from reduced boar broth), 8 crushed juniper berries, marjoram, thyme, lemon rind, and the remaining garlic. Boil until well reduced, then strain over the diced sealed boar fillet. Cool.

Mix the diced boar fillet, pork tenderloin, pistachios, truffles and broken up foie gras into the forcemeat. Stuff the head so that when it is sewn together along the lower jaw it regains its original shape. Seal the remaining opening at the neck with a piece of soaked bacon rind and sew to the skin of the boar's head. Wrap the head firmly in roasting film or a cloth.

Use the wild boar bones and vegetables to make a light broth. Strain and season well. Cook the boar's head in the broth at a maximum temperature of 176° – at higher temperatures the skin will split. Test with a needle to ascertain when it is cooked through. Make sure that the head is completely covered with broth throughout the cooking time, adding more liquid as the broth evaporates. Leave the head to cool in the broth.

During cooking the head will contract slightly, regaining (almost) its original shape. Of course when you carve the head the slices will be of different sizes, which can be annoying when you want to carve equal portions. This can be overcome by cutting away some of the rind on the underside before stuffing. In this case you should bind up the head with a strip of linen, applied like a bandage. But do not bind too tightly so that the stuffing can expand slightly during cooking. (Secure the bandage with thread.)

Cooking time: about 3–3¼ hours.

It is traditional to glaze the boar's head with a brown chaudfroid sauce or brown aspic. This goes well with the flavor and enhances the frightening appearance of the head. This recipe can also be adapted to make a rolled pâté. Serve with rose-hip sauce and apples, mushrooms or glazed chestnuts, braised in white wine.

The Outsiders among Pâtés

Timbales, parfaits, mousses – all are dishes to set the pulse of the serious gourmet racing. If we disregard for the moment Antoine Carême's large timbales, these are the smallest of the great pâté family. But are they really pâtés? This is a difficult question to answer for while these outsiders all have some feature in common with the pâté or terrine, be it the shape, the forcemeat or the filling, some of them differ widely from the accepted form of the terrine or pâté. So should they be included within the scope of this book? As with other types of pâtés, when correctly prepared they are the finest of delicacies and their refined method of preparation is proof that they are closely related to pâtés. Yet, compared with large pies or galantines, many of these recipes are relatively easy to make.

Mousse, a delicate foam

In French the word simply means "foam." In German the mousse is defined as a foam loaf, not a particularly apt description, for these, the lightest of all pâtés, do not even have their shape in common with a loaf. They are pâtés made with aspic. The basic ingredient is always a fine purée of vegetables, poultry, ham, game, poultry liver, fish or shellfish, and this is combined with gelatin and whipped cream. This purée can be easily made in a blender or food processor. The mousse can be made in molds of a variety of shapes, but is usually served unmolded. It is not essential to cover them with a layer of aspic even though this has one definite advantage: the tender, creamy mousse tastes particularly fresh under its aspic (which should naturally harmonize with the flavor of the mousse) and it is well protected against absorbing flavors from other foods, in the refrigerator for example. It should be unnecessary to add that, with mousses, fresh, high-quality ingredients are as essential as they are with pâtés.

Parfait (the French word means complete, perfect) is the term used to describe the finest stuffings made either with aspic, that is, bound with gelatin, or with egg white and poached in water. The term very accurately describes this very fine and tender dish and is almost synonymous with the term mousse. There is not really much difference between a poached parfait and a terrine cooked without its coating of pork fat. Their light consistency and the opportunity they offer for variation makes them a favorite of the new, light style of cuisine. Experiments have been carried out and new creations invented from ingredients which were once

Poultry liver mousse, a very tender delicacy made from turkey liver and foie gras. It is excellent served with papaya stewed in sugar, vintage Tokay and a dash of pepper.

thought unsuitable for pâté making. Think of the light, airy hors d'oeuvre made from puréed vegetables. Fish and shellfish too are an ideal basis for these light forcemeats and offer a wide range of possible combinations with vegetables.

Timbales are molds with a filling of some kind and the master chef and pâtissier, Antoine Carême, whom we have already mentioned, invented some extremely complicated timbales. Cooked or uncooked ingredients arranged in layers in a charlotte mold, poached and then unmolded were real works of art and a favorite highlight of menus in nineteenth-century France. Some of these creations are still popular today, like the Timbale *à la milanaise*.

The first timbales must have been pies in the shape of a kettle drum (the French word *timbale* means kettle drum) which were baked blind, that is, without the filling. In the course of time these changed in shape to become conical. These were filled with forcemeat and baked, or filled with stewed meat. Eventually the best-loved and finest timbales came to omit the pastry altogether. Fine forcemeats, usually bound with egg or egg white, were poured into small, individual molds greased with butter. Any type of meat or fish suitable for pâté making is also suitable for a timbale. But you can also make wonderfully tender timbales with puréed vegetables, and, served with a suitable sauce, these make an excellent hors d'oeuvre. And they have one definite advantage: they are quick to make. More exquisite still are the filled timbales. The outside is a tender forcemeat, filled with a fine stew and sealed with forcemeat. They are poached in a water bath. You will often find timbales on many menus, which unfortunately prove to be stews served in small individual dishes. Here any relationship with pâtés ends.

Assorted tartlets

No one can say precisely where they came from or how long they have been made. They have more in common with pies than many others of the same family. They are small tartlets, baked blind, in basic pie or sometimes puff or yeast pastry. Beyond this they become less easy to define. The rest relies upon the cook's imagination. Even the shape of the tartlet can be varied, but they should always bear some resemblance to a small tart. They can be plain or fluted, round, oval or square in shape. The size should always be adequate for one serving. They can be filled with stew while still warm, covered with forcemeat and baked, or covered with sauce and browned under the broiler. Or, if preferred, they can be filled with cold ingredients and served cold.

Poultry Liver Mousse

Mousse de foies de volaille

Illustrated on page 130
$\frac{3}{4}$ lb turkey or chicken liver
$\frac{1}{4}$ lb fresh pork fatback
$\frac{1}{2}$ cup port wine
$1\frac{1}{2}$ tablespoons Armagnac
1 teaspoon salt
$\frac{1}{2}$ bay leaf
1 small sprig each thyme and lemon balm
freshly ground white pepper
2 tablespoons butter
$\frac{3}{4}$ lb fattened (or prepared) goose liver
1 envelope unflavored gelatin
3 tablespoons chicken broth
$\frac{1}{2}$ cup cream
1 cup liquid aspic made with
chicken broth
1-quart mold or 6 6-oz individual molds

Remove all skin and blood vessels from the liver. Coarsely dice the pork fat and place in a bowl with the liver. Add the port wine, Armagnac, salt, herbs and pepper. Cover and leave to marinate overnight in the refrigerator.

Drain off the marinade and quickly fry the liver and fat in the hot butter, shaking the skillet continuously. Remove from the skillet and leave to cool. Add the drained marinade to the cooking juices, reduce to a thick liquid and leave to cool.

Purée the chilled liver and fat in a food processor with the reduced marinade. Sieve the prepared goose liver through a fine strainer. Over ice, beat into the turkey liver forcemeat. Dissolve the gelatin in the warmed chicken broth and stir it into the forcemeat. Add the cream. Add extra seasoning if necessary. Transfer to the mold, or molds, coated with aspic. Leave to cool in the refrigerator and cover the top with aspic. Leave until completely set. To unmold the mousse stand in hot water for a few moments and slide the delicate mousse very gently onto a flat dish.

Broccoli Torte

Tourte de brocoli

sherry wine aspic for coating
$\frac{1}{2}$ lb venison fillet, fried and well seasoned
then thinly sliced
2 slices carrot
2 slivers of truffle
$\frac{3}{4}$ lb broccoli, cleaned
$\frac{1}{2}$ teaspoon salt
freshly ground white pepper
$\frac{1}{8}$ teaspoon nutmeg
thyme and basil
2 envelopes unflavored gelatin
6 tablespoons brown game broth
1 cup lightly whipped cream
1 lb puff pastry
1 egg yolk for glazing

Coat two deep soup plates with sherry wine aspic and leave to set. Arrange the thinly sliced venison fillet in a circle over the aspic. Place a slice of boiled carrot and a piece of truffle in the center of each circle.

Cook the broccoli in salted water until soft, drain and leave to cool. Purée in a blender and, if necessary, push through a fine strainer. Add salt, pepper, nutmeg and herbs to taste. Dissolve the gelatin in the hot game broth and stir into the broccoli purée, which should be at room temperature. Then gradually beat in the lightly whipped cream and transfer to the soup plates coated with aspic and venison. Smooth the tops and

leave the mousse in the refrigerator to set.

Roll out the puff pastry to about $\frac{1}{4}$-inch thick and cut a $1\frac{1}{2}$-inch wide ring of pastry the same size as the plate to go around the mousse. It can be either plain or fluted. Roll out the remaining pastry once more very thinly. Cut two rounds the same size as the rings and transfer to a baking sheet. Brush with egg yolk, top with the rings of pastry and brush these too with egg yolk. Leave to stand for 15 minutes and then bake in a preheated 425° oven for 10–12 minutes. Unmold the broccoli mousses into the cooled pastry bases.

1 **Coating with aspic jelly** (the technical term for this is *chemiser*). Pour cool aspic carefully into the mold, making sure no air bubbles form. This will only be possible if the aspic itself is free of bubbles.

2 **Stand the mold in iced water.** The water should come almost to the top of the mold. Leave the aspic until it begins to set – the length of time needed for this will depend on the temperature of the liquid aspic.

3 **Pour off the aspic:** it should leave behind an even layer about $\frac{1}{8}$ inch thick. If the layer is too thin refill the mold with liquid aspic and return to the iced water.

Smoked Fish Mousse

Mousse de poisson fumé

Smoked salmon mousse
5 oz smoked salmon fillet
$\frac{1}{2}$ cup velouté sauce made with fish broth
salt and freshly ground white pepper
1 envelope unflavored gelatin
5 tablespoons beef broth
$\frac{1}{2}$ cup whipped cream
Smoked trout mousse
5 oz smoked trout fillets
$\frac{1}{2}$ cup velouté sauce made with fish broth
salt and freshly ground white pepper
1 envelope unflavored gelatin
5 tablespoons beef broth
$\frac{1}{2}$ cup whipped cream

light fish aspic for coating
1 (2-oz) jar caviar
1-quart mold

Cut up the smoked salmon and purée slowly in a blender with the velouté sauce. Sieve through a fine strainer and season. Dissolve the gelatin in the hot broth and add to the purée. Before the mixture sets, whisk in about a quarter of the whipped cream and then fold in the rest with a wooden spoon.

Prepare the smoked trout mousse in exactly the same way.

Coat the mold with the fish aspic and leave to set in the refrigerator. Fill first with the salmon mousse. Make a hollow along the center and fill with caviar, leave to stand for a while and then add the trout mousse. Bang the mold repeatedly on a damp cloth to prevent air gaps. Smooth the top and leave to chill in the refrigerator. Cover the top with fish aspic and allow to set.

To unmold the mousse, dip the mold into hot water for a few seconds, slide the mousse carefully onto a flat dish and serve with caviar.

This smoked fish mousse with caviar filling is a real luxury coated in a delicate fish aspic. The coating of aspic not only protects the mousse and keeps it fresh, but should also bring out its flavor. So it is important for the flavors of the mousse and its coating to harmonize well, but the flavor of the aspic should not dominate that of the mousse.

Carrot Mousse

Mousse de carottes

5 oz carrots
½ cup velouté sauce made with chicken broth
1 envelope unflavored gelatin
3 tablespoons beef broth
salt and ground white pepper
½ cup whipped cream
light aspic made with chicken broth and sherry or white wine for coating
6 6-oz molds or custard cups

Boil the carrots until soft, then dice and slowly purée them in a blender with the velouté sauce. Sieve through a fine strainer. Dissolve the gelatin in the hot broth. Whisk into the carrot mixture and season. Before the mixture begins to set whisk in about a quarter of the whipped cream, then gradually fold in the rest with a wooden spoon. Coat the molds with aspic and leave to set. Add the carrot mousse before it begins to set, smooth the top and leave to set in the refrigerator. If you use fluted molds the aspic layer will need to be slightly thicker; they will also need warming for longer if they are to unmold easily, which will mean losing some of the aspic.

Unmold the mousses and garnish with a blanched parsley leaf and a slice of carrot. Serve with a tomato and green peppercorn sauce. *Serves 6.*

Goose Liver Mousse

Mousse de foie gras

5 oz fattened (or prepared) goose liver
¼ teaspoon pâté salt
ground white pepper
1 tablespoon Armagnac
2 tablespoons port wine
½ tablespoon butter
⅓ cup jellifying chicken broth
⅓ cup velouté sauce made with chicken broth
1 envelope unflavored gelatin
2 tablespoons beef broth
½ cup whipped cream
Muscatel wine aspic for coating
6 slices truffle
6 6-oz molds

Cut the prepared goose liver into thick slices, season and cover with the Armagnac and port wine. Leave to marinate in the refrigerator for at least 2–3 hours. Wipe the liver dry, fry until semi-cooked in the butter and drain on paper towels. Reduce the chicken broth and marinade to a thick liquid and strain over the liver. Sieve the liver and velouté sauce through a fine strainer. Dissolve the gelatin in the hot beef broth. When the liver mixture is at room temperature whisk in the gelatin mixture. Check the seasoning. Before the mixture begins to set, whisk in about a quarter of the whipped cream and then gradually fold in the remainder with a wooden spoon. Coat the molds with aspic, place a slice of truffle in the bottom of each and leave to set. Fill the molds with the goose liver mousse and leave to set in the refrigerator.

Unmold the mousses and serve with sliced kiwi fruit, sprinkled with pink peppercorns. *Serves 6.*

Individual mousses are more time-consuming to make for each mold has to be coated with aspic. But they look very attractive and in their aspic coating will keep fresher longer. Instead of small molds you can use custard cups, but they must taper toward the base so that they unmold easily.

Ham Mousse

Mousse de jambon

¾ lb cooked ham
I cup velouté sauce made with veal broth
salt and freshly ground white pepper
2 envelopes unflavored gelatin
6 tablespoons beef broth
I cup whipped cream
white wine aspic for coating
6 6-oz molds

Cut up the ham, grind then purée it in a blender with the velouté sauce. Sieve through a strainer and season. Dissolve the gelatin in the hot broth and add to the purée. Before the mixture sets whisk in about a quarter of the whipped cream and then gradually fold in the remainder with a wooden spoon. Coat the molds with aspic and leave to set. Fill with the ham mousse, smooth the tops and leave to set in the refrigerator. Cover the tops with aspic and leave to set.

Unmold the mousses and serve with an asparagus sauce. *Serves 6.*

Tomato Mousse

Mousse de tomates

2 cups diced, peeled and seeded tomatoes
¼ cup tomato catsup
2 tablespoons tomato juice
3 tablespoons tomato paste
salt, sugar and cayenne
1½ envelopes unflavored gelatin
3 tablespoons hot beef broth
I cup whipped cream
white wine aspic for coating
6 6-oz cups

Sieve half the diced tomato through a fine strainer, add the tomato catsup, tomato juice and tomato paste and season with salt, sugar and cayenne. Dissolve the gelatin in the hot broth and whisk into the tomato mixture. Before the mixture sets whisk in about a quarter of the whipped cream and then gradually fold in the remainder with a wooden spoon. Finally, fold in the remaining diced tomato. Coat the molds with aspic and leave to set. Fill with tomato mousse, smooth the tops and leave to set in the refrigerator. Cover with some more aspic and leave to set until firm.

Unmold the mousses and serve with a salad of shrimp, tomatoes and asparagus tips. *Serves 6.*

Jumbo Shrimp Mousse

Mousse de crevettes

¾ lb cooked jumbo shrimp, shelled and deveined
I cup velouté sauce made with fish broth
salt and freshly ground white pepper
2 envelopes unflavored gelatin
6 tablespoons hot beef broth
I cup whipped cream
light fish aspic for coating
2–3 tablespoons chopped dill
6 6-oz molds

Purée the shrimp and velouté sauce in a blender. Sieve through a strainer and season. Dissolve the gelatin in the hot broth and stir into the shrimp purée. Before the mixture sets whisk in about a quarter of the whipped cream, then gradually fold in the remaining cream with a wooden spoon. Coat the molds with aspic, sprinkle with dill and leave to set. Fill with the shrimp mousse, smooth the tops and leave in the refrigerator to set.

Unmold the mousses and serve with a lemon sauce. *Serves 6.*

Timbales or cup molds

This term covers a whole range of creations which resemble pâtés in some way, but it also covers other dishes which have little in common with them. Originally the term referred to piecrust pies in the shape of a small kettle drum (*timbale* in French). They were usually baked blind, that is, without their filling and then filled with some kind of stew. They were usually big enough to serve 4–6 people. Over the years the kettle drum shape changed to a cup shape and became smaller to serve one or two. These smooth or fluted molds were thinly lined with pastry (basic pie is best), filled with dried peas, covered with a pastry lid and baked. The lid was removed while still hot, the pie was filled, and the lid replaced before serving hot. But that is only one of many possibilities. Timbales can also be baked with the filling and served hot with a sauce or cold as individual hors d'oeuvre. Many fine timbale recipes use pasta dough, crêpes or macaroni arranged carefully in the mold as a casing. Today, at least with individual timbales, the pastry is often omitted altogether and the molds are lined with a fine forcemeat. They are filled, sealed with more forcemeat and poached in a water bath, then unmolded for serving.

Partridge Timbale with Morels in Cream

Timbale de perdreaux aux morilles à la crème

4 partridges, each weighing about $\frac{1}{2}$ lb
6 juniper berries, crushed
1 clove garlic, crushed
grated orange and lemon rind
$\frac{1}{4}$ oz pâté salt
2 egg whites, lightly beaten
$\frac{3}{4}$ cup flour panada
$1\frac{3}{4}$ cups whipped cream
$\frac{3}{4}$ oz dried morels
1 cup partridge or game essence
1 cup cream
salt and freshly ground white pepper
1 heaping tablespoon finely chopped chives
butter for greasing molds
4 8-oz timbale molds or cups of the same size

Bone the partridges. Cut the carefully trimmed meat, to give about $\frac{3}{4}$ lb, into strips and sprinkle with the crushed juniper berries, crushed garlic, orange and lemon rind and pâté salt. Cover with plastic wrap and chill. When the meat has had time to absorb the flavor of the seasoning grind twice through the finest blade of the grinder. Over ice, gradually beat in the lightly beaten egg whites and then the sieved panada. Sieve the forcemeat through a strainer, beat in the whipped cream a spoonful at a time and continue beating until it is fully incorporated and the forcemeat smooth and silky.

Leave the dried morels in water to swell slightly, thoroughly wash to remove any dirt and then soak in fresh water. Boil for about 25 minutes in the soaking water and partridge essence, drain, leave to cool and chop. Reduce the cream until thick, strain into the morel juice and season. Add the morels and chives, stir in and leave to cool. Grease the timbale molds or cups generously with butter and cover the bottom and sides evenly with about three quarters of the forcemeat. This is quite easy with a pastry bag and plain tube. Pipe a spiral of forcemeat over the bottom and up the sides of each mold and smooth flat with a round-bladed knife. Fill with the stewed morels and cover with the remaining forcemeat.

Cook for about 15 minutes in a water bath, regulating the oven so that the water temperature does not exceed 176°. If you use cups allow an extra 5–6 minutes.

Pistachio Timbale with Sautéed Pheasant

Timbale de pistaches au sauté de faisan

$\frac{3}{4}$ lb lean boneless pork
salt and ground white pepper
2 egg whites
$\frac{3}{4}$ cup flour panada
1 cup pistachios
$\frac{1}{2}$ cup milk
1 cup whipped cream
1 cup cream
1 cup pheasant essence
$\frac{1}{4}$ lb lean pheasant meat
1 tablespoon oil
butter for greasing molds
4 8-oz timbale molds

Cut the trimmed pork into strips and season it. Grind twice through the finest blade of the grinder. Gradually beat in the lightly beaten egg whites and then the sieved panada. Purée the pistachios with the milk in a blender and work into the forcemeat. Sieve the forcemeat through a fine strainer and beat in the whipped cream a spoonful at a time.

Reduce the cream until thick, then strain it into the hot pheasant essence and season. Dice the pheasant meat and seal it in oil. Remove from the skillet, drain and add to the sauce. Stir in well and leave to cool. Coat the buttered timbale molds with about three-quarters of the forcemeat. Fill with the sautéed pheasant and cover with the remaining forcemeat.

Cook in a water bath for about 15 minutes, regulating the heat so that the water temperature does not exceed 176°. *Serves 4.*

Salmon Timbale with Frog's Legs

Timbale de saumon au sauté de cuisses de grenouilles

$\frac{3}{4}$ lb salmon fillet
salt and ground white pepper
2 egg whites, lightly beaten
$\frac{3}{4}$ cup flour panada
$1\frac{3}{4}$ cups whipped cream
2 tablespoons diced shallots
$1\frac{1}{2}$ tablespoons butter
7 pairs frog's legs
3 tablespoons white wine
1 cup veal broth
1 cup cream
lemon juice
butter for greasing molds
4 8-oz timbale molds

Cut the salmon into strips, season and chill. Grind twice through the finest blade of the grinder and work in the lightly beaten egg whites and then the sieved panada. Sieve the forcemeat through a strainer and add the whipped cream a spoonful at a time.

Soften the diced shallots in the butter. Fry the frog's legs, add the wine and broth and simmer for 8 to 10 minutes. Bone the frog's legs and cut them into small pieces. Reduce the broth by about three quarters and strain. Reduce the cream until thick, strain into the broth, add the frog's legs and season with salt and lemon juice. Coat the molds with the forcemeat, add the filling and cover with the remaining forcemeat. Cook in a water bath for about 15 minutes with water at 176°. Serve the salmon timbales on a bed of steamed spinach. *Serves 4.*

Pike Timbale with Shrimp in Dill Sauce

Timbale de brochet aux crevettes en sauce à l'aneth

1 tablespoon butter
2 shallots, sliced
$\frac{3}{4}$ lb pike fillet
salt and ground white pepper
$\frac{1}{8}$ teaspoon each nutmeg and
English mustard powder
2 egg whites, lightly beaten
$\frac{3}{4}$ cup flour panada
$1\frac{3}{4}$ cups whipped cream
$1\frac{1}{4}$ cups cream
1 tablespoon lemon juice
5 oz shelled shrimp, deveined
2 tablespoons chopped dill
butter for greasing molds
4 8-oz timbale molds

Melt the butter, soften the shallots without allowing them to color and leave to cool. Remove any bones from the pike fillet, cut into strips, season with salt, pepper, nutmeg and mustard, sprinkle with the shallots and chill. Grind twice through the finest blade of the grinder. Gradually beat in the lightly beaten egg whites and then the sieved panada. Sieve the forcemeat through a fine strainer and beat in the whipped cream a spoonful at a time.

Reduce the cream until thick, strain, season with salt, pepper and lemon juice, add the shrimp and simmer for a few minutes. Finally add the dill and leave to cool. Grease the timbale molds generously with butter. Cover the bottoms and sides with about three-quarters of the forcemeat, fill with the shrimp mixture and cover with the remaining forcemeat. Cook, in a water bath, for about 15 minutes with water at 176°.

Smoked Salmon Timbale with Mussels

Timbale de saumon fumé aux moules

$\frac{1}{2}$ lb smoked salmon fillet
$\frac{3}{4}$ cup whipped cream
2 tablespoons diced shallots
1 teaspoon butter · $\frac{1}{4}$ cup cream
5 oz bottled mussels, drained
1 tablespoon freshly grated horseradish
salt and ground white pepper
butter for greasing molds
4 6-oz timbale molds

Use only tender, best quality smoked salmon, to give the forcemeat a delicate

flavor. Finely dice the salmon, chill thoroughly and purée in a food processor. Over ice, gradually beat in the whipped cream.

Soften the diced shallots in the butter. Reduce the cream until thick and strain over the shallots. Add the mussels and horseradish, season, stir well and leave to cool. Generously grease the timbale molds with butter and cover the bottoms and sides with about three-quarters of the forcemeat. Fill with the mussel mixture and cover with the remaining forcemeat.

Cook, in a water bath, for about 15 minutes with water at 176°. *Serves 4.*

Fish forcemeats for individual timbales have one great advantage: they make a very light and airy hors d'oeuvre with great possibilities for variation. Unfilled fish or shellfish timbales are served with a suitable sauce. Hollow timbales can be filled with a forcemeat of the same fish or with shrimp as in the Pike Timbale recipe above .

Broccoli Timbale with Walnut Sauce

Timbale de brocoli à la sauce aux noix

¾ lb broccoli, cleaned
1 tablespoon butter
1 cup chicken broth
salt, ground white pepper and nutmeg
2 eggs
3 tablespoons cream
butter for greasing molds
4 6-oz timbale molds

Cut the broccoli into small pieces and cook until soft in the butter and broth with salt, pepper and nutmeg to taste. Purée, sieve though a strainer, beat in the eggs and cream and check seasoning. Transfer the purée to the buttered molds and cook for 20–25 minutes in a 400° oven. *Serves 4.*

Carrot Timbale with Herb Sauce

Timbale de carottes à la sauce aux herbes

1¼ lb carrots, cleaned
1½ tablespoons butter
1 cup chicken broth
salt, sugar and nutmeg
3–4 eggs
5 tablespoons cream
butter for greasing molds
4 6-oz timbale molds

Cut the carrots into small pieces and cook in the butter and broth with salt, sugar and nutmeg to taste. Purée, sieve through a strainer, beat in the eggs and cream and check seasoning. Transfer to the buttered molds and cook in a preheated 400° oven for about 20–25 minutes. *Serves 4.*

Cauliflower Timbale with Spinach Sauce

Timbale de chou-fleur à la sauce d'épinards

¾ lb cauliflower, washed
1 tablespoon butter
1 cup chicken broth
salt and nutmeg
2 eggs
3 tablespoons cream
butter for greasing molds
4 6-oz timbale molds

Cook the cauliflower in the butter and broth with salt and nutmeg to taste until soft. Purée, sieve through a strainer, beat in the eggs and cream and check seasoning. Transfer to the buttered molds and cook in a preheated 400° oven for about 20–25 minutes. *Serves 4.*

Lobster Parfait

Parfait d'écrevisses

1 lb rock lobster tail meat
1 teaspoon salt
freshly ground white pepper
1 egg white, lightly beaten
½ cup flour panada
½ cup light cream
1 cup whipped cream
2 tablespoons chopped dill
butter for greasing mold
1-quart pâté mold
light fish aspic and
chopped dill to finish

Cut half of the lobster meat into pieces, sprinkle with the seasoning and chill. Grind twice through the finest blade of the grinder. Over ice beat in the egg white and then the

Chicken Parfait with Chicken Liver and Mushrooms

Parfait de volaille aux foies de volaille et cèpes

¾ lb lean chicken meat
pâté salt and white pepper
⅛ teaspoon ground ginger
⅛ teaspoon cardamom
1 egg white, lightly beaten
¾ cup flour panada
1½ cups whipped cream
5 oz chicken livers
5 oz mushrooms, washed
1–2 tablespoons oil
butter for greasing mold
1-quart pâté mold
Madeira wine aspic
3 tablespoons chopped parsley

sieved flour panada, adding a little at a time. Sieve the forcemeat through a strainer and add the light cream and then the whipped cream a spoonful at a time. Finally stir in the dill.

Dice the remaining lobster and stir into the forcemeat. Grease the mold with butter and line with roasting film. Fill with the forcemeat and smooth the top. Bang the mold several times on a damp cloth, seal and cook for 40 minutes in a water bath, with the water at 176°.

Unmold the lobster parfait, cover with light fish aspic and sprinkle with a little chopped dill.

Cut the chicken into strips, sprinkle with the pâté salt, pepper and spices and chill for at least 2–3 hours. Grind twice through the finest blade of the grinder. Over ice, first beat in the lightly beaten egg white and then gradually add the sieved panada. Sieve the forcemeat through a strainer and beat in the whipped cream a spoonful at a time.

Remove all skin and blood vessels from the chicken livers and cut into small pieces. Dice the mushrooms. Quickly fry the chicken livers and mushrooms separately in hot oil, drain and fold into the forcemeat. Line the buttered mold with roasting film, add the forcemeat and smooth the top. Fold the overhanging film over the forcemeat, cover the mold and cook, in a water bath, for about 40 minutes, with water at 176°.

When cool unmold the parfait, carefully

remove the film, cover with Madeira wine aspic, sprinkle well with parsley and cover again with Madeira wine aspic. Leave in the refrigerator to set and then arrange over a bed of diced Madeira aspic.

Pheasant Parfait with Foie Gras and Morels

Parfait de faisan au foie gras et morilles

2 lb pheasant or other game bones and
trimmings
5 tablespoons oil
1 small carrot, coarsely chopped
1 onion, coarsely chopped
2 quarts water
bouquet garni ($\frac{1}{2}$ sprig parsley, white of
1 leek, 1 piece celery, 1 bay leaf)
1 teaspoon salt
12 juniper berries, crushed
6 white peppercorns
$1\frac{1}{2}$ cloves garlic, crushed
5 oz trimmed pheasant meat
1 teaspoon pâté salt
grated rind of $\frac{1}{2}$ orange and $\frac{1}{2}$ lemon
1 egg white, lightly beaten
$\frac{1}{4}$ cup flour panada
$\frac{3}{4}$ cup whipped cream
$\frac{3}{4}$ oz dried morels
5 oz goose liver, marinated in
$2\frac{1}{2}$ tablespoons brandy
butter for greasing mold
2-cup pâté mold

Roast the bones and pheasant meat
trimmings in the oil with the carrot and
onion, adding a little cold water from time
to time. Transfer to a saucepan and add the
remaining water. Bring to a boil, skim and
simmer for 2–3 hours. About 45 minutes
before the end of the cooking time add the
bouquet garni, salt, 8 juniper berries, the
peppercorns and 1 garlic clove. Strain
through cheesecloth and reduce to about 3
cups.

Remove any skin and ligaments from the
pheasant and cut into strips. Sprinkle with
the pâté salt, remaining juniper berries and
garlic and the orange and lemon rinds.
Grind twice through the finest blade of the
grinder. Over ice, beat in the lightly beaten
egg white a little at a time. Sieve the chilled
panada and gradually work into the
mixture. Sieve the mixture and beat until
smooth and silky. Work in the whipped
cream a spoonful at a time. Chill the
forcemeat thoroughly after each stage.

Soak the dried morels in water until they
begin to swell, wash thoroughly and soak in
2 cups fresh water. Then boil in the soaking
water and an equal quantity of pheasant
broth for 25 minutes. Leave to cool.
Remove the morels from the pan and reduce
the liquid until a thick essence. Cut the
morels into large pieces, return to the
essence, bring to a boil and leave to cool.

Cut up the goose liver and work into the
forcemeat with the morels and essence.

Grease the mold with butter, line carefully
with roasting film and fill with the
forcemeat. Fold over the overhanging film
and cover the mold.

Cook in a water bath for about 35
minutes with water at 176°. Serve with a
rose-hip sauce, delicately flavored with
Armagnac.

Mushroom Tartlets

½ cup cream
½ lb mushrooms, sliced and braised
salt
ground white pepper
2 tablespoons diced onion
1½ tablespoons butter
½ lb fresh bulk spinach
nutmeg
2 tablespoons broth · 4 tartlet cases
2 tablespoons Hollandaise sauce

Reduce the cream until thick, strain and bring back to a boil with the mushrooms. Season. Soften the onion in the butter, add the spinach and cook for a few minutes. Season with salt, pepper and nutmeg and add the broth. Fill the tartlet cases first with the spinach and then the mushrooms, cover with Hollandaise sauce and brown under the broiler. *Serves 4.*

Veal and Asparagus Tartlets

1 cup cream
¼ cup velouté sauce made with veal broth
¼ lb boneless veal, cooked (braised) and diced
¼ lb mushrooms, cooked and sliced
salt and ground white pepper
4 tartlet cases
12 asparagus tips, boiled
¼ cup Mornay sauce

Reduce the cream and strain into the velouté sauce. Add the veal and mushrooms, warm through and season with salt and pepper. Fill the tartlet cases with the mixture, top each with 3 asparagus tips, and cover each with a tablespoon of Mornay sauce. Brown under the broiler. *Serves 4.*

Salmon and Egg Tartlets

¼ cup mayonnaise
salt and ground white pepper
lemon juice
5 oz salmon fillet, cooked and diced
4 tartlet cases
4 fried eggs
4 heaping teaspoons caviar

Season the mayonnaise with salt, pepper and lemon juice and stir in the salmon. Fill the tartlet cases with the mixture, top each with a fried egg and garnish with the caviar. *Serves 4.*

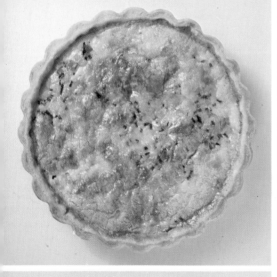

Cheese and Bacon Tartlets

2 slices bacon, fried, drained and crumbled
2 tablespoons diced cooked ham
¼ cup diced Emmental cheese
½ cup diced onion softened in butter
4 tartlet cases
¼ cup cream
1 egg · 1 egg yolk
1 tablespoon grated Parmesan cheese
salt
sweet paprika
1 teaspoon finely chopped chives

Mix together the bacon, ham, cheese and onion and arrange in the tartlet cases. Beat the cream with the egg, egg yolk, Parmesan, salt, paprika and chives, pour over the ingredients in the tartlet cases and bake for about 10 minutes in a preheated 425° oven. *Serves 4.*

Liver and Apple Tartlets

8 slices fattened goose liver, weighing about ¾ oz each
salt and ground white pepper
flour
1 tablespoon oil
4 tartlet cases
8 slices apple, poached in 1 cup cream
6 tablespoons Madeira sauce
12 large green grapes, peeled and poached
2 slices bacon, cut into fine strips, fried and drained

Season the goose liver with salt and pepper, dip in flour and fry each side in the oil. Line the tartlet cases with the apple slices, add the goose liver, cover with Madeira sauce and garnish with the grapes and bacon. *Serves 4.*

Mussels in Cream Tartlets

2 tablespoons diced onion
1 tablespoon butter
3 tablespoons diced celery
3 tablespoons diced carrot
a little white wine
1 cup cream
½ lb bottled mussels, drained
1 teaspoon each chopped dill and parsley
salt and ground white pepper
4 tartlet cases

Soften the onion in the butter, add the celery and carrot and soften them also, then add the wine and braise for a few minutes. Reduce the cream and strain into the vegetables. Add the mussels and herbs, season and warm through. Use to fill the tartlet cases. *Serves 4.*

Artichoke Tartlets

2½ oz canned artichoke hearts
2 tablespoons cream sauce
salt and ground white pepper
1¼ cups veal forcemeat
4 tartlet cases
truffle strips for garnish

Purée the artichokes and warm through in the cream sauce. Season with salt and pepper. Pipe a ring of veal forcemeat into the tartlet cases and fill the center with the artichoke purée, then cover with the remaining forcemeat. Bake for about 8 minutes in a preheated 425° oven. Garnish with strips of truffle. *Serves 4.*

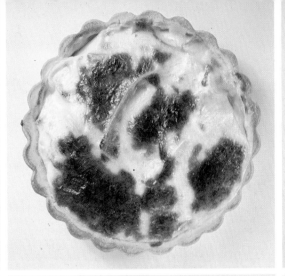

Leek Gratin Tartlets

½ cup cream sauce
2 tablespoons grated Parmesan cheese
1 tablespoon whipped cream
¼ lb leeks, chopped and braised
3 slices bacon, cut into fine strips, fried and drained
salt and ground white pepper
4 tartlet cases
2½ oz Swiss cheese, sliced

Warm the cream sauce, fold in the Parmesan cheese, cream, leeks and bacon and season. Line the tartlet cases with the cheese slices, cover with the leek mixture and brown under the broiler. *Serves 4.*

Sea Bass Tartlets

12 slices sea bass, each weighing about ⅓ oz
6 tablespoons velouté sauce made with fish broth
½ teaspoon chopped basil
salt and ground white pepper
a little white wine
4 tartlet cases
¼ cup each shredded carrot, celeriac and green of leek, lightly braised in butter and a little fish broth

Poach the sea bass in fish broth. Warm the velouté sauce and season with basil, salt, pepper and wine. Line the tartlet cases with the shredded vegetables, top each with 3 slices sea bass and cover with the basil sauce. *Serves 4.*

Macaroni Tartlets

1 cup boiled macaroni
¼ cup diced cooked ham
1 cup sliced mushrooms, braised
1 tomato, peeled, seeded and diced
4 tartlet cases
6 tablespoons Madeira sauce
1 tablespoon grated Swiss cheese

Mix together the macaroni, ham, mushrooms and tomato and spoon the mixture into the tartlet cases. Cover with the Madeira sauce, sprinkle with cheese and brown under the broiler. *Serves 4.*

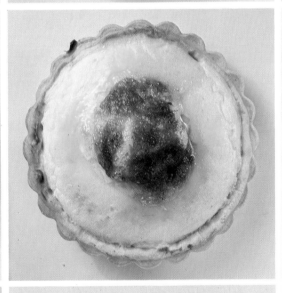

Chicken Tartlets

½ cup cream
2 tablespoons velouté sauce made with chicken broth
½ cup finely diced cooked chicken
1 cup finely diced cooked mushrooms
salt and ground white pepper
¾ cup chicken forcemeat
4 tartlet cases
4 teaspoons Hollandaise sauce

Reduce the cream and strain it into the velouté sauce. Add the chicken and mushrooms and season. Pipe a ring of chicken forcemeat into the tartlet cases and bake for 8 minutes in a preheated 425° oven. Fill the center with the chicken and mushroom mixture, cover each with 1 teaspoon Hollandaise sauce and brown under the broiler. *Serves 4.*

Chanterelle Tartlets

2 tablespoons diced shallots
1½ tablespoons butter
½ lb small canned chanterelles
salt and ground white pepper
1¾ cups cream
1 tablespoon chopped parsley
8 quail breasts, fried
reduced quail broth
4 tartlet cases

Soften the shallots in the butter, add the drained chanterelles, cook for a few minutes and then season. Reduce the cream until thick, strain and add the chanterelles and parsley. Season. Brush the quail breasts with the reduced broth. Fill the tartlet cases with the chanterelles, and top with the quail breasts. *Serves 4.*

Bouchées, Patties and Vol-au-vents

This is a chapter on puff pastry pies, even though they were not all originally made in this type of pastry. But today they all have something in common. They are baked as pastry cases, that is, blind, and filled with a hot filling before serving. There are also more recent recipes with cold fillings, but puff pastry is in fact much more suitable for hot fillings. It has a better flavor hot than cold, especially if not made entirely with butter. When hot it is flaky and light and entirely suited to its warm filling.

Bouchées, as the name implies, were originally small – almost miniature – pies, which could be eaten in one mouthful. (The French word *bouche* means mouth, i.e. mouthful.) These are still made for special occasions, but have unfortunately been largely replaced by the somewhat larger individual patties. It is much easier to make one patty per person for an hors d'oeuvre or *entremet*, and the larger size means less chopping for the filling. So the term "Bouchée" on a menu must not be taken too literally, and you must be prepared to eat them with a fork. Regardless of whether you choose to make bouchées or patties, both are the quickest to make of the pie family. The pastry cases can be baked well in advance, freeze well (although freezing is not always necessary) and when warmed through are as crisp and tasty as they are when freshly made. You can also buy them ready made from the baker or from a supermarket. But ready-bought cases do not have that special all-butter flavor. To save time you can also use ready-bought fillings, which are available in a variety of qualities and prices. But of course this would not suit the tastes of a real gourmet.

Patties are small puff pastry pies which are rather more difficult to define, but they too have their history. They are thought to have originated in the medieval courts of Les Baux and Orange in Provence. It is certainly true that the troubadours appreciated good food and in this land of milk and honey with its wealth of vegetables, meat and fish there was every opportunity

for culinary discoveries of this kind. The edible patty case used to be made with pie pastry, baked blind and covered with a pastry lid which helped keep the delicate filling warm. But there were also recipes which used potato dough, a dough from groats or pasta dough. These patties are closely related to the filled timbales. Weber's cookery lexicon of 1911 even gives a quick method of making a patty of this type: "Grate the crust off a small roll, cut across the center, remove the bread from the inside of the roll and fry in lard." Today puff pastry patties are often made without a lid. They are baked in a wide range of sizes and shapes, ranging from the small individual patty to a large quiche. Round, oval or square, any shape is possible and so of course is any filling, provided it is delicious and warm.

The story of the invention of the patty case entirely merits the word "story." Like many other inventions in the history of cooking, they are attributed to the famous French chef, Carême. He was the first to try making a patty with puff pastry instead of the traditional basic piecrust. When his assistant opened the oven he is said to have shouted, "*Maître, il vole au vent*" (Master, it's flying into the air). For the flat pastry had risen into a large dome. The master chef and the words of his assistant are still commemorated today in the name *vol-au-vent*, for the English equivalent of patty case comes nowhere near the descriptive quality of the French term. Puff pastry is a highly individual piecrust, which takes a long time to prepare and whose use is almost entirely restricted to the unpretentious bouchée or patty. But they can also be a great showpiece on any table and, with the right filling, a great delicacy.

Today, even the filling has become a matter of some debate with nouvelle cuisine turning its back on the rich sauces which complement the ingredients of the filling so well. It is, of course, possible to make new style fillings for patties, but these omit the cream or velouté sauce. Just think of the great classic garnishes (the garnish in this case is the main ingredient bound by the sauce) such as *Mirabeau* or *Financière*. We don't have to stick to these classic fillings, but for puff pastry patties only the best is good enough.

A fine lobster filling which can be used in puff pastry patties of any shape or size, from bouchées to vol-au-vents. This delicate pastry is the best for these fine sauces.

1 **First cut out the rings.** Roll the puff pastry to ⅛-inch thick and cut into rings with a sharp 2¾-inch cutter and a 1¾-inch cutter. Roll out the remaining pastry to about ⅛-inch thick and cut out bases to match.

2 **Transfer to a baking sheet** moistened with water. Brush the rings with egg yolk, avoiding getting any egg on the sides. Place the side with the egg yolk onto the base and press down gently.

Puff Pastry Patties

Success in baking bouchées, and particularly the larger patties and vol-au-vents, depends primarily on the quality of the puff pastry. It must rise evenly. Ready-bought pastry rarely rises crookedly for, in the first instance it contains a highly stable mixture of fats and secondly it is turned mechanically. This guarantees even rolling with pastry layers of even thickness, and these are essential if it is to rise evenly during baking.

For small quantities you can buy frozen puff pastry in a block (good for rolling) or in ready-rolled rectangular sheets. These are too thin to use for large patties and should be used for nothing larger than small bouchées. But if you stick two sheets of pastry together with egg white or water and roll them quickly together with the rolling pin, this gives pastry of the right thickness. Halve the rectangle of pastry and cut to size with a sharp knife to give square patties. These have the advantages of greater stability for they tend to rise more evenly in baking and they also use all the pastry. If you want a pastry made with butter you will have to make your own, sticking strictly to the basic rules (pages 16–17). In addition, the butter puff pastry must be worked when it is as cool as possible, for butter becomes softer much quicker than vegetable fats, and is therefore slightly more difficult to handle.

When using puff pastry, whether home-made or frozen, there are a few essential points which must be followed to give good results.

● Never roll out the pastry in one direction only, but where possible roll alternately from left to right and then from top to bottom. If the pastry is rolled in one direction only your round patty will be oval in shape when you take it from the oven.

● Puff pastry, especially when made with all butter, should be as cool as possible for handling. Ideally it should be rolled on a sheet of marble in a cool room. It is a good idea to open a window if the weather is cool or to cover the worktop with a cloth and ice cubes.

● Always roll the thick rings first. They have to rise most and should be cut out while the pastry is still perfect. Use sharp cutters to prevent squashing the edges of the pastry together.

● Leftover pastry is good enough for the bases. Keep them thin to leave room for a lot of filling. If you use re-rolled leftovers they will not rise so much.

● Go carefully with the egg yolk! When brushing with egg yolk or putting the patties together do not allow any egg yolk to run down the sides. The pastry will stick together where there is any egg yolk and prevent even rising.

● Before baking puff pastry needs to stand for at least 15 minutes in a very cool place. This allows the pastry to settle and makes for more even rising in the oven.

● Dampen the baking sheet with water, but do not grease it. The pastry itself contains enough fat to prevent sticking. The water turns to steam in the hot oven and helps the pastry rise. You can increase the steam by splashing half a cup of water into the oven and immediately closing the door. This will increase the amount of steam considerably.

● Puff pastry needs uninterrupted heat if it is to rise. Never open the oven door during the

3 **Prick with a fork** to prevent any air bubbles forming in the base during baking. Brush the tops of the rings with egg yolk, again making sure not to get any egg yolk down the sides.

4 **Rolls of foil for even rising.** Professional chefs use metal tubes, but aluminum foil folded double or triple is almost as good. They should fit closely to the inside edge of the pastry.

5 **To make the lids** roll any leftover pastry to ⅛-inch thick. Cut out with a plain or fluted 2½-inch cutter. Brush with egg yolk and lightly mark a diamond pattern in the pastry with a fork for decoration.

first 5 minutes of baking. This could make the steam condense and affect the rising of the pastry.

● The oven should be preheated to 425°. It is advisable to have the oven hotter still, at 475° for the first 5 minutes. This will make the pastry rise quicker. Then reduce the heat to 425°. This will prevent the patties either falling or burning.

● Small pastry lids need a much shorter baking time. So remove them from the oven earlier, unless you are baking them on the same baking sheet as the patties.

Puff pastry cases are in a manner of speaking an edible container for a variety of hot dishes. They rightly deserve their popularity as the round vol-au-vents or bouchées. Less familiar are the variously shaped patties. These can be square, round, oval or baked in a variety of other shapes.

The main thing once more is to obey the basic rules of the game, and then there is no reason why you shouldn't be able to make successful patties in flower or fish shapes.

Puff pastry is best frozen after baking. It is a good idea to make the filling in advance too and to freeze it in suitable sized portions. Then you can make an excellent hors d'oeuvre in a matter of minutes. But baked pastry cases will also keep for a long time out of the refrigerator, providing they are kept in a dry room and away from strongly flavored foods. Puff pastry is very sensitive to other flavors, but you can overcome this problem by wrapping tightly in aluminum foil.

Lobster Filling

Ragoût d'homard

3 tablespoons oil
1 lb lobster and shrimp shells
1¼ cups mixed diced carrot and onion
¼ cup brandy
⅓ cup tomato paste
1 quart fish broth
1 piece each celery and leek
¼ onion
¼ bay leaf
1 sprig thyme
2 tablespoons each flour and butter
worked to a paste
a little salt and cayenne
½ lb cooked lobster meat, diced
¼ lb mushrooms, cooked

Heat the oil and sauté the lobster and shrimp shells. Add the diced carrot and onion and continue frying. Add the brandy, stir in the tomato paste and add the broth. Add the leek, celery, onion, herbs, salt and cayenne and simmer for 20 minutes. Strain.

Reduce the lobster broth by half, bind with the flour and butter paste and season to taste. Strain again, add the lobster and mushrooms and warm through without allowing to boil. *Serves 4.*

Bouchées à la reine

5 oz mushrooms
3 tablespoons lemon juice
1 cup velouté sauce made with chicken
broth
¾ cup cream
salt and ground white pepper
1 teaspoon Worcestershire sauce
¾ cup diced cooked veal

Wash and trim the mushrooms. Bring a little water to a boil with 2 tablespoons of the lemon juice and braise the mushrooms for 5 minutes. Drain and cut into quarters. Bring the velouté sauce to a boil and add the strained, reduced cream. Simmer until the sauce thickens, stirring continuously. Season the sauce with salt, pepper, Worcestershire sauce and the remaining lemon juice. Add the mushrooms and veal and warm through but do not allow to boil. *Serves 4.*

Basic White Sauce

Velouté Sauce

3 tablespoons butter
1½ tablespoons finely chopped onion
¼ cup flour
1½ quarts fat-free cold broth (veal,
chicken, fish or vegetable)
2 cups cream
salt and ground white pepper

Normally veal broth is used to make the sauce as this goes well with most flavors. But for best results use the original broth, i.e. for a chicken filling use chicken broth.

1 **Make a roux (butter and flour liaison).** Soften the finely chopped onion in the melted butter. Sprinkle with flour and stir in quickly. Cook for 5 minutes, stirring continuously.

2 **Add the broth.** Add the cold broth a spoonful at a time, whisking in with a wire whisk. Bring to a boil, scraping the bottom of the pan continuously to prevent lumps forming and the sauce sticking to the pan.

Shrimp Patty

Croustade de langoustines

5 tablespoons butter
$\frac{3}{4}$ lb shelled jumbo shrimp
$\frac{1}{4}$ cup finely chopped shallots
1 tablespoon flour
2 cups chicken broth
$\frac{1}{2}$ teaspoon salt
$\frac{1}{8}$ teaspoon cayenne and ground ginger
1 cup cream
1 egg yolk
2 tablespoons chopped dill
8–10 asparagus tips, freshly boiled or
canned
$\frac{3}{4}$ lb puff pastry

Melt the butter, quickly seal the shrimp, remove from the skillet and drain on paper towels. Soften the shallots in the remaining butter. Sprinkle with flour and cook for a few minutes. Dilute with the chicken broth and reduce to about 1 cup. Season with salt, cayenne and ginger and sieve through a strainer. Reduce the cream until thick and also sieve into the sauce. Bind with the egg yolk. Add the dill, shrimp and asparagus tips and heat through, without allowing the mixture to boil. Transfer to the warm patty case. The patty case requires a base $\frac{1}{8}$-inch thick and 9 inches in diameter and a ring about $\frac{1}{3}$-inch thick. The rim will rise perfectly if you roll out the pastry to the right size and then cut out the ring. You will need 1 lb pastry for this method. You will need 5 oz pastry for the ring and more or less the same quantity for the base. A second method uses less pastry: roll out $\frac{3}{4}$ lb puff pastry until 15 inches in length and about $\frac{1}{3}$-inch thick. Cut 2 strips 1-inch wide. Press the remaining pastry back into a ball and

roll again to make the thin bases. Arrange the thin strips around the base to make a rim and press the ends firmly together. Fold a piece of aluminum foil over several times to give extra strength, shape the 2-inch wide strip into a ring and line the rim of the patty. Brush the top of the ring with egg yolk and leave to stand for at least 15 minutes. Bake in a preheated 425° oven for 15–20 minutes. After baking loosen the foil immediately from the rim and remove.

3 **Skim the sauce.** Simmer the sauce for 30 minutes. The scum which rises to the surface removes all impurities from the sauce and must be removed continuously until it no longer forms.

4 **Strain the cream into the sauce.** In a separate pan reduce the cream until thick, stirring continuously, and then strain into the sauce through a hair strainer to catch any lumps. Simmer for a further 15 minutes.

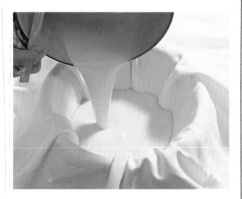

5 **Strain the sauce through cheesecloth.** When thick pour the sauce into a bowl lined with cheesecloth. Lift the cloth, twisting both ends to allow the sauce to drain through.

Vegetable Filling

Ragoût de légumes

6–8 medium-sized dried morels
1 cup shelled fresh peas
salt
¼ lb small young carrots
pinch of sugar
½ cup cream
1 cup velouté sauce made with chicken
broth
freshly ground white pepper
¼ lb asparagus tips, freshly boiled or
canned

Soak the morels in cold water, wash thoroughly and soak again in fresh water. Bring the soaking water (without the morels) to a boil, then add the morels and simmer gently over a low heat for 20–25 minutes. Cook the peas in a little salted water for about 15 minutes. Trim the carrots and cook in water with a little salt and sugar for about 20 minutes. Drain the morels and vegetables, catching the broth in a bowl. Reduce 2 tablespoons of the vegetable broth with the cream to half the quantity, stirring continuously. Add the velouté sauce and simmer until the sauce thickens, stirring continuously. Season with salt and pepper. Add the morels, peas, carrots and asparagus and heat through without allowing to boil. *Serves 4.*

Chicken Filling

Ragoût de poulet

6–8 medium-sized dried morels
1 cup velouté sauce made with chicken
broth
½ cup cream
1 teaspoon Worcestershire sauce
2 teaspoons lemon juice
salt and freshly ground white pepper
¾ lb cooked chicken breast meat

Soak the morels in cold water, wash thoroughly and soak again in fresh water until soft. Bring the soaking water to a boil, add the morels and simmer over a very low heat for 20–25 minutes. Drain thoroughly and chop. Bring the velouté sauce to a boil. Reduce the cream until thick, stirring continuously. Strain into the sauce and simmer until thick, stirring continuously. Season with Worcestershire sauce, lemon juice, salt and pepper. Chop the chicken and add to the sauce with the morels. Heat through without allowing the mixture to boil. Garnish with lemon wedges. *Serves 4.*

This filling is a sort of basic recipe and can be used with other types of poultry, turkey, pigeon or guinea fowl for example. Nor need you stick to morels: button, field or flat mushrooms go just as well with poultry.

Sweetbread Filling

Ragoût de ris de veau

1 lb sweetbreads
white of 1 leek
1 onion, stuck with 2 cloves
1 bay leaf
3 tablespoons butter
5–6 tablespoons port wine
1 cup reduced veal broth
¼ cup finely chopped shallots
1 cup cream
salt and ground white pepper

Leave the sweetbreads in a bowl under cold running water until they are completely white. Remove the skins. Transfer to lukewarm water, bring to a boil, pour off the water and transfer to cold water. Bring to a boil once more in fresh salted water. Cut up the leek and, when the liquid has boiled, add to the pan with the onion and bay leaf. Simmer for 5 minutes. Leave the sweetbreads to cool in the broth. Remove any remaining skin and break into small pieces. Fry quickly in 2 tablespoons of the butter over a high flame. Add ¼ cup port and ¾ cup veal broth and reduce by half, stirring frequently. Meanwhile soften the shallots in the remaining butter, add the remaining port and veal broth and simmer for a while. Add the reduced, strained cream and reduce until the sauce thickens, stirring continuously. Season with salt and pepper. Strain the sauce and check seasoning, add the sweetbreads and warm through once more without allowing the mixture to boil. Garnish with parsley. *Serves 4.*

Shrimp Nantua Filling

Ragoût d'écrevisses Nantua

5 oz cooked sweetbreads
3 oz mushrooms
flour
3 tablespoons butter
1 cup velouté sauce made with fish broth
2 tablespoons shrimp butter
salt and freshly ground white pepper
2 teaspoons lemon juice
½ cup veal forcemeat with diced truffles
¼ lb cooked shelled shrimp, deveined
strips of truffle for garnish

Break the sweetbreads into small pieces. Trim and quarter the mushrooms. Dip the sweetbreads and mushrooms in flour and fry quickly in hot butter over a high flame. Drain thoroughly on paper towels. Bring the velouté sauce to a boil and whisk in the shrimp butter. Season with salt, pepper and lemon juice. Take some of the veal forcemeat in the palm of your hand and shape into small balls with a teaspoon. Simmer the balls in water for about 5 minutes. Drain and add to the sauce with the sweetbreads, mushrooms and shrimp. Heat through without allowing the mixture to boil. Garnish the filled patties with strips of truffle. *Serves 4.*

If preferred the veal forcemeat can be replaced with small balls of lobster forcemeat.

Jumbo Shrimp Filling

Ragoût de crevettes roses

8 jumbo shrimp (about ½ lb)
salt
small sprig each dill and parsley
3 oz small mushrooms
about 3 tablespoons lemon juice
1 cup velouté sauce made with fish broth
1 tablespoon shrimp butter
freshly ground white pepper
⅛ teaspoon cayenne
pinch of sugar
dill for garnish

Wash the shrimp thoroughly under cold water. Bring a little water to a boil with salt and the herbs and simmer the shrimp for about 10 minutes. Wash the mushrooms. Bring a little water to a boil with 1 tablespoon of the lemon juice and braise the mushrooms in it for about 5 minutes. Remove the shrimp from the liquid, shell, devein and cut into pieces. Bring the velouté sauce to a boil and whisk in the shrimp butter. Season with salt, pepper, cayenne, the remaining lemon juice and sugar. Add the shrimp and drained, halved mushrooms and heat through without allowing the mixture to boil. Garnish with dill.

For special occasions add ½ cup lobster forcemeat in small balls. *Serves 4.*

Scallop Filling

Ragoût de coquilles Saint-Jacques

¾ lb scallops
½ cup finely chopped onion
¼ cup butter
1 teaspoon curry powder
3 tablespoons sherry wine
1 cup cream
1–2 teaspoons chili sauce
2 teaspoons mango chutney
salt
flour
1 banana
chopped pistachios and slices of pimiento
for garnish

Thaw and drain the scallops, if frozen. Soften the finely chopped onion in 1½ tablespoons of the butter, stir in the curry, dilute with the sherry and bring to a boil. Add the reduced, strained cream, season with chili sauce, mango chutney and salt and reduce to a thick sauce, stirring frequently. Meanwhile, wipe, dry and chop the scallops, dip in flour and fry in 1 tablespoon butter. Strain the sauce, check seasoning, add the scallops and warm through. Peel and slice the banana, coat lightly in flour and quickly brown in the remaining butter. Fold gently into the scallop mixture. Garnish with chopped pistachios and slices of pimiento. *Serves 4.*

Shrimp and Dill Filling

Ragoût d'écrevisses à l'aneth

1 lb asparagus
1½ quarts water
salt
pinch of sugar
2½ tablespoons lemon juice
¼ lb mushrooms
1 cup velouté sauce made with fish broth
freshly ground white pepper
1 tablespoon chopped dill
½ lb cooked shelled shrimp, deveined
dill for garnish

Peel the asparagus from the tips downwards, cut off the woody stems and tie together with thread. Bring the water to a boil with the salt, sugar and 1 tablespoon lemon juice and cook the asparagus for 20–30 minutes, depending on thickness. Remove from the pan, drain and cut off 8 tips. (You can use the liquid as the basis for a soup, adding the rest of the asparagus, finely chopped.) Wash the mushrooms. Bring a little water to a boil with 1 tablespoon of the remaining lemon juice and simmer the mushrooms in it for 5 minutes. Drain and halve. Bring the velouté sauce to a boil, season with salt, pepper and the rest of the lemon juice, stir in the dill, check seasoning, add the shrimp, asparagus and mushrooms and warm through without allowing the mixture to boil. Garnish with dill. *Serves 4.*

Snails in Riesling Sauce Filling

Ragoût d'escargots

3 dozen canned snails
¼ lb mushrooms
¼ cup finely chopped shallots
1 tablespoon butter
1 tablespoon brandy
¾ cup Riesling wine
2 tablespoons snail juice (from the can)
1 cup plus 1 tablespoon cream
1 clove garlic
salt
1 teaspoon chopped herbs (thyme, basil and marjoram)
1 teaspoon chopped parsley
freshly ground white pepper
1 egg yolk

Drain the liquid from the snails. Wash the mushrooms and cut off the stems. Soften the shallots in the butter. Add the snails and mushroom caps and cook for a few minutes. Add the brandy, bring to a boil and then add the wine and 2 tablespoons snail juice. Reduce by half, stirring continuously. Add the reduced, strained cream and reduce to a thick sauce, stirring continuously. Crush the garlic with a little salt. Season the filling with the garlic, herbs, salt and pepper. Beat the egg yolk into the extra tablespoon of cream and use to thicken the sauce. Do not allow the mixture to boil after this point. *Serves 4.*

Open Mushrooms with Sweetbread Filling

Ragoût de cèpes au ris de veau

¼ cup finely chopped shallots
3 tablespoons butter
1 tablespoon brandy
1 tablespoon Madeira wine
1 cup reduced veal broth
¾ cup cream
salt and ground white pepper
½ lb cooked sweetbreads
flour
½ lb open mushrooms
1 teaspoon chopped parsley
slices of truffle for garnish

Soften the shallots in a little of the butter. Add the brandy and Madeira, then the veal broth and reduce by half, stirring constantly. Reduce the cream until thick, strain into the sauce and reduce until thick, stirring continuously. Season with salt and pepper. Cut 4 slices of sweetbread and keep to one side for the garnish, then break the remaining sweetbreads into pieces. Dip in flour. Cook the mushrooms in the remaining butter, add the floured sweetbreads and cook for a few minutes. Add to the sauce and warm through without allowing the mixture to boil. Sprinkle with parsley and garnish with sliced sweetbread and truffle. *Serves 4.*

Large Patty Shell

Vol-au-vent

If you follow the basic rules for puff pastry this is nowhere near as difficult as it looks. To make a 12-inch diameter patty shell (inclusive of rim) you will need about $1\frac{1}{4}$ lb puff pastry. You should use new pastry for the base, top and rim with the original layers of pastry still intact, but trimmings can be used for the decoration. After working this pastry together into a ball you should, however, leave it to stand for a few minutes. Leave the assembled patty shell to stand in the refrigerator for 30 minutes before baking in a preheated $425°$ oven.

1 **Line a dome shape** (in this case a bombe mold) with aluminium foil, pressing the foil as smoothly as possible to the mold. Fill lightly with shredded paper and fold over the excess foil.

2 **Roll out a sheet of pastry $\frac{1}{8}$-inch thick.** Place the foil dome on the pastry. With a pastry wheel or knife cut around the dome leaving a rim 2-inches wide. Brush with egg yolk.

3 **Cover with the pastry lid.** It should be rolled to $\frac{1}{8}$-inch thick. Fold in half or, simpler still, roll around the rolling pin to prevent tearing. Press gently into shape over the foil dome.

4 **Cut off any excess pastry** to leave a rim of about 2 inches. Before cutting press the two sheets of pastry firmly together with your thumbs to make sure they stick well together. Smooth out any creases.

5 **Decorate the case.** Roll out the leftover pastry to $\frac{1}{16}$-inch thick and cut into tapering strips with either plain or fluted edges. Brush the top of the case with egg yolk and decorate with the strips. Cover the extreme top with 3 rounds of pastry, cut to varying sizes.

6 **Make the rim.** Roll fresh pastry and cut a long strip about $2\frac{1}{2}$-inches wide and $\frac{1}{8}$-inch thick, then cut to length. Brush the rim of the case with egg yolk and place the strip around the rim, pressing the ends firmly together.

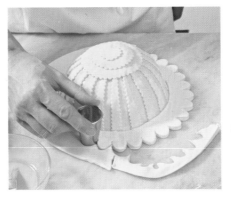

7 **Trim the rim; it can be either plain or fluted.** You have three layers of pastry one on top of the other here, which can be cut into semi-circles with a cutter or plain with a knife. If preferred you can cut notches around the rim with a sharp knife.

8 **Cut the lid off the case,** holding the case firmly with the other hand. Hold a cutter over the opening; it should be slightly larger than the opening. This will allow you to remove the foil and shredded paper without damaging the pastry case.

Pies: the English Pâtés

England, with its old English pies, is quite a special case. The English usually refer to basin pies, either completely encased in pastry or with just a pastry lid, as puddings, and these feature as one of the favorite national dishes. As they are usually cooked in water – especially when made with suet pastry – the term pudding is most appropriate. But there are also a large number of pies which are baked in the oven. Let us concentrate for the moment on pies, which are popular not only in Great Britain but throughout the whole Anglo-Saxon world. To present the full picture we must mention that the English possess numerous sweet pie recipes to complement their savory pies.

According to the English the pie was invented around the fifteenth century. But many would claim that the Ancient Romans had a hand in their invention when they conquered southern England and left behind many of their eating and cooking habits. It has been proved that these included the art of piemaking. But one fact is certain; over the centuries English cooks and housewives have perfected the art. Recipes have been handed down from generation to generation with continual refinements. English settlers took the tradition with them to the New World and today traditional pies, albeit with slight variations, are as popular in the eastern United States as in the mother country.

They can be baked in either pie molds or basins. For many pies the baking pan is lined with pastry, filled with the filling and topped with pastry. Or you can fill the pan with the filling alone and top it with a pastry lid. Sweet and savory pies are easily distinguished in England, for traditionally the top of a savory pie is decorated whereas sweet pies come without decoation.

When a visitor to Great Britain takes a stroll around an average supermarket, he will find all kinds of pies on sale. This could give the impression that pies are an important basic foodstuff for the British. This is not the case, of course, but the wide choice available does show the popularity of these dishes. Unlike France, pies are thought of as an everyday dish, as good, wholesome food. In certain respects this is correct. Mass-produced pies such as steak and kidney pies, chicken pies, Cornish pasties, pork pies and veal and ham pies, are eaten as fast-food by millions of working people who have neither the time nor the inclination to cook for themselves. But it would be wrong to assume that today's savory pies are of poorer quality or less tasty than the penny pies of the nineteenth century or the pies sold at the Pie Corner near Smithfield meat market during the reign of Elizabeth I.

Of course the flavor of mass-produced pies cannot compare with homemade pies. In the Duchy of Cornwall in Southwest England, Cornish pasties, for example, can vary considerably in flavor despite the fact that they rely upon relatively simple ingredients such as meat, potato, seasoning and broth. But alongside such homely dishes there are also very special pies filled with steak and oysters. The basic rules of piemaking still apply for both homely and special pies; a good dish can only be made with the best ingredients.

Whereas in France the taste for pies was almost entirely restricted to the nobility prior to the nineteenth century, in the history of the British Isles puddings and pies were enjoyed by both rich and poor alike. Of course in Britain – as anywhere else – these varied considerably between rich and poor. The rich ate venison, partridge or even lark pies while the poor had to content themselves with far less expensive ingredients. For special court banquets pies were made in the north of England of such a size that they could not be transported by road but were sent south to London by sea. They created monstrosities, like those produced even earlier in France, with pastry which had to be malleable and was therefore inedible. The only consideration was for them to look attractive.

At one time pie molds or basins were not used in Great Britain. The filling was surrounded with pastry, pressed into shape by hand and then baked on a baking sheet in the oven. But now it is becoming increasingly common for cooked or uncooked fillings, meat or otherwise, to be served in a dish. The dish may be lined with pastry in some cases, but the pie is always completed with a pastry lid before baking or steaming.

A recent innovation is the ovenproof steaming basin which is lined with suet pastry, filled and covered with more pastry. These pies are usually steamed like puddings. Although potatoes have been eaten in England since the sixteenth century when Sir Walter Raleigh brought them back from America, they were unpopular at first and of little commercial value. But their popularity increased when it was discovered that they could be used to great advantage in pies. People began covering pies with a layer of mashed potato and also including it in the filling.

Steak and Kidney Pie

Illustrated on page 154

This is the oldest and best loved of all the English pies. It is equally traditional when made as Steak and Oyster Pie: for this simply replace the kidney with 8–12 oysters.

1½ lb lean flank steak
½ lb lamb kidney
½ cup port wine
2 tablespoons beef drippings
1¼ cups diced onion
¼ cup flour
1¾ cups beef broth
½ teaspoon dried mixed herbs
1 teaspoon salt
freshly ground white pepper
1 teaspoon sugar
1 lb suet pastry (recipe page 14)
1 egg yolk for glazing
1-quart casserole or deep pie dish

Cut the steak into 1-inch cubes. Soak the kidney thoroughly in water, remove the fat and cut into cubes also. Heat the port wine, flambé it and reduce by half. Heat the beef drippings in a large skillet, brown the meat and kidney in several batches and remove from the skillet. Soften the onion in the remaining fat, sprinkle with the flour and cook for a few minutes. Return the meat and kidney to the pan and dilute with one-third of the port and broth. Bring to a boil, stirring continuously, add the remaining port and broth, bring back to a boil and add the herbs, salt and pepper. Over a moderate heat cook for 1½–2 hours until the meat is tender. Check seasoning. Bring the sugar to a boil with a little water, stir into the meat and leave to cool.

Roll out the pastry to ⅛-inch thick, cut a strip about ¾-inch wide and arrange on the rim of the dish. Carefully fill the dish with the meat. Brush the pastry rim with egg yolk, top with a pastry lid and press the edges firmly together. Cut off any excess pastry, work into a ball and use for decorations for the pastry lid, which you have previously brushed with egg yolk. Brush the top of the pie again with egg yolk and make an opening to allow the steam to escape.

Bake for about 25 minutes in a preheated 425° oven.

Chicken Pie

1 chicken, weighing about 3¼ lb
¾ cup coarsely diced onion
1 clove
salt
6 slices white bread, crusts removed
milk
1 egg
½ teaspoon chopped thyme
½ tablespoon chopped parsley
nutmeg and ground white pepper
5 oz fresh pork fatback, sliced
2 hard-cooked eggs, sliced
¾ lb puff pastry
1 egg yolk
1-quart casserole or deep pie dish

Bone the chicken and keep the leg and breast meat and the liver to one side.

With the remaining meat, bones, onion, clove, salt and 1 quart water, make a broth. Reduce to 1¼ cups and strain.

Soak the bread in a little milk and squeeze out well. Coarsely chop the chicken leg meat and liver, about ½ lb, and mix with the bread, egg, herbs, salt, nutmeg and pepper. Slice one of the chicken breasts and use to line the bottom of the dish. Cover with the pork fat and then cover with half the filling. Arrange one hard-cooked egg over the filling, top with the remaining filling and then with the remaining egg and sliced chicken breast. Cover the dish with puff pastry, glaze with beaten egg yolk and make an opening to allow steam to escape. After baking pour the hot broth into the pie through a funnel.

Bake for 55–70 minutes in a preheated 350° oven.

One of the traditional pies and a favorite lunch dish. The chicken pie can also be eaten cold. There are several variations on this recipe and it is often adapted to use up any leftovers, but of course this cannot compare with the original recipe.

Squab Pie

4 squab breasts
¾ lb apples
5 oz bacon slices
juice of ½ lemon
2 tablespoons sugar
1 teaspoon cinnamon
salt and ground white pepper
6 tablespoons butter
¾ lb puff pastry
1 egg yolk for glazing
½ cup cream
1-quart casserole or deep pie dish

Thinly slice the boned squab breasts. Peel, core and thinly slice the apples. Line the dish with bacon slices, add a layer of apple and sprinkle with lemon juice, sugar and cinnamon. Cover with half the squab breasts, season with salt and pepper and dot with butter. Add a second layer of apple and squab breast and season. Dot with butter and top with the remaining bacon.

Cover with a pastry lid, decorate with any leftover pastry and make an opening for the steam to escape. Glaze with egg yolk. After 35 minutes baking pour the heated cream into the pie through a funnel. Bake in a preheated 425° oven for 15 minutes, then reduce the heat to 350° and bake for 35 minutes longer. *Serves 4.*

Squab Pie, an ineresting recipe which combines the smoky flavor of the bacon with squab, apple and sugar. It is said to have originated in the Middle Ages when combinations of such ingredients were quite common.

Eel Pie

3 lb eel
root vegetables (1 carrot, a little parsley,
leek and celery)
1½ teaspoons salt
freshly ground pepper
nutmeg
flour
6 tablespoons butter
1 cup diced shallots
¾ cup dry sherry wine
1 tablespoon lemon juice
2 tablespoons chopped parsley
1 lb suet pastry (recipe page 14) or ¾ lb
puff pastry
1 egg yolk for glazing

It is advisable to get your fish merchant to kill the eels for you. To skin them, cut through the skin below the head. Hold the head firmly with one hand and with the other pull off the whole skin at one go. Clean and fillet the eel and cut the fillets into pieces about 3 inches in length. Boil the head, fins and skin with the root vegetables in about 1½ quarts water for 20 minutes. Skim the broth, strain into a fresh pan and reduce to 2 cups.

Season the pieces of eel with a mixture of salt, pepper and a little nutmeg and dip in flour. Heat the butter in a skillet and fry the eel for a few minutes over a high flame until sealed all over. Remove from the skillet and keep to one side. Soften the shallots in the butter. Add the sherry and lemon juice and return the eel to the skillet. Cover with the lightly salted broth. Simmer over a gentle heat for 10 to 15 minutes.

Arrange the eel in layers in a dish. The square shape of the eel pieces makes a square dish preferable. Cover with the broth and sprinkle with the chopped parsley. Cover the pie with pastry. Brush the top with egg yolk, decorate and make an opening to allow the steam to escape. Even with a pie of this sort it is a good idea to use a funnel to prevent the liquid spilling onto the top.

Bake for 35 to 40 minutes in a preheated 400° oven. *Serves 4 to 6.*

Eel Pie Island Pie is the original name of this pie for it originated from a small island of the same name in the Thames River. This island has been famous for its fine eel pies since the seventeenth century. Early recipes, like many other English pie recipes, include hard-cooked eggs. For the pie crust either suet or puff pastry can be used. But puff pastry should be kneaded to prevent it rising too much.

Stick a thin strip of pastry around the rim of the pie dish with water or egg white. In England special pie dishes are used, but any ovenproof dish with a rim to which the pastry will stick can be used.

Cover the pie with pastry. Brush the strip of pastry with egg yolk. Roll up the pastry lid and unroll over the dish. Press the edges firmly together with the handle of a large spoon. Use any leftover pastry for decoration.

Steak and Mushroom Pudding

To make a real English suet pudding you will need a proper pudding basin, a basin with a lip around the top. The cloth is tied into place below this lip. Metal basins are unsuitable because they do not allow the pudding to expand sufficiently during cooking. A successful pudding also requires the steam which comes through the cloth. This recipe for 4 will fill a 1-quart basin. The same method can be used for other fillings, steak and kidney for example. The ingredients are used uncooked and finally covered with broth.

1½ lb flank steak
½ lb mushrooms, halved
1¼ cups diced onion
½ cup flour
¾ cup beef broth
1½ teaspoons salt
½ teaspoon freshly ground pepper
lard for greasing
1 lb suet pastry (recipe page 14)

Remove any skin and gristle from the steak and cut into ¾-inch cubes. Mix the meat, mushrooms and onion in a bowl. Add the flour and toss to coat. Season the broth well with salt and pepper.

Grease the pudding basin, line with suet pastry and fill with the meat and mushroom mixture. Pour in the broth. Cover with pastry and press the edges firmly together or pinch between finger and thumb. Cover first with greased parchment paper and then, as shown in the illustrations, cover tightly with a cloth. Place a wire rack or an inverted plate in the bottom of a large kettle, stand the basin on the rack and fill the pan with water to just below the cloth. Simmer gently over an even heat for 4 to 4½ hours, replenishing the water as it evaporates. *Serves 4 to 6.*

1 **Roll out the pastry to ¼-inch thick.** Grease the basin lightly with lard and line with pastry leaving a ½-inch rim of pastry overhanging the top of the basin. Cut off excess pastry. Fill with the uncooked ingredients.

2 **Cover the filled dish with pastry.** First pour the broth over the filling and brush the pastry rim with egg yolk or white. Roll out the remaining pastry into a circle, place over the pudding and seal the edges firmly.

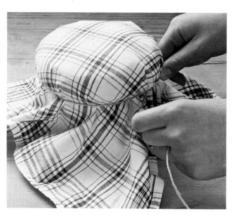

3 **Seal the pudding with a cloth.** Cut a round piece of parchment paper to fit the basin, grease and place over the pudding. Cover with the cloth and tie with string below the rim of the basin.

4 **Tie up the cloth.** Knot together the opposite corners on top of the pudding. It is essential that the string remains tight below the rim of the basin and the cloth remains firmly in place throughout the cooking time.

Veal and Ham Pie

4 cups flour
1 cup (½ lb) butter
1 teaspoon salt
⅓ cup water
1 egg
butter for greasing pan
6 hard-cooked eggs
1 egg yolk for glazing
12 × 5-inch loaf pan
Madeira wine aspic to finish

Veal and ham filling
1½ lb lean boneless veal, diced
1½ cups diced cooked ham
2 tablespoons chopped parsley
5 tablespoons brandy
6 tablespoons chicken or beef broth
grated rind and juice of ½ lemon
1 teaspoon dried sage
2 teaspoons salt
freshly ground pepper

Work the butter, salt, water and egg into the flour to give a smooth dough.

Grease the loaf pan with butter. Roll about two-thirds of the pastry to ¼-inch thick and cut into a rectangle to fit the pan. Then line the pan with pastry. Mix together the ingredients for the veal and ham filling, add just under half of it to the pan and make a hollow along the center. Cut the narrower end off the hard-cooked eggs so that they can fit closely together and arrange them in a row down the center of the pie. Cover with the remaining filling, pressing it down as firmly as possible. Roll out the remaining pastry, cut to make a lid and cover the pie. Press the edges together with the handle of a wooden spoon. Decorate with cut-outs from the leftover pastry, make an opening to allow the steam to escape, insert a funnel and brush the pie with egg yolk. Bake for about 1¼ hours in a preheated 350° oven.

When cool fill the pie with Madeira wine aspic.

Serve the pie with a mustard sauce, made from mayonnaise and whipped cream, seasoned with mustard, salt and green peppercorns. There are many variations on this veal pie. For example, the eggs can be replaced with 8–10 bottled black walnuts. *Serves 8 to 10.*

1 **Place the eggs in a row over the filling.** Cut off the narrow ends to ensure that the eggs fit closely together and that every slice cut contains equal amounts of egg white and yolk. Fill the pie with the remaining filling, pressing down as firmly as possible.

2 **Make a wavy edge.** This looks attractive and also makes a good seal. Brush the rim of the pastry with egg yolk and cover with the lid. Cut to leave a ½-inch rim and press together with the handle of a wooden spoon.

Venison Pasties

1 lb boneless leg of venison
¾ cup finely diced carrots
¾ cup finely diced celeriac
½ cup finely diced onion
pared rind of 1 lemon
1 bay leaf
1 sprig fresh thyme
5 juniper berries, crushed
3 tablespoons peanut oil
1 cup port wine
1 teaspoon salt
freshly ground pepper
2 tablespoons currant jelly
1½ lb pie pastry
1 egg yolk for glazing
3 tablespoons butter

Carefully remove all skin and gristle from the venison and cut into ½-inch cubes; make sure that they are no larger than this. Place in a bowl and mix with the carrot, celeriac and onion. Add the lemon rind, bay leaf, thyme and juniper berries. Cover with the oil and port wine, cover the bowl and leave to marinate in the refrigerator for at least 48 hours.

Pour off most, but not quite all, of the marinade. Remove the lemon rind, bay leaf, thyme and juniper berries. Season with salt and pepper and stir in the currant jelly. Roll out the pastry to ¼-inch thick and cut into 8 7-inch rounds. Place 4 of the rounds on a baking sheet and cover with the meat mixture leaving the edges free. Brush the edges with egg yolk. Cover the pasties with the remaining rounds of pastry and press the edges together with the tines of a fork. Brush the tops with egg yolk, decorate with leftover pastry and make an opening in the center for the funnel. Bake for 30 minutes in all, 5 minutes at 400°, then at 350° until cooked.

After baking pour the warm butter into the hot pasties through the funnel opening. The pasties are best served hot, possibly with a hot game sauce. *Makes 4.*

In England Venison Pasties are a luxury. They are usually made according to current international cooking methods and thus are no different from French or German game pies. The pasties on this page are something of an exception; they are typical homemade pasties, but no less tasty for all that.

Cornish Pasties

"The devil is afraid to come to Cornwall, for fear he should be baked into a pasty," so goes an English saying. In fact Cornish people are renowned for their pasties and are not fussy what goes into the filling. But a real Cornish pasty can be a great delicacy. Originally they always contained beef or lamb and potato. Sometimes a carrot or one other vegetable may be added. The pastry is usually a nice crumbly pie pastry, but Cornish Pasties can also be made with puff pastry or even yeast pastry. Recently pasties with mackerel filling have been introduced around the Cornish coast.

2 cups flour
salt
¾ cup softened butter, diced
1 egg

Filling
⅔ cup finely diced lean boneless beef or lamb
1¼ cups finely diced potatoes
1 shallot, finely chopped
1 teaspoon chopped thyme
¼ cup beef broth
salt and freshly ground pepper
1 egg yolk for glazing

Sift the flour onto the work surface and make a well in the center. Add the salt, soft diced butter and the egg. Gradually work in the flour and then work all the pastry ingredients together to give a smooth dough. Chill for 15–20 minutes until firm.

Mix together the meat, potato, shallot, thyme and broth and season with salt and plenty of pepper. Cut the pastry into 4 equal pieces and roll each into a 7-inch circle. Divide the filling between the circles, placing it in the center. Brush the edges with egg yolk. Fold the pastry over the filling like a turnover and press the edges firmly together with a fork. Brush the tops with egg yolk.

Bake for 30–35 minutes in all, first for 10–15 minutes at 400°, then at 375° until cooked. *Makes 4.*

They were the sandwiches of the Cornish people, a poor man's pie which could weigh as much as 2 pounds and which they took with them to work. Clever wives put their husband's initials in one corner so that they would be able to recognize their own half-eaten pastry, for they were usually big enough for two meals.

Pirozhki and Kulebyaka

A hearty *Na zdorovye* to the thousands of different pies which go under the name of *pirozhki* in Mother Russia. A refined *à votre santé* to the *coulibiac*, the elegant French relation of the original Russian *kulebyaka*. There are a wide variety of Russian pies, both large and small. The smaller varieties – served as an hors d'oeuvre or with soup or cocktails – are called *pirozhki* (*piroggi* in Poland). The larger pies are called *pirog*, which is Russian simply for tart: savory, well-filled quiches which are a meal in themselves. These include the great delicacy known as *kulebyaka*. The filling may be cabbage, which is preferred hot in Russia – or for special occasions fish, such as fresh salmon, and a delicate fish velouté sauce. Sometimes they are filled country-style turnovers made with yeast dough, or they may be made with a light brioche dough. They may be typically Russian or classically French with Russian origins.

Kulebyaka is one of the Russian national dishes, whereas the *coulibiac* is one of the best dishes that classic French cuisine has to offer. It is said to have been invented by the great Auguste Escoffier (1846–1935), based on an original Russian recipe, to honor a visit by the Russian ballet to Monaco. His was a real gourmet recipe which has remained a favorite over the years, made with salmon braised in wine, and the reduced broth mixed with fish velouté, egg yolk and seasoning, spread over the salmon, and left to cool. Escoffier then rolled yeast dough until very thin to make a layer of fine crêpes or blinis. This was covered with a mixture of rice and hard-cooked eggs in a chicken sauce topped with a layer of salmon and further layers of blinis and rice mixture. The whole thing was wrapped in pastry, shaped into a loaf, decorated with pastry and baked to make the *coulibiac*. It was eaten warm with melted butter poured into the opening in the top. It is a complicated, time-consuming specialty admittedly, but worth the trouble. The taste is incomparably delicious.

But the Russian *kulebyaka* – which come in a host of variations – are less time-consuming, for they are made without the blinis. There are no hard and fast rules about *kulebyaka*; the main thing is that it should contain plenty of salmon.

But there are also *kulebyaka* with cabbage filling, a special dish in country districts – and they are indeed special for, despite their modest filling and unpretentious method of preparation, they have a delicious flavor.

The many Russian *pirozhki* should not be regarded as the poor relation in the pie family. They amply repay closer attention.

Working from the outside inwards: first of all they are generally turnovers made of yeast or pie pastry, less frequently with puff pastry. The filling may be meat, fish, rice, egg or cabbage or any other suitable type of stuffing. For example there are Tvorogom *pirozhki* which have a cheese filling. Or there are the delicious *chebureki*, fried turnovers with a lamb filling. These were originally a Tartar dish, which they took with them from the Crimea to Central Asia. There are also *pyrishki* – bite-sized and delicious. These are usually made with yeast dough, occasionally with puff pastry, but always filled with meat or mushrooms, onion, cabbage or cheese – and served with a clear chicken soup. In fact many types of *pirozhki* are traditionally served with soup, with the filling echoing the main ingredient of the soup. This means that with a fish soup you would only serve *pirozhki* with a fish filling.

And then there are *pelemeni*, boiled turnovers, which are a cross between turnovers, stuffed dumplings and ravioli. We cannot leave these without saying a little more about walnut-size meatballs wrapped in pastry. According to the original recipe they should be frozen, for they are Siberian turnovers and in the Siberian winter freezing is no problem. They are cooked frozen in salted water. After draining they are sprinkled with chopped parsley or dill and eaten with sour cream or warm butter, and in many villages with a dash of vinegar too.

For many generations now Siberian peasant women have made *pelemeni*. The icy winters ensure that they keep for as long as necessary, so they were made in huge quantities and kept for use as required or to feed unexpected guests. For example, the farmers took a few *pelemeni* with them when they went out to cut hay for the cattle. And they helped fight off the gnawing hunger produced by the cold.

When a Russian describes someone as being an artist at making *pirozhki*, this is the highest praise that can be given. For they are almost as fond of *pirozhki* as they are of vodka. Of course the best thing is to have the two together if it can be arranged. And it can often be arranged, especially with the famous hors d'oeuvre table known as *zakouska* which precedes special celebration menus. This so-called hors d'oeuvre – adapted from Baltic cooking over 200 years ago – is so rich and delicious that many guests overeat ann have no appetite left for their meal. This is due to the fact that *zakouska* is usually served in a separate room and guests – not knowing what is to follow on the dinner menu – happily eat their fill. Together with a variety of vegetable and fish dishes, *kulebyaka* and *pirozhki* are an essential feature of any *zakouska*. And this goes for the vodka too.

Russian Salmon Kulebyaka are the absolute tops among a host of Russian pies. Auguste Escoffier adapted this recipe and made it, under the name *coulibiac*, a feature of classic French cuisine.

Russian Salmon Turnover

Kulebyaka

1¾ lb salmon fillet, skinned
salt
freshly ground white pepper
3 tablespoons chopped dill
½ cup butter
2 cups diced onion
¾ cup rice
1 cup meat broth
nutmeg
½ lb mushrooms, cooked and chopped
2 hard-cooked eggs
¾ cup velouté sauce made with fish broth
1 tablespoon chopped parsley
brioche dough made with 4 cups flour
1 egg yolk mixed with 2 tablespoons
cream for glazing

Remove any bones from the salmon and cut into ¾-inch slices. Sprinkle with 2 teaspoons salt, pepper to taste and 1 tablespoon dill and chill.

Heat 2 tablespoons of the butter, soften ½ cup of the diced onion, then add the rice and glaze it. Add the meat broth, season with salt and nutmeg and cook in a preheated 350° oven, for about 18 minutes until the rice is tender. Transfer the rice to a baking sheet, cover with buttered parchment paper and leave to cool.

Heat another 2 tablespoons butter, soften the rest of the diced onion and leave to cool.

Mix the cool rice with the fried onion, mushrooms, eggs, velouté sauce, the parsley, the rest of the dill and the remaining butter and check seasoning. Roll half the brioche dough into a rectangle and cover with one-quarter of the rice mixture, leaving a ¾-inch rim. Continue with layers of marinated salmon and rice mixture, pressing each layer down gently. You should eventually have 4 alternate layers of rice and 3 of salmon. Roll out the remaining dough into a slightly larger rectangle. Brush the rim of the base with the egg and cream mixture, cover with the lid and press the edges firmly together. Cut off any excess pastry. Cut the leftover pastry into decorations, brush the top of the pie with egg and cream and add the decorations. Cut an opening, insert a funnel and brush the top of the *kulebyaka* once more with the egg and cream mixture to give a good brown finish after baking.

Bake for about 40–45 minutes in a preheated 400° oven. *Serves 8.*

Russian Cabbage Turnover

Kulebyaka

2 lb head white cabbage
2 cups diced onions
3 tablespoons butter
1 cup water
3 hard-cooked eggs, chopped
3 tablespoons chopped dill
2 tablespoons chopped parsley
1 tablespoon salt
sugar
freshly ground white pepper
pie pastry made with 5 cups flour
2 egg yolks for glazing

Quarter the cabbage, cut out the central core and coarsely chop the leaves. Blanch the cabbage in a kettle of boiling salted water for 5 minutes, then leave to drain thoroughly. Fry the onions in the butter until golden. Add the cabbage, cover with the water and bake in a covered pan in a preheated 350° oven, for 30–40 minutes. When the cabbage is tender remove the lid to allow the liquid to evaporate. Drain the cabbage and leave to cool slightly. Mix in the chopped eggs and herbs and season with salt, sugar and pepper.

Roll out half the dough, fill with the cabbage mixture and cover with a lid, as in the recipe left.

Place the *kulebyaka* on a greased baking sheet and chill for about 15 minutes before baking in a preheated 425° oven for about 30 minutes. *Serves 8.*

If preferred you can fill the *kulebyaka* with red cabbage, replacing the dill with caraway.

The traditional loaf shape too can be varied, and the pastry made as a pie. The same quantities of pastry and filling are sufficient for a 10-inch pie pan. Line the pan with two-thirds of the pastry, add the filling and cover with the remaining pastry. Decorate, make an opening for the funnel and bake.

1 **Cut the ⅛-inch thick base** (about half the pastry) into a rectangle. Add the filling to make a loaf shape, leaving a 1-inch rim. Roll out the remaining pastry and, using the rolling pin to help you, lay it over the filling.

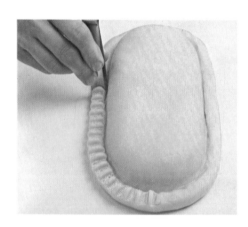

4 **Decorate the rim with a pastry crimper** or the tines of a fork. Brush the rim with egg yolk so that the raised parts of the rim alone will brown during baking.

6 **Cabbage Kulebyaka should come out of the oven brown and crisp.** Chill for at least 15 minutes before baking to help the turnover keep its shape and prevent the seams splitting during baking. Serve with sour cream.

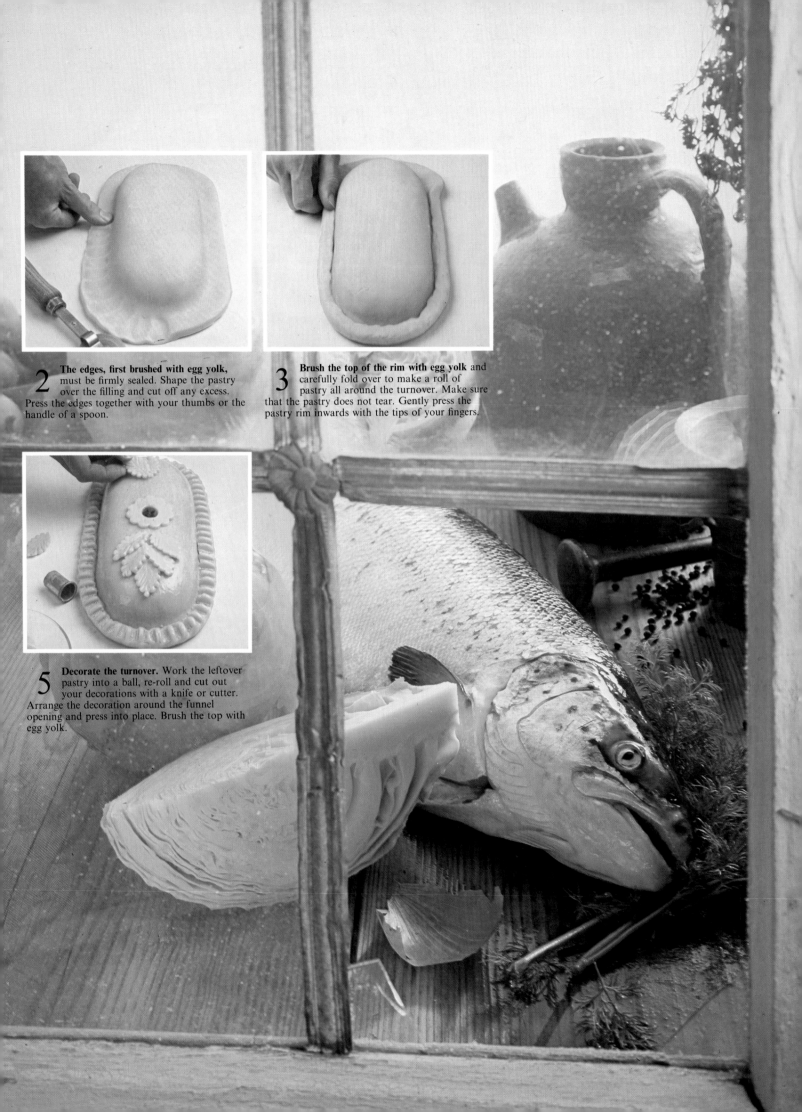

2 The edges, first brushed with egg yolk, must be firmly sealed. Shape the pastry over the filling and cut off any excess. Press the edges together with your thumbs or the handle of a spoon.

3 Brush the top of the rim with egg yolk and carefully fold over to make a roll of pastry all around the turnover. Make sure that the pastry does not tear. Gently press the pastry rim inwards with the tips of your fingers.

5 Decorate the turnover. Work the leftover pastry into a ball, re-roll and cut out your decorations with a knife or cutter. Arrange the decoration around the funnel opening and press into place. Brush the top with egg yolk.

Cheese Tarts

Vatruzhki

3 cups flour
½ teaspoon baking powder
1 teaspoon salt
7 tablespoons softened butter
3 eggs
1 cup plus 1 tablespoon sour cream
2 cups low-fat cottage cheese
freshly ground pepper
1 teaspoon sugar
1 egg yolk for glazing

Sift the flour and baking powder into a bowl, make a well in the center, add ½ teaspoon salt and the soft butter and work in a little of the flour. Then add one egg and 1 cup sour cream and beat with a wooden spoon to give a smooth dough. Shape into a ball, wrap in wax paper and chill for at least 45 minutes.

To make the cheese filling, sieve the cheese through a strainer and stir in the remaining sour cream, eggs and salt, the pepper and sugar. Chill for at least 45 minutes.

Roll out the pastry to ⅛-inch thick and cut into equal numbers of 4½-inch and 4-inch rounds. Place 1–2 tablespoons of the cheese mixture in the center of each of the larger rounds and cover with a smaller round. Brush the edges with egg yolk. Fold up the edge of the lower round and pinch into small pleats. Brush the tops with egg yolk.

Bake for about 20 minutes in a preheated 400° oven. *Serves 6 to 8.*

Pirozhki

Pirozhki

There is no standard size for these small turnovers just as there is no standard pastry cutter. As a guide you can use the size given in old Russian cookbooks which say "cut to the size of a side-plate." Pirozhki can be made either with pie (page 12) or yeast pastry. The Vatruzhki pastry with sour cream in the preceding recipe is excellent for pirozhki. The quantities in the following filling recipes are for about 1 lb pastry. This is rolled to about ⅛-inch thick and cut into rounds or rectangles. Top with the filling and brush the rims with egg yolk. Fold over and seal firmly so that no filling can escape during baking. Press the edges together with a fork. Brush the tops with egg yolk and, if you are using yeast pastry, leave to rise thoroughly before baking. The baking time will depend on the size of the pirozhki, averaging about 15–25 minutes in a preheated 400° oven, depending on the type of filling.

Mushroom and Chicken Filling

½ lb mushrooms
2 tablespoons butter
1 cup diced cooked chicken meat
3 hard-cooked eggs
salt and pepper
chopped parsley

Cook the chopped mushrooms for a few minutes in butter. Mix with the diced chicken and eggs and season.

Pork and Beet Filling

½ lb ground pork
⅓ cup diced shallots
3 tablespoons butter
¾ cup cooked rice
⅔ cup diced cooked beet
1 tablespoon chopped parsley
salt, pepper and caraway
1 cup sour cream

Fry the ground pork and shallots in the hot butter, breaking up the meat with a fork. Mix with the rice, diced beet and parsley. Season with salt, pepper and caraway. Top the filling of each pirozhki with a teaspoon of sour cream.

Sauerkraut Filling

$\frac{3}{4}$ cup diced onion
5 tablespoons pork drippings
14 oz sauerkraut · salt
$\frac{1}{2}$ cup white wine
1 tablespoon chopped dill
4 hard-cooked eggs, chopped

Soften the onion in the hot drippings. Add the sauerkraut and braise for 20 minutes. Add the salt and wine, and braise for a further 10 minutes. Stir in the dill and chopped eggs.

Herb Cheese Filling

1 cup cottage cheese · 1 egg
1 tablespoon sour cream · salt
3 tablespoons chopped herbs (parsley, dill, lovage, thyme)

Stir the cheese with the egg, cream, salt and chopped herbs.

Smoked Salmon Filling

$\frac{1}{2}$ cup diced onion
$\frac{1}{2}$ lb smoked salmon fillet, cut into strips
1 tablespoon finely chopped dill
pepper

Mix the diced onion with the salmon, cut into strips, the dill and pepper. Add salt only if necessary.

Ham and Rice Filling

$\frac{1}{4}$ cup butter · $\frac{1}{2}$ cup finely diced onion
1 clove garlic, crushed
1 cup diced cooked ham
salt, pepper and chopped parsley
$\frac{3}{4}$ cup cooked rice

Heat the butter and soften the onion and garlic in it. Add the ham and fry for a few minutes. Add salt, pepper and parsley and stir in the rice.

Lamb Filling

$\frac{1}{2}$ cup finely diced onion
$\frac{1}{2}$ cup chopped mushrooms
3 tablespoons butter · $\frac{1}{4}$ lb ground lamb
salt, pepper, garlic salt
2 hard-cooked eggs, chopped

Quickly soften the onion and mushrooms in the hot butter, stir into the lamb and season with salt, pepper and garlic salt. Stir in the chopped eggs.

Pâtés from Around the World

Can anyone be familiar with all the pâtés that exist around the world? Can anyone know all their names? It is all but impossible to make even an approximate list. Regrettably, many will have to go unmentioned here, for our subject is an infinitely wide area in the world of cooking. Pâtés are found in South America and Finland, in China and Italy and in Germany too. All we can do is offer a brief look at some of these, starting with those which are baked or fried, and then going on to look at ones which are cooked in a variety of other ways, by steaming or cooking in soup, for they are all a form of pâté.

It is not known whether the Spanish conquistadors took the delicious pies known as *empanadas* with them to Latin America or whether they are a traditional Indian dish. But it is certain that these explorers succeeded in passing on some of their eating habits to the indigenous native population to produce a happy combination of native and Spanish cooking. There is no doubt about the Spanish origin of the Galician *empanada*, a local specialty whose wonderful flavor long ago conquered the hearts of gourmets throughout the length and breadth of Spain. In Santiago de Compostela they are made as both large and individual pâtés. The golden-brown piecrust hides a delicious meat or fish filling. Sometimes bread dough is used for the piecrust and sometimes *hojaldre*, a puff pastry made with pork lard. They are almost always cooked in a paella pan and are usually eaten cold rather than hot. Because the people of Santiago love their pies above all else they have even erected a monument to them in the middle of the cathedral which is dedicated to James the Apostle, the patron saint of Spain. Here a stylite is portrayed biting greedily into a typical Santiago pie (see photograph). In La Coruna, a coastal town on the northwest tip of Spain, live, as every expert knows, the famous seafood *empanada* bakers. The sea provides an abundance of ingredients fresh from the net, fish and shellfish which other Europeans can only dream about. The *empanadas* eaten in Chile, Uruguay and Argentina do not vary greatly from the Spanish *empanadas*. They are among the most delicious specialty dishes of these countries and are usually served as an hors d'oeuvre, but are also popular as an *entremets* or as a snack to be taken on journeys or picnics. They are usually

Home cooking of the best possible kind is an *empanada* from Galicia. There the freshest fruits of sea and land are baked in pastry. This is a prime example of the many national pâtés which are often promoted to join the ranks of international cuisine.

filled with meat, mixed with raisins, olives, onion and vegetables. And they are often highly seasoned, with cayenne for example, or chopped chilies.

In Finland too they know how to bake an excellent meat filling in pastry and these go by the almost unpronounceable name of *Lihamurekepiiras*. To suit the country's cold climate these are filling pies, with a lot of sour cream in the pastry. They are a close relative of the Russian *pirozhki*, and are usually served with more sour cream and cranberry sauce. But there are also a wide range of country-style pâtés which are baked for particular celebrations once a year, like the *Pâté de Paques du Berry*, a French Easter pâté with eggs baked into it, or the *Torta pasqualina*, an Italian Easter favorite.

Rissoles are usually made with 4 inch rounds of either pie or brioche pastry filled with a *salpikon*, a fine stew, or less often with a forcemeat of some kind. And then comes the stage which gives such cakes their own individual character – they are deep fried in hot oil.

With pancake rolls, which can be enjoyed in Chinese restaurants throughout the world, we come to a close relative of the rissole. Here a dough, which may sound rather complicated at first, is made into small, thin crêpes, filled with all kinds of meat and vegetables, rolled and fried in fat. Experts claim that the best pancake rolls are made in Fukien on the south coast of China, and here too the best soy sauce is prepared, the essential accompaniment to pancake rolls. The wide variety of dim sums, steamed envelopes of pastry, which are made throughout the country, make China a promised land for many who love fine food. There is nothing unusual in a Chinese restaurant offering 50 different sorts of these savory dumplings on the same menu. This is a totally new experience for Europeans, but something which the Chinese take for granted.

But if you ask a Swabian or an Italian what they would prefer, it would certainly not be dim sums. Their favorite pâté-type dish would be *Maultaschen*, triangles of pasta dough, filled with ground meat or ham, onion, spinach and seasoning which are boiled in broth. For the Swabians at least. Italians on the other hand, especially in Piedmont, swear by their ravioli, filled envelopes of dough which are eaten with tomato sauce and grated Parmesan cheese.

Empanadas, the Spanish pie

Empanadas are typical of many other types of national pâtés. Wherever they are made they have been adapted to suit the country and its local products. In northern Spain where the empanada originated recipes vary greatly from one region to another, or at

It is not only in their external appearance that empanadas are indistinguishable. Whether filled with potatoes, like these Colombian empanadas, or with best beef, the hotness of the chilies makes it difficult to distinguish.

least, the fillings vary greatly. Some contain pork or vegetables or, as in the case of the *Empanada Gallega*, chicken, onion and peppers. Or there are the fish and shellfish fillings found all along the Atlantic coast. They are usually baked to serve 4 to 6 and are a popular lunch or snack dish. But in South America empanadas are even more popular than in the mother country. The former Spanish colonies have introduced new varieties with new fillings and in new shapes. With a multitude of new products, vegetables and seasonings, each country with a Spanish population has produced its own specialties, sometimes with extremely simple fillings such as vegetables or leftovers. But there are also extremely rich fillings, in Argentina for example, where best beef is seasoned with the best spices. *Empanada de Horno* is one such specialty, whose filling includes hard-cooked eggs and olives.

Calamari Empanada

¼ cup olive oil
1 cup diced onion
2 cloves garlic, crushed
2 green or red peppers
3 tomatoes, peeled
2 fresh chilies
2 squid, weighing about 14 oz
1 cup red Rioja wine
1 cup fish broth or water
1–2 teaspoons salt
2 teaspoons sweet paprika
a little fresh rosemary, thyme and sage
1 lb mussels, in the shell
½ lb shelled shrimp, deveined
yeast dough made from 4 cups flour
2–3 tomatoes, sliced
1 egg yolk for glazing

Heat the oil in a skillet and soften the onion and garlic. Cut the peppers into strips and add to the skillet with the peeled tomatoes. Carefully remove the seeds from the chilies and finely chop them. Add to the vegetables and cook for about 10 minutes. Clean the

Squid and mussel empanada is a specialty of the Restaurante Ricardo in Noya on Galicia's Atlantic coast. The cook uses a light yeast pastry. She rolls out half the pastry and uses it to line a paella pan. This is topped with the prepared filling, a highly seasoned mixture of green peppers, tomatoes, squid and mussels covered with a layer of sliced tomato. A second sheet of yeast pastry seals the empanada before firm finger pressure gives a wavy edge to seal the two layers of pastry.

The cook believes, rightly enough, that sophisticated decoration would do nothing to improve the flavor and sticks to a simple crisscross pattern made from thin rolls of pastry.

squid, removing the ink sac without damaging it, and take out the cuttle bone (you will use only the top of the head with the tentacles and tail which are cut into rings). Add the squid to the vegetables and then the red wine and broth. Season with salt, paprika and herbs. Simmer for about 20 minutes over a moderate heat, adding more broth if necessary. Scrub the mussels thoroughly and boil for 5 minutes in salted water, then remove the shells. Stir into the filling with the shrimp. Line the pan with yeast dough, add the filling, cover with sliced tomato and sprinkle with salt. Cover with dough, decorate, glaze with egg yolk and leave to rise for 10 minutes before baking for 25–30 minutes in a preheated 400° oven. *Serves 6.*

Spanakópitta

3 cups flour
1 cup wholewheat flour
2 (0.6 oz) cakes compressed yeast
1 cup water
1 egg
½ cup plus 3 tablespoons olive oil
salt
2 lb fresh bulk spinach
2 onions, finely diced
1 clove garlic, crushed
a little pepper and nutmeg
2 sprigs dill, chopped
¾ lb feta cheese
1 egg yolk for glazing
12-inch quiche pan

Mix the flour and wholewheat flour in a bowl and make a well. Crumble the yeast into the well and dilute with the lukewarm water. Leave to stand for 10 minutes, then add the egg, 3 tablespoons olive oil and 1 teaspoon salt and work all the ingredients together to give a fine, uniform dough.

Wash the spinach, shake dry and chop, but not too finely. Heat the remaining oil in a large saucepan. Soften the diced onions. Add the crushed garlic and spinach and cook for a few minutes until the spinach wilts. Salt lightly, for the cheese can sometimes be extremely salty, and season with pepper and nutmeg. Stir in the dill and crumbled feta cheese.

Roll out two-thirds of the pastry and use to line the pan, leaving a rim of about ½ inch. Prick the bottom several times with a fork and fill with the cooled spinach mixture. Brush the pastry rim with egg yolk, roll out the remaining pastry and use to cover the pie. Pinch the edges firmly together and cut off any excess pastry. Brush the top with egg yolk and use any leftover pastry for decoration. Make an opening in the center to allow the steam to escape. Leave to rise for 15–20 minutes, then bake in a preheated 400° oven for 40–45 minutes. *Serves 6.*

Spanakópitta is a vegetarian pâté from Greece, filled with spinach and sheep's milk cheese, highly seasoned with fresh dill. An excellent variation can be made with pie pastry. But to appreciate fully the hearty flavor, use a yeast dough or, as in the recipe above, a wholewheat flour yeast dough. The Greeks use the same filling to make small pies which look just like the Indian Samosa (page 173), and are also made by folding strips of pastry. These are called *Spanakotrigona* and the pastry is similar to our pasta dough, made without eggs and rolled almost as thin as pasta dough. The pastry for Chinese pancake rolls is very similar and could be used instead. They are baked in the oven until brown and crisp.

Rissoles

These are an ideal snack for any sort of occasion, but are also a traditional appetizer. It is not certain how far back their history can be traced, but in French the term *rissoler*, to cook until brown (in fat) has been around for a long time. It is also associated with the French word *roussâtre* (reddish), which is fairly appropriate for, when cooked, rissoles do in fact have a reddish tint to them. The common factor among all rissoles is that they are deep fried, and they are usually similar in shape. They are made from rounds of pastry, folded over to a half-moon shape before coating with egg and bread crumbs. There are fewer standard recipes for the fillings, for they can be varied in any number of ways, but it should be strong enough in flavor not to be masked by the fried pastry. They can be made with puff pastry but a pie pastry usually gives better results. Roll the pastry to about $\frac{1}{8}$-inch thick and cut into 4–$4\frac{1}{2}$ inch rounds. Place 2–3 tablespoons of filling in the center of each, brush the edges with egg yolk and fold over. Press the edges firmly together, coat in bread crumbs and deep fry.

Curry Filling

2 tablespoons oil
$\frac{1}{2}$ cup diced onion
1 clove garlic, crushed
$\frac{1}{2}$ lb boneless lamb, diced
$\frac{1}{2}$ teaspoon salt
2 teaspoons curry powder
1 teaspoon tomato paste
$\frac{1}{2}$ bay leaf
$\frac{1}{2}$ cup broth
1 tart apple, diced

Heat the oil and soften the diced onion. Add the garlic, lamb, salt, curry powder, tomato paste and bay leaf and fry, stirring from time to time. Add the broth and diced apple and cook for about 10 minutes. Leave to cool and use to fill the rissoles.

Samosa

2 cups flour
$\frac{1}{4}$ cup oil
salt
$\frac{1}{2}$ cup warm water
2 onions, finely chopped
2 teaspoons grated fresh ginger
1 clove garlic, crushed
1 fresh chili, finely chopped
$\frac{1}{2}$ teaspoon crushed coriander
2 teaspoons curry powder
1 tablespoon tomato paste
1 tablespoon lemon juice
$\frac{1}{2}$ lb lean boneless lamb, very finely chopped
$\frac{1}{2}$ cup veal or beef broth
1 tablespoon coarsely chopped mint
oil for deep frying

To make the pastry, sift the flour onto the worktop and make a well in the center. Add 2 tablespoons of the oil and 1 teaspoon salt with half the water. Working around the mixture from the center outwards, mix the ingredients together by hand. Gradually work in the remaining water, adding a little more if necessary. As with all water-based pastries the type of flour will determine the exact quantity of water needed. Knead the dough for about 10 minutes until completely uniform with the consistency of pasta dough. Cover with plastic wrap and leave to stand for 1–2 hours.

Heat the remaining oil in a skillet and soften the onions. Add the ginger, garlic and chili and cook for a few minutes before adding the coriander, curry powder, $\frac{3}{4}$ teaspoon salt, the tomato paste and lemon juice, and finally the very finely chopped lamb. Fry over a hot flame, stirring continuously. Add the broth, cover the pan and simmer over a low heat until all the liquid has evaporated. Sprinkle with the coarsely chopped fresh mint and leave to cool. Roll out the pastry and cut into strips. Fill and deep fry the samosas in oil at 350°.

Filling for singaras, a vegetarian variation:

Peel and dice 2 boiled potatoes. Mix with 2 tablespoons diced cooked carrot and season with 1 tablespoon lime juice, a finely chopped fresh chili, 2 teaspoons curry powder and a little cumin and salt.

Like all deep-fried pies, samosas, pies from India, are best served hot. Singaras are a vegetarian variation, which are made with a spicy potato filling. Both can be made with a ready-bought strudel or Chinese pancake pastry.

Fill the strips of pastry. Roll out the pastry thinly as for pasta and cut into strips $2\frac{1}{2}$ × 8 inches. Place 1 tablespoon of cold filling at one end.

Fold the end of the pastry diagonally across the filling. Then fold over the other end and continue folding the pastry diagonally until you have used the whole strip. Stick the end in place with egg white.

Dim Sums, pies from China

Every day these small individual pâtés are eaten in their millions, and like most of the dishes of great Chinese cooking, they are little culinary masterpieces. They are filled envelopes of pastry which are steamed or deep-fried in fat like pancake rolls. They come originally from the old traditional cooking of Canton and the name can be translated either as "what the heart desires" or as "stopgap." Both are appropriate. There are hundreds of recipes for dim sums and the wealth of Chinese cooking makes for a wide variety of fillings. There are also a number of different pastries. Dim sums are often served between the separate courses of a Chinese meal, but can also be served in many variations as a meal in themselves, usually served for the lunch diner in a hurry nowadays. Waitresses push trollies laden with steaming bamboo baskets from table to table. They open the lids one after another patiently listing the separate ingredients of each. These usually range from simple Chinese cabbage with pork to the refined mixture of mushrooms and shrimp. But they are also sold on the streets by itinerant cooks who pile their three-wheeler

bikes with large bamboo baskets. Each basket holds a different kind of dim sum with traditional fillings. Most types can be made at home, nor are they very difficult. Before steaming they will keep for 1–2 days in the refrigerator and can even be deep-frozen. The Chinese housewife can often buy the pastry ready-made, so that it only requires to be filled and cooked. For steaming you can't do any better than the traditional bamboo baskets. They are inserted into a large pan with water below the level of the internal strainer. The dim sums should not stand in water. Several baskets, covered at the top with a lid, can be cooked together. This is rather similar to the layered method of cooking which is used in modern pressure cookers. Of course it is hardly doing justice to these delicious morsels to describe such peaks of Chinese cooking in the usual brief, telegrammatic style of the recipe, but anyone who is used to handling food and possibly has a little experience in Far Eastern cooking, will know exactly how to proceed with the following recipes for fillings. Truly delicious examples of Chinese cuisine at its best.

A specialist in pancake roll pastry. The housewife doesn't need to concern herself with the time-consuming making of these rounds of pastry. But it is no easy matter even to cook them. It is a dough of flour, water and salt with a very low fat content, which may be lard or oil. The fat helps keep the pastry malleable so that it folds easily. The pastry is dipped into a skillet for a few seconds and then removed, leaving behind an extremely thin layer of pastry. After a minute at the most it is cooked and is removed from the pan with the speed and dexterity of a true artist, using only the fingers.

Siew Mai For about 20 pancakes make a dough using 1 cup flour, 1 egg and a pinch of salt. To make the filling, cover ½ oz tongu mushrooms with boiling water, leave to soak for 30 minutes, then drain and finely chop. Mix with ⅔ cup finely chopped raw shrimp, ⅓ cup finely chopped pork tenderloin and ¼ cup finely chopped pork fatback. Add ½ tablespoon cornstarch, and salt, pepper, sugar, and monosodium glutamate to taste, and a little sesame oil. Cut the dough into thin 2½-inch squares, cover with the filling and squeeze together to leave an opening at the top. Steam for 8 minutes.

Fan Goa Pau These dim sums are made in the same way as Siew Mai, but have a different filling. Soak 2 tongu mushrooms, drain and chop. Finely chop 1½ oz pork tenderloin, 1 oz water chestnuts (canned) and 3 oz raw shrimp. Shred 3 oz Chinese cabbage and blanch. Mix these ingredients with 1 tablespoon chopped scallion, ½ tablespoon chopped coriander leaves or parsley, ½ tablespoon cornstarch and salt, pepper, sugar, and monosodium glutamate to taste, and a little sesame oil.

A selection of dim sums made by Mr. Li. Each type has its own shape, its own special pastry and its own particular filling. Mr Li is the chef at the Mayflower Restaurant on Singapore's Shenton Way and is known throughout the city for the best dim sums with the most varied fillings. At his restaurant you can choose between traditional recipes and refined new creations. The delicious fillings come wrapped either in a thin egg-pancake dough, delicate yeast pastry or a pastry made with lard and cornstarch, which when steamed looks like frosted glass. As with many Western terrines or galantines, the wrapping is sometimes completely omitted even here, and the filling cooked in small balls.

Har Kau To make about 20 dim sums, mix 1 cup Chinese wheat flour with ¼ cup cornstarch, stir in ½ cup boiling water, leave to cool slightly and then work in 1 teaspoon lard. For the filling finely chop ¾ lb raw shrimp, 1 oz pork fatback and ¼ lb bamboo shoots and mix with ½ teaspoon cornstarch, ½ teaspoon sesame oil and salt, pepper, sugar and monosodium glutamate to taste. Use the mixture to fill thin 3-inch rounds of dough and press together at the top. Sprinkle with a little seasame oil and steam for 5 minutes.

Glossary and Ingredients List

A

Abatis
French term for poultry giblets.

Abats
general French term for variety meat.

Agnolotti
egg-pasta ravioli with meat and vegetable filling, served with meat sauce, butter, grated cheese. From Piedmont.

Alsace timbale
molds lined with goose liver purée, filled with forcemeat of goose liver, smoked tongue, mushrooms and truffles in Madeira sauce and topped with liver purée. Served with Madeira sauce.

Armagnac
well-known brandy from south-west France. Contains at least 38 percent alcohol and matures in oak casks. Its flavor is the ideal complement for meat pâtés.

Aromatics
seasoning ingredients such as roots, herbs or spices.

Artichoke
thistle-like vegetable from southern Europe.

Aspic
term for a meat or fish gelatin.

Aspic jelly
clarified liquid that will set, used to coat pâté, or served, diced, with pâté. Aspic jelly preserves, keeps forcemeat fresh longer, brings out flavor. Carcass or bones of meat used for pâté are boiled with water and seasoning. It jellies easier if you include bones that contain a lot of gelatin. Usually flavored with wine: Madeira, port, sherry, Tokay, Muscatel or strongly-flavored white wine.

Aspic powder
ground gelatin, sometimes sold mixed with herbs.

B

Ballotines
small galantines of stuffed poultry legs which retain the original shape, poached in broth.

Beans
almost all varieties can be used for pâtés or included in pie fillings.

Béchamel sauce
white sauce made from flour, butter, milk or veal broth, and possibly herbs. A basic sauce, which can also be used to bind pâtés.

Beef marrow pâtés
small brioche molds lined with pie pastry filled with forcemeat of moistened bread, ground almonds, egg, egg yolk, beef marrow, salt, pepper, and cayenne. Baked and served hot.

Beef and potato pie
English pie. A precooked mixture of meat, potato, onion, broth and flour, placed in small oval dishes, covered with gravy, topped with mashed potato and browned under the broiler.

Bénédictine
French herb liqueur.

Bindings for pâtés *page 18*

Bouchées
puff pastry patty shells, usually baked blind before filling with fine forcemeat. Generally small enough to be eaten in one bite. Still feature in fine cuisine today but have been largely replaced by bigger vol-au-vents. Served as an hors d'oeuvre or entremets.

Bouchées à l'américaine
American-style patty shells of puff pastry with a filling of lobster à l'Américaine.

Bouchées à la bouquetière
puff pastry patty shells with mixed vegetable filling of carrots, turnip, peas, cauliflower, in a Hollandaise sauce or fine cream sauce.

Bouchées à la chasseur
puff pastry patty shells with a filling of game, mushrooms and truffles in Madeira sauce.

Bouchées à la dieppoise
puff pastry patty shells with a filling of shrimp and mussels in white wine sauce.

Bouchées à la financière
puff pastry patty shells filled with cock's combs, chicken kidney, sweetbreads, mushrooms, chicken meat balls, olives and sliced truffles in sauce financière.

Bouchées à la reine
puff pastry patty shells with a filling of mushrooms, chicken velouté with cream, diced cooked veal, Worcestershire sauce, lemon juice and seasoning.

Bouchées Montgelas
puff pastry patty shells with a filling of foie gras, mushrooms, smoked tongue and truffles in Madeira sauce.

Bouchées Nantua
puff pastry patty shells with a filling of shrimp, mushrooms and truffles in Nantua sauce.

Bouquet garni *page 42*
bunch of herbs and spices, e.g. parsley, chervil, chives, tarragon, thyme, bay leaf, marjoram and onion, often tied in cheesecloth. Ingredients are interchangeable. Used to season soups, sauces and broths.

Broccoli
green cabbage vegetable, best suited for vegetable pâtés.

Burgundian lark pie
classic French pie, also named after chefs Rousette or Racouchot. Instead of the rare lark, the French now use farm-raised quail. The dish is lined with pastry, covered with thin slices of pork fatback and topped with 12 larks or 4 quail surrounded by forcemeat. The forecemeat is made from the gizzards, livers, lark innards, pork, pork fatback, boiled ham, truffles, seasoning and Madeira marinade (from the birds). The birds are covered with more forcemeat and topped with a pastry lid.

C

Calf's brain pie
puff pastry turnover filled with mixture of calf's brains, mushrooms, butter, onion, cream, salt, pepper and lemon rind. Sometimes made into long pie.

Carolines
choux pastry éclairs filled with foie gras.

Carrot mousse *page 134*
carrots boiled until soft and puréed with chicken velouté.

Carrot
popular vegetable for pâté fillings or as a mousse.

Cauliflower
used for vegetable pâtés or as ingredient for pie fillings.

Champagne rabbit pie
pastry-lined mold filled with forcemeat and rabbit meat marinated in pink champagne. Flavored with champagne brandy. Filled with aspic jelly made from rabbit bones when cool.

Champignons
(button mushrooms), the most popular mushrooms for pâtés and terrines.

Chanterelle tartlets *page 143*

Chanterelle terrine *page 90*
terrine de chanterelles, fine veal forcemeat with chanterelles.

Chaudfroid sauce *page 98*
term applied generally to any dish which is prepared warm, but eaten cold (*chaud* = warm, *froid* = cold).

Chebureki *page 163*
fried turnovers with lamb filling from Tartar cooking.

Cheese and onion pasties
small, English pies made with cheese puff pastry. Filling is made of cheese, onion, milk, and bound with cornstarch.

Cheese pirozhki
baked turnovers of pie pastry filled with mixture of eggs, butter, salt, pepper and grated cheese.

Chicken liver mousse   *page 132*
mousse de foies de volaille.

Chicken pie   *page 156*

Citrus fruit
mainly orange and lemon (juice and rind), used to season forcemeats and broths. Lime goes well with game meat and birds.

Cock's combs
used for special fillings (à la financière) for patty shells.

Cognac
French brandy from Charente. Indispensable for flavoring broths for pâtés.

Confit d'oie   *page 101*
specialty of south-west France where geese are reared for foie gras, but popular throughout France. Can also be made with duck or turkey.

Corail
lobster roe, used to color fish pâtés.

Cornish pasties   *page 161*

Cou d'oie farci   *page 126*
stuffed neck of goose.

Coulibiac
Escoffier's grand cuisine adaptation of the large Russian pie filled with salmon, a rice mixture and blinis.

Country-style terrine
meat, poultry or variety meat forcemeats with diced fat. Also known as *pâté de campagne, terrine du chef, pâté de la maison.* Wrapped in pork fatback.

Cream mussel tartlets   *page 142*
filled with mussels in an onion-celery-carrot mixture.

Croustade à la financière
puff pastry pie with a filling of goose liver poached in butter, cock's combs, chicken kidneys, truffles, seasoning, and a basic brown sauce flavored with brandy.

Croustade de langoustines   *page 149*
a shrimp pie.

Croustades
usually blind-baked puff or pie pastry cases. Filled and served as appetizer or entremets. Once they always had a pastry lid but seldom nowadays. Size ranges from individual to large quiches.

Croûtes
thick slices of white bread, hollowed out, fried in butter and then filled.

D

Darioles gallic style
small pâtés made in molds lined with aspic jelly. Filling of cock's combs, chicken kidneys, mushrooms and truffles in mayonnaise. Unmolded when set.

Demiglace   *page 93*
highly-flavored brown sauce, reduced, and flavored with Madeira. A basic sauce.

Dim sum   *page 174*
Chinese titbits, for snack or cocktail dish. Various fillings wrapped in pasta-like pastry are steamed in bamboo baskets. Can also be boiled, braised or steamed in broth. Also served as a lunch dish in special restaurants. Numerous variations.

Dim sum beef meat balls with ginger
walnut-sized balls of pasta-like dough filled with beef forcemeat, salt, soda, cornstarch, sugar, pork fatback, coriander leaves, fresh ginger, seasoning and scallion.

Dim sum char siew pau
steamed rolls of baking-powder pastry with pork filling; often made with yeast dough.

Dim sum hoeng sai kau
rolled lard pastry envelopes filled with mixture of tongu mushrooms, shrimp, pork, pork fatback, bamboo shoots, salt and coriander leaves.

Dim sum pockets with bamboo shoots
balls of dough, pressed together in waves at the seams, filled with shrimp, pork, pork fatback, bamboo shoots, groundnut oil, sugar, monosodium glutamate, sesame oil, cornstarch and chopped coriander leaves or chives.

Duck pie Amiens
boned duck with skin baked in pastry-lined mold, with forcemeat of duck liver and gizzard, bacon, mushrooms, seasoning (mainly bay leaf), juniper spirit, fried onion purée and beaten egg. Fill with aspic jelly made from giblets when cooked.

Duckling terrine Nantes
small boned duckling with skin, marinated in potato spirit with mild fennel and fresh mint then stuffed with forcemeat of duck and chicken livers, pork and marinade. Baked in terrine lined with pork fatback, surrounded with more forcemeat. Covered with aspic jelly made from giblets when cooked.

Duxelles
thick, brown mushroom-based sauce poured over meat or poultry dishes or used as filling for puff pastry pies.

E

Easter patties Berry
served as appetizer to precede Easter lamb. Square pan lined with pastry and filled with alternate layers of forcemeat (pork and veal marinated in white wine, ground, and flavored with brandy and nutmeg) and hard-cooked eggs, ending with a layer of forcemeat. Covered with pastry and baked. Served at room temperature.

Eel
river fish used whole in pâtés or as outside casing. It is used for pies in England.

Eel pie   *page 157*

Eel terrine   *page 78*
terrine d'anguille.

Eggplant
(aubergine/*melanzane*), with lamb and herbs makes a good filling for hot pies.

Empanada   *page 170*
pie from Galicia. Case of pasta-like dough or *hojaldre* (puff pastry) with filling of meat, seafood such as shrimp, or fish. Almost always baked in a paella pan.

Empanada gallega
Spanish chicken pie. Filling of cooked chicken, fried onion, garlic, sweet peppers, ham and tomatoes, spread on a round of pastry, topped with a second round and pressed together. Edges are turned upwards. Baked and served hot or lukewarm.

Empanadas fritas
small turnovers of lard pastry, with filling of beef, onion, garlic, sweet peppers, cumin, olives and hard-cooked egg. Deep-fried in fat and served hot.

Entrées
(from the French for "start"), cold or hot hors d'oeuvre. Most pâtés are served as an entrée.

F

Farce
forcemeat, finely chopped or puréed mixture of meat, game, poultry, fish or vegetables. Includes lightening or binding agents.

Fattened chicken
(*poularde*), young, fattened chicken with firm, white flesh. Basis for good stuffings. Best quality from France, e.g. Bresse or Landes chickens.

Fattened liver
alternative name for foie gras.

Fish
for fish pâtés and terrines quality is very important. Specially recommended: pike, salmon, eel, perch, trout.

Fish balls   *page 37*
made from fish forcemeat and cooked in broth. Used as filling for patty shells.

Fish broth
made with fish bones and trimmings, sliced onion, parsley, mushroom peelings, peppercorns, water and white wine. Used for poaching galantines and making sauces.

Fish forcemeat   *page 34*
made with fish fillet and bread or flour panada, with egg white and cream.

Fish velouté
basic white fish sauce.

Flour panada   *page 36*
popular lightening agent for delicate meats such as poultry and veal, but also used for fish and vegetables. Basic recipe: $\frac{1}{2}$ cup milk, 2 tablespoons butter, seasoning, $\frac{1}{2}$ cup flour, 1 egg. Made like choux pastry and pushed through a strainer when cool.

Foie gras en brioche   *page 106*
goose liver in brioche pastry.

Foie gras mousse   *page 134*
mousse made from goose liver, marinated in Armagnac and port wine and lightly fried.

Frying fat
for deep-frying of pies. The fat should have a high burning-point, like oil or vegetable fats.

Fungi
almost every variety can be used for pâtés. Used most frequently in veal or poultry forcemeats.

G

Galantine
fine forcemeat enclosed in boned meat, including skin, cooked in an appropriate broth, e.g. duck in duck broth. A simpler and more usual modern method is to make a roll after stuffing, rather than trying to recreate original shape.

Galantine de canard   *page 118*
rolled pâté of duck.

Galantine de canard sauvage   *page 120*
rolled pâté of wild duck.

Galantine de coquilles Saint-Jacques   *page 121*
rolled scallop pâté.

Galantine de foie gras
rolled goose liver pâté. Foil or cloth is lined with pork fatback, then covered with a forcemeat of liver trimmings, onion, salt, pepper, bay leaf, thyme, Madeira, pork, pork fatback, reduced béchamel sauce, bread crumbs, egg and brandy. Forcemeat is dotted with diced truffle, fat and pistachios, topped with fattened goose liver and rolled. Poached in veal broth, then cut into slices and glazed with aspic jelly.

Galantine de gibier à l'épicure
Italian rolled game pâté. Forcemeat of venison, hare, pork, pork fatback (part diced and marinated in brandy) and marinade spread on cloth or foil, topped with venison breast and rolled. Poached in broth of vegetables, thyme, bay leaf, cloves, peppercorns, red wine, salt, water and powdered gelatin. Aspic jelly made from broth and used to cover galantine.

Galantine de pigeon à l'ancienne
old-fashioned Dutch rolled pigeon pâté. Pigeons stuffed with forcemeat of poultry livers poached in butter, pork, veal, seasoning, Armagnac, Madeira, eggs, goose liver marinated in Madeira, diced truffles, and breast meat marinated in Armagnac. Poached in bone broth. Sliced and covered with aspic.

Galantine de poulet   *page 123*
rolled chicken pâté.

Game
excellent for pâtés, especially hare and game birds, for it is low in fat, high in protein and of good flavor. Can also be used frozen for pies, unlike other meats: it contains little liquid to be lost during thawing. For a fine forcemeat only the best is good enough.

Game broth   *page 42*
made from game bones and trimmings, vegetables, tomato paste, water, bouquet garni of celery, leek, parsley, bay and thyme, shallots, garlic, juniper, peppercorns and salt.

Game terrine with truffles   *page 54*
terrine de gibier aux truffes.

Gefillte fish
Jewish dish of stuffed fish. One of the most famous international dishes. Usually two freshwater fish are used, for example trout, pike, carp. Skinned fish with bones, stuffed with forcemeat of fish, onion, seasoning, egg and matzo flour. Cooked in fish broth which is then reduced to jelly and used for coating. Served with horseradish.

Genoese vegetable pie
pastry filled with exotic vegetables in velouté and baked.

Goose liver
(foie gras), usually refers to fattened goose liver, which come from 13–18 pound geese, force-fed for 21 days. Livers weigh $1\frac{1}{2}$–$2\frac{1}{4}$ pounds. From gray Gascony or Périgord geese or white Alsace geese. Imported from the Eastern bloc and Israel.

Goose liver and apple tartlets   *page 142*
filled with seasoned and floured pieces of goose liver fried in oil, and topped with sliced apple.

Goose liver parfait
(*parfait de foie gras*), goose liver mixed with a pork forcemeat. Goose liver mousse is often referred to as parfait.

Guinea fowl
(*pintade*), gives excellent meat for forcemeats.

H

Halibut pie
rectangle of puff pastry covered with forcemeat of mushrooms, chopped sweet green pepper, salt, pepper, thyme, nutmeg and ginger, topped with seasoned and fried halibut fillets, and then more mushroom forcemeat dotted with butter. Pastry folded over, sealed and baked. Served with shrimp sauce.

Ham mousse   *page 135*
mousse de jambon.

Hare pâtés
made from various recipes. The fillets are usually marinated and included whole.

Hare pie
hare cooked in butter, white wine, brandy and seasoning with glazed onions and mushrooms, transferred to a pie dish, covered with seasoned gravy and puff pastry. Served hot with remaining gravy.

Herbs   *page 24*
pâtés and terrines are usually seasoned with dried herbs, but fresh herbs are substituted where they complement the dish. Fresh herbs can be used in fish pâtés and pies, aspics, sauces, hot patties.

Hure de sanglier farcie
stuffed wild boar's head. Highly complicated galantine, with a long tradition.

J

Jumbo shrimp mousse   *page 135*
mousse de crevettes.

Jus
(French for broth), defatted meat juice. For forcemeats it is usually made with bones and trimmings of meat used.

K

Khatshapuri
Georgian cheese loaf, an unusual pâté in the shape of a quiche or loaf of yeast dough. Filled with a mixture of mild Camembert, Gouda and sheep's milk cheeses, butter, egg and parsley.

Kneaded pastry
one of the many names for pie pastry.

Kulebyaka *page 164*
Russian salmon or cabbage pies.

Kulebyaka with chicken
baked yeast pastry rectangle filled with layers of chicken forcemeat (chicken cooked in butter, chopped onion, sliced mushroom, chicken broth, chopped hard-cooked egg and parsley) and fried blinis.

L

Lamb galantine
rolled boned shoulder of lamb stuffed with forcemeat of sliced calf's liver, fried onion, lamb, pork fatback, eggs, seasoning, parsley, brandy and diced smoked tongue. Poached in slightly jellied lamb broth.

Le poirat berrichon
pear pie from Berry region of France. Two-crust pie filled with pears marinated in brandy, sugar and a little pepper. Served chilled. Variation made with half apples, half quinces.

Leek tartlets gratin *page 143*

Leverpostej
Danish liver pâté. Forcemeat of pork liver, pork fatback, onion, eggs, puréed anchovy fillets, seasoning, béchamel sauce, whipped cream and meat broth baked in mold lined with pork fatback.

Lihamurakepiiras
Finnish pâtés, sour cream pastry filled with forcemeat of mushrooms, ground meat and cheese (Cheddar). Eaten with sour cream.

Liver pâté
all pâtés with liver as main ingredient. The absolute tops for gourmets: pâté de foie gras.

Livonian caldunis
yeast dough turnovers filled with forcemeat of pork, suet, pepper, allspice, mace and salt. Cooked in boiling salted water. Served with brown butter and Parmesan.

Livonian salmon pirozhki
turnovers made from pastry of flour, water, egg, brandy and plenty of butter. Filled with rice mixture, with slices of salted salmon, chopped onion and butter. Baked.

Lobster
delicately flavored, expensive shellfish, popular for parfaits and used in pieces in fish pâtés. Also used as filling for patty shells.

Lobster terrine with vegetables *page 84*
terrine de langouste aux légumes.

Lorraine boar's head pie
can also be made as a terrine. Forcemeat of fresh pork sides, beaten egg, white cheese, plum brandy and seasoning, mixed with boar's head meat marinated in Aligoté white wine and plum brandy. Mold lined with pie pastry, topped with forcemeat, slices of boar's liver, more forcemeat, then pastry lid. Decorated and baked.

Lorraine cheese tarts *page 142*
quiche lorraine.

Lorraine goose pâté
mold lined with heavy, but smooth pie pastry. Forcemeat of pork, veal, egg, bread crumbs, plum brandy and seasoning added and topped with goose, veal and breast of pork, all in pieces and marinated in Mosel wine. Covered with pastry and baked. Aspic jelly made with goose trimmings and veal bones poured into pâté while still warm.

M

Macaroni tartlets *page 143*
à la milanaise, filled with macaroni, ham and mushrooms.

Madeira aspic jelly
extremely popular aspic jelly for filling pâtés or served diced with pâté.

Marinade
pâté ingredients used whole, or for the forcemeat, are often marinated, sometimes for up to 3 days depending on the recipe. Basis of marinade is usually wine, mainly southern wines such as port, Madeira, sherry, but also red and white wine.

Maultaschen
specialty from Swabia. Triangles of pasta dough filled with ground meat or ham, onion, spinach and seasoning are boiled in broth.

Meat forcemeat
meat filling for pâtés, pies or meat balls.

Meat jelly
clarified meat broth which jellyfies on cooling due to inclusion of calves' feet or gelatin.

Mirabeau pies
puff pastry patty shells filled with sole, cooked in butter, broken into pieces and bound with anchovy sauce.

Mogador patties
once a specialty in the Parisian restaurant of the same name. Diced chicken and smoked tongue are bound with a chicken cream sauce and used as a filling for patty shells with alternate layers of puréed goose liver; served warm.

Montgelas filling
for patty shells. Goose liver and smoked tongue are poached separately in Madeira and mixed with fried mushrooms and Madeira sauce.

Moorland sheep pie
mold lined with pastry, covered with forcemeat made from moorland sheep, pork, pork fatback, seasoning, reduced broth, and diced smoked tongue and ham, and topped with pieces of leg or loin of lamb seasoned with sauce from shallots, Kümmel liqueur, reduced broth and seasoning. Covered with more forcemeat and pastry, decorated and baked.

Morels
after truffles the most popular fungus for pâtés and fillings.

Mousse *page 131*
pâtés with aspic added, whose main ingredient may be a fine purée of vegetables, poultry, ham, game, chicken liver, fish or shellfish. Made with gelatin and whipped cream and unmolded to serve.

Mousseline farce
forcemeat for mousse.

Mushroom tartlets *page 142*

Mushroom terrine *page 90*
terrine de cèpes.

N

Nantes patties
puff pastry patty shells filled with cooked seafish mixed with mushrooms fried in butter and fish velouté. Served with mushroom gravy.

O

Onions *page 23*
for fine pâtés and terrines the more delicately-flavored shallot is used, or possibly mild seasoning onions. Yellow onions and garlic are used where a stronger flavor is appropriate. Red onions are milder and can be used more freely. The same is true for scallions.

Ox tongue
smoked, popular diced in pâté fillings.

Oyster
delicately flavored shellfish, made into pâté or included whole.

Oyster pasties
braised oysters in rounds of pie pastry, shaped into turnovers and cooked in hot butter.

Oyster pie
old English recipe, oysters cooked in a stewed beef filling.

P

Panada *page 36*
used for lightening forcemeats. Can take the form of a flour panada (like choux pastry) or a cream béchamel sauce.

Pancake rolls *page 174*
thin pancakes or crêpes of special dough, filled with bean sprouts, Chinese mushrooms, chicken, pork, shrimp, bamboo shoots and seasoning.

Paotze
small Chinese balls of pasta dough filled with pork (like dim sum).

Parfait
term for fine forcemeats which include either aspic or egg white and are poached in a water bath. Ideal basic ingredient: vegetables, also fish and shellfish.

Parfait d'écrevisses *page 140*
shrimp parfait.

Parfait de faisan au foie gras et morilles *page 141*
pheasant parfait with goose liver and morels. Forcemeat made from seasoned pheasant, egg white, flour panada, whipped cream, pieces of goose liver marinated in brandy and morels in their juice.

Parfait de volaille au foies de volailles et cèpes *page 140*
chicken parfait with chicken liver and flap mushrooms

Parisian pie
1. Forcemeat of marinated pork, pork fatback, eggs, shallots, seasoning, thyme and bay in pastry-lined mold with alternate layers of diced meat. 2. Shredded beef fillet, marinated in white wine and brandy and flavored with herbs and shallots, in pastry-lined mold with balls of beef, veal and panada forcemeats. Covered with pastry and baked.

Partridge
ideal meat for forcemeats. Breasts of young partridge are good for using whole.

Pâté
French for pie or pâté.

Pâté d'alouettes
lark pâté. Boned birds, stuffed with truffles and goose liver, rolled into balls. Baked in pastry case with forcemeat made from sieved liver. Filled with aspic jelly after baking.

Pâté de venaison *page 50*
venison pâté. Same recipe can be used for antelope pâté.

Pâté d'artichauts *page 86*
artichoke pâté. Forcemeat of veal and pork with artichoke hearts. Baked in yeast dough.

Pâté de bécasses
woodcock pâté. Boned woodcock stuffed with forcemeat of innards, lightly fried chicken liver and woodcock legs mixed with pork forcemeat. Baked in pastry case with more woodcock forcemeat, and pork forcemeat mixed with Madeira wine, pâté seasoning and diced foie gras. When cold filled with aspic jelly made from woodcock bones.

Pâte brisée
French term for pie pastry.

Pâté de caille *page 54*
quail pâté. Forcemeat of quail meat, pork, pork fatback, seasoning, quail broth, chopped pistachios and truffle baked in pastry case with foie gras and fried quail breasts.

Pâté de chevreuil *page 48*
venison pie.

Pâté à la contade
original name of pâté de foie gras, named by its inventor Jean-Pierre Clause after his master, the Maréchal de Contade.

Pâté à la corniaule
takes its name from the Corniaule area near Vichy. A pâté made from kid served on April 23 for the feast of St George. Kid is marinated for 24 hours in local wine (from *gaillard noir* grapes) with wild thyme, juniper berries, onion and garlic. Forcemeat made from kid's liver, pork fatback, wood mushrooms, salt, seasoning, shallots, lightly fried in butter. Mold lined with pastry, filled with forcemeat and marinated kid, covered with pastry and baked.

Pâté d'escargots *page 85*
snail pâté. Forcemeat of fried, sliced shallots, white bread, egg white, light and whipped cream, veal, thyme, marjoram and seasoning, mixed with snails fried in butter, and broth made with Pernod, brandy, veal broth, snail liquid and seasoning. Baked in pastry case.

Pâté de faisan en croûte
pastry-lined oval mold filled with layers of sliced pork fatback, pheasant forcemeat (pheasant meat (marinated and fried), pork, pork fatback, goose liver and meat glaze), marinated pheasant breast meat, pheasant and chicken livers and halved truffles. Covered with pastry and baked. Filled with Madeira aspic jelly when cold.

Pâté de foie gras *page 101*
goose liver pâté. Invented by Jean-Pierre Clause in 1762. Fattened goose liver from Alsace wrapped in pastry and baked, without truffles.

Pâté de foie truffé *page 108*
truffled liver pâté. Forcemeat of calf's liver, pork liver and pork, with diced, fried liver, ham and truffles added.

Pâté de jambon *page 61*
ham pâté. Pork forcemeat around a piece of pork tenderloin.

Pâté de lièvre
hare pâté, with a forcemeat of hare and pork. Includes hare fillets wrapped in pork fatback.

Pâté de marcassin *page 50*
wild boar pâté with a forcemeat of boar's leg and pork loin.

Pâté de perdrix *page 53*
partridge pâté. Forcemeat of partridge legs, pork, fat and seasoning with diced foie gras, truffles, smoked tongue and pistachios.

Pâté de poularde, chaud ou froid *page 67*
chicken pâté, hot or cold. Served warm with Madeira sauce, or cold filled up with Madeira aspic jelly.

Pâté de saumon *page 77*
salmon pâté. Forcemeat of salmon fillet, white bread, egg white, cream and diced truffles.

Pâté de tartouffes
potato pâté. Mold lined with pastry of flour, egg, butter, salt and water, filled with alternate layers of thinly sliced potato and onion (dotted with lard and goose fat) and season. Covered with pastry, baked and served hot.

Pâté de volaille au foie gras *page 69*
poultry pâté with goose liver. Forcemeat of seasoned guinea fowl, duck and pork fillet. Includes fried guinea fowl breasts and truffled goose liver.

Pâté seasoning *page 22*
mixture of seasoning for all types of stuffings.

Patties capuchin
puff pastry patty shells filled with scrambled egg, braised sweetbreads and chopped truffle.

Patties à la Kaunitz
Austrian puff pastry patty shells filled with mixture of diced blanched sweetbreads and diced mushrooms fried in butter, diced truffle, balls of veal forcemeat, and Madeira sauce.

Patties nimois
puff pastry patty shells filled with lamb, smoked bacon, chicken liver, basil and brandy, fried and then lightly crushed.

Pelemeni *page 163*
a kind of pâté of egg-pasta dough with meat filling, cooked in salted water. Served hot with chopped parsley or dill, melted butter or sour cream. Originally from Siberia.

Peppers
sweet, mostly used in fillings for empanadas.

Perch
one of the best freshwater fish, equally good for forcemeats or used in fillets.

Petites terrines de champignons en couche *page 89*
individual mushroom terrines. Forcemeat as for *terrine de champignons à la maison*, of veal or poultry. Cooked in buttered molds and covered with white or green chaudfroid sauce.

Petits pâtés de foie en brioche *page 107*
individual liver brioches. Forcemeat as for
terrine de foies de volaille. Brioche molds lined
with pastry, filled with forcemeat, and topped
with pastry. Filled with port wine aspic jelly
when cold.

Pheasant
game bird, excellent for pâtés.

Pie *page 151*
filled pastry case, with or without a lid.

Pie or kneaded pie pastry *page 12*
known as *pâte brisée* in France. Suitable for
all pies. Basic recipe: 5 cups flour, 1¼ cups
butter, 1 teaspoon salt, ½–¾ cup water, 1 egg.

Pie pastry with shortening *page 12*
basic recipe: 4 cups flour, ¾ cup shortening, 1
teaspoon salt, ¾–1 cup water.

Piecrusts *pages 10–17*

Pie alla ferrarese
pastry-lined mold filled with forcemeat of
mushrooms, fried sweetbreads, chicken, salt,
pepper, wine, boiled short macaroni, broth,
béchamel sauce, cheese and butter. Covered
with pastry and baked.

Pies *page 155*
English dish pies, usually with only pastry lid,
less frequently with dish completely lined with
pastry.

Pigeon terrine *page 73*
terrine de pigeon au basilic.

Pike
(*brochet*), ideal fish for forcemeats. Can be
used for pie fillings or fish balls.

Pirozhki
term covers a variety of Russian pâtés, served
with soup or as appetizer.

Pirozhki fillings *page 167*
flap mushrooms with chicken; pork and beet;
sauerkraut; herb cheese; smoked salmon; ham
and rice; lamb.

Pirozhki Smolensk style
filling of buckwheat groats, toasted in a pan,
seasoned and boiled until thick, mixed with
melted butter, finely chopped hard-cooked
egg, chopped onion and parsley. Spread on
squares of yeast dough, rolled and baked.

Pirozhki tworogom
pirozhki filled with herb cheese.

Pistachios
fruit of pistachio tree. Popular ingredient for
pâtés, partly for their lovely green color.

Poisson en brioche *page 78*
fish pâté in brioche dough.

Pork
by far the most popular meat for pâté fillings.
Pork is also added to most kinds of game
pâtés to make the meat less dry.

Pork fatback
for most terrines and pâté fillings best quality
fresh pork fatback is used. Can also be
marinated. To line and cover molds.

Pork pie
English pork pie. Hot pastry of flour, lard,
water and eggs, covered with pork tenderloin
forcemeat, rolled, brushed with egg yolk and
baked. Filled with pork aspic jelly when cold.

Port
famous Portuguese wine, mainly used to
flavor aspic jellies.

Poultry liver
the liver (unfattened) of all types of poultry is
a popular ingredient for forcemeats. If
included in pieces in pâtés, it is usually diced
and fried first.

Poultry pie with goose liver *page 69*
pâté de volaille au foie gras.

Poultry tartlets *page 143*
small tartlets filled with cooked poultry and
poultry forcemeat, covered with Hollandaise
sauce and browned.

Poultry velouté
basic white poultry sauce.

Pudding *page 158*
English term; also refers to steamed meat pies.

Puff pastry *page 16*

Punta di vitello ripieno *page 128*
Italian-style stuffed breast of veal.

Q

Quail
the smallest game bird of the field fowl
family, also available from quail farms. For
fine forcemeats and used in pieces
(particularly breasts).

Quark puff pastry
can be used instead of traditional puff pastry,
but has slightly sour taste. 2 cups flour, 1
teaspoon baking powder, ½ lb (1 cup) quark,
½ lb (1 cup) finely chopped cold butter, salt.
Work together, chill and use as for puff
pastry.

Queen patties *page 148*
the most popular of the puff pastry pâté
shells; filled with various fillings, but usually
with *ragoût fin*.

R

Rabbit
popular for pies in both the domestic and
wild varieties. As with hare the fillets are
often included whole.

Ragoût de cèpes au ris de veau *page 152*
filling of mushrooms with sweetbread and
truffles.

Ragoût de coquilles Saint-Jacques *page 151*
scallop filling.

Ragoût de crevettes roses *page 151*
filling of jumbo shrimp and mushrooms.

Ragoût d'écrevisses à l'anèth *page 152*
shrimp and dill filling.

Ragoût d'écrevisses Nantua *page 151*
shrimp filling Nantua.

Ragoût d'escargots *page 152*
filling of snails in Riesling sauce with shallots
and mushroom caps.

Ragoût d'homard *page 148*
lobster filling.

Ragoût de légumes *page 150*
filling of morels, green peas, spring carrots in
chicken velouté with cream and asparagus
tips.

Ragoût de poulet *page 150*
filling of diced morels in chicken velouté with
cream and cooked, diced chicken breast.

Ragoût de ris de veau *page 150*
filling of pieces of sealed sweetbread in a port-
veal-broth-cream sauce with parsley.

Raised game pie
English game pie. Mold lined with hot water
pastry, covered with slices of pork fatback
and forcemeat of hare, rabbit and pheasant,
and topped with strips of fried pheasant
breasts, rabbit and hare fillet. Covered with
pastry. Filled with aspic jelly after baking.

Rastegai
pâté with *vesiga*, the dried back tendon of the
sturgeon. Sold in European specialty shops.
Vesiga is soaked and cooked in meat broth,
then finely chopped, mixed with chopped
hard-cooked egg and fish velouté, transferred
to rounds of yeast pastry, shaped into
turnovers and baked.

Ravioli
envelopes of Italian pasta in various shapes,
filled with meat or vegetables and cooked in
broth or tomato sauce. Served with grated
Parmesan. A specialty of Genoa.

Ravioli alla genovese
envelopes of Italian pasta with filling of veal
and pork, calf's brains and sweetbreads, egg,
bread, Parmesan and turnip, seasoned with
nutmeg.

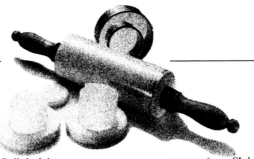

Red deer pie
prepared as for venison pie, the fillet being sealed and included whole.

Reduced broth or essence
concentrated broth made from trimmings of the main meat used, with root vegetables, and often diluted with wine. Added to forcemeat to bring out the flavor of ingredients used whole – for example by brushing onto fillets.

Reims pie
pastry-lined mold filled with lean meat forcemeat topped with strips of pork marinated in Champagne with juniper berries. Covered with pastry and baked.

Rice croustade capuchin
rice cooked in meat broth, pressed into cup molds and cooled, then breaded and deep-fried. Centers removed and filled with scrambled egg and grated Parmesan.

Rillettes de porc
the original terrine recipe, preserved pork. French specialty. Chopped fat pork fried in lard with onions, herbs and seasoning, chopped, boiled until soft, seasoned with paprika, mixed with liquid lard and bottled. Use to spread on bread.

Rissoles (turnovers)
rounds of pie or brioche pastry, topped with forcemeat of meat, fish, poultry or shellfish, folded into half-moons and deep-fried.

Rissoles with beef marrow
puff pastry turnovers with a filling of poached beef marrow, with Madeira sauce reduced until thick. Coated in bread crumbs and deep-fried.

Rissoles à la bohémienne
brioche pastry turnovers with a filling of goose liver and truffles bound with meat glaze.

Rissoles cendrillons
Cinderella rissoles. Brioche pastry turnovers with filling of chicken and truffles in puréed goose liver. A totally undeserved name.

Rissoles à la chalônaise
pie pastry turnovers filled with chicken, mushrooms and truffles in velouté sauce.

Rissoles Indian style
puff pastry turnovers with filling of lamb (fried), onion, flour, curry, tomato paste and chopped apple.

Rissoles Lucy
turnovers with a filling of crushed, smoked sprats and blue-vein cheese.

Rissoles de poisson
puff pastry turnovers with filling of seasoned ground fish in thick béchamel and egg yolk. Coated in bread crumbs and deep-fried.

Rissoles Pompadour
pie pastry turnovers filled with smoked tongue, mushrooms, truffles and meat glaze.

Rolled pâté   *page 116*
another term for galantine where filling is spread over boned poultry such as duck or pheasant and then rolled up, with no attempt to keep the original shape. Quick method for making galantines.

Roman pies
batter made from 1 cup flour, 1 cup milk, 1 tablespoon oil, salt, nutmeg. Traditional pie irons are heated in fat, dipped into batter, fried in fat until golden brown, and filled with filling to taste.

Roux   *page 148*
binding agent for forcemeats.

Rub-in pastry   *page 13*
pie pastry, for which fat and flour are rubbed together to form crumbs before the other ingredients are added.

S

Salmon
(*saumon*), ideal for pâtés, either fresh or smoked. Equally good as a forcemeat or used in fillet form.

Salmon and fried egg tartlets.   *page 142*

Salmon terrine   *page 82*
terrine de saumon, truffled salmon forcemeat, wrapped in salmon fillets. Almost a galantine.

Salpiçon
(*ragoût fin*), meat, poultry, game, fish or vegetables, finely diced and bound with a little gravy. Used as patty shell or quiche filling.

Samosa   *page 173*
savory Indian crêpes. Flour-oil-water pastry cut into thin rounds (saucer-sized), halved, topped with filling and pressed together into triangles. Filling of garlic, ginger, onion, oil, curry, ground beef or lamb, mint and coriander.

Sea bass medallion tartlets   *page 143*

Sea trout
freshwater fish of the salmon family. Makes a particularly delicate fish pâté.

Seafood pie
American pie of chicken, scallops, oysters, fish, onion, celery, lobster and sherry. Covered with pie crust.

Seasonings   *page 19*

Shallots   *page 23*

Shepherd's pie
cooked, ground lamb mixed with onion, carrot and seasoning (mint, rosemary, marjoram and parsley) in baking dish, topped with mashed potato, beaten with egg and egg white and seasoned, and baked.

Shrimp
made into fillings for pâtés, terrines, parfaits and timbales and also used whole. Also popular in patty shells.

Singara   *page 163*

Smoked fish mousse   *page 133*
mousse de poisson fumé, with caviar filling.

Snipe
a much sought-after game bird for pâtés, but protected in some countries.

Spanakopitta   *page 171*
Greek pie with spinach and feta cheese filling. Yeast pastry.

Spirits
used to flavor forcemeats. Added to the broth, alcohol boiled out to leave only the flavor.

Squab pie   *page 56*
English pie which ideally combines sweet and savory ingredients.

Steak and kidney pie   *page 156*
the best-known of all the English pie recipes.

Steak and mushroom pudding   *page 158*
steamed suet pie.

Strasburg goose liver pâté
a pâté de foie gras. Basically a terrine of truffled goose liver, marinated in Madeira and brandy, and goose liver forcemeat.

Suet pastry   *page 14*

Sulzpastete
German term for mousse.

Sweetbreads
popular variety meat for pies and also for patty shell fillings.

T

Tartar Caldunis
Pastry turnovers filled with mixture of tender, finely chopped beef and finely diced suet. Boiled in salted water or light broth.

Tartlets
small, blind-baked pie pastry shells, occasionally puff or yeast pastry. Filled with *ragoût fin* (*salpiçon*) and served hot. Or first lined with forcemeat, then baked and filled.

Tartlets Agnes Sorel
pastry shells coated with chicken forcemeat and baked, then filled with chicken, mushrooms and truffle in velouté with cream. Covered with more chicken forcemeat and browned. Decorated with smoked tongue and truffle slices and a dash of Madeira sauce.

Tartlets aiglon
filling of fresh goose liver and mushrooms braised in butter with brandy-flavored liver forcemeat.

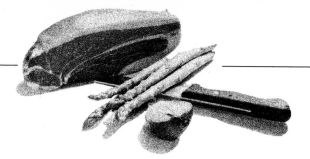

Tartlets Argentueil
filling of cooked chicken breast and puréed asparagus, decorated with buttered asparagus tips.

Tartlets danoises
Danish, pastry shells filled with salmon purée, topped with mayonnaise, sprinkled with cheese and browned.

Terrine *page 39*
pâté without piecrust. The forcemeat is cooked in terrines (porcelain or ceramic dishes), usually lined with thin slices of pork fatback.

Terrine d'abatis d'oie *page 70*
duck giblet terrine. Forcemeat very low in fat content.

Terrine de brocoli *page 87*
broccoli terrine. Alternate layers of broccoli and celery forcemeat. Covered in chaudfroid sauce.

Terrine de campagne *page 60*
country-style terrine. Forcemeat of rabbit and pork, flavored with herbs and brandy.

Terrine de canard *page 71*
duck terrine.

Terrine de canard au poitrine de canard truffée *page 72*
duck terrine with truffled breast of duck. A breast of duck is stuffed with truffles and included in the terrine.

Terrine de canard sauvage au foie de canard *page 59*
wild duck terrine with duck's liver. Forcemeat of wild duck and pork with breast of duck included.

Terrine de champignons à la maison *page 88*
house-style mushroom terrine with veal forcemeat.

Terrine de dindon truffé *page 72*
truffled turkey terrine with turkey and pork forcemeat.

Terrine de faisan au foie gras *page 58*
pheasant and goose liver terrine. Forcemeat of pheasant and pork with pistachios and diced truffles. Pheasant breasts and goose liver included in pieces.

Terrine de foie gras *page 120*
goose liver terrine.

Terrine de foie de veau *page 108*
calf's liver terrine. Forcemeat as for *pâté de foie truffé*, but with pork to replace the pork liver.

Terrine de foies de volaille *page 122*
Poultry liver terrine with pork and pork fatback.

Terrine de lapin *page 57*
rabbit terrine with forcemeat of rabbit and pork and back fillets of rabbit included whole.

Terrine de légumes au foie gras *page 87*
vegetable and goose liver terrine with a chicken forcemeat.

Terrine maison aux haricots verts *page 65*
house-style terrine with green beans. Forcemeat of pork, chicken breast and calf's liver.

Terrine de Nérac
mold lined with bacon, filled one-third full with a forcemeat of partridge, pork fatback, chicken liver and Armagnac and topped with partridge breasts, fried and flambéed in Armagnac, slices of foie gras and truffle. Covered with remaining forcemeat and bacon.

Terrine de pintade au ris de veau et morilles *page 74*
guinea fowl terrine with sweetbreads and morels.

Terrine de pintadeaux *page 74*
terrine of young guinea fowl. Forcemeat of guinea fowl and pork tenderloin, with guinea fowl breast, flavored with Armagnac, included whole.

Terrine de poisson du chef *page 77*
chef's own fish terrine. Forcemeat of pike or turbot fillets; flap mushrooms, lobster claws, green beans, carrots, sea trout and turbot included.

Terrine de poulet au foie de volaille *page 68*
chicken terrine with liver.

Terrine de ris de veau *page 63*
sweetbread terrine with forcemeat of veal and pork.

Terrine de sanglier *page 52*
wild boar terrine.

Terrine de sanglier "Rioja" *page 52*
wild boar terrine with game liver marinated in Rioja wine and Armagnac.

Terrine de sole au foie gras *page 81*
sole terrine with goose liver.

Terrine de truites arc-en-ciel et truites saumonées *page 80*
rainbow and sea trout terrine.

Terrine de truites saumonées au parfait d'huîtres *page 72*
sea trout terrine with oyster parfait. Forcemeat of sea trout. Includes oyster forcemeat with carrot sticks and green beans.

Terrine de turbot au basilic frais *page 72*
turbot terrine with fresh basil.

Terrine de veau aux champignons de couche *page 64*
veal and mushroom terrine.

Thrush pâté
(*pâté de grives*), a delicate pâté from Languedoc. The boned birds are stuffed with truffled foie gras and baked in a forcemeat of pork, pork fatback and game liver, flavored with Armagnac.

Tim sum
name in Singapore for titbits known as dim sum in China.

Timbale de brochet aux crevettes en sauce à l'anèth *page 138*
pike timbale with shrimp in dill sauce.

Timbale de brocoli à la sauce aux noix *page 139*
broccoli timbale with walnut sauce. Forcemeat of puréed steamed broccoli, eggs, cream and seasoning.

Timbale de carottes à la sauce aux herbes *page 139*
carrot timbale with herb sauce. Forcemeat of carrots braised in butter, broth and seasoning and whisked with egg and cream. Cooked in molds.

Timbale de chou-fleur à la sauce d'épinards *page 139*
cauliflower timbale with spinach sauce. Forcemeat of cauliflower braised in butter and chicken broth, puréed with eggs and cream.

Timbale de perdreaux aux morilles à la crème *page 136*
partridge timbale with morels in cream.

Timbale de pistaches au sauté de faisan *page 137*
pistachio timbale with sautéed pheasant, with pork forcemeat.

Timbale de saumon au sauté de cuisses de grenouilles *page 137*
salmon timbale with frogs' legs. Served on steamed spinach.

Timbale de saumon fumé au moules *page 138*
smoked salmon timbale with mussels.

Timbales *page 136*
small metal molds, also known as darioles. Originally pastry pâté cases baked blind in cup molds, and still made in this way occasionally. But usually cooked in water bath without the pastry case.

Tomato mousse *page 135*
mousse made with sieved tomatoes and catsup.

Tongue
one of the best parts of slaughtered animals, also game. Particularly popular is smoked ox tongue used in pieces.

Torta pasqualina
Italian Easter pie. Light pastry filled with seasoned artichoke purée, spinach, possibly chicory in light ricotta cheese and milk sauce with hard-cooked eggs, and baked.

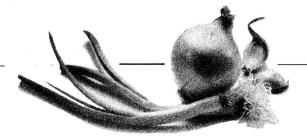

Tourte de brocoli *page 132*
broccoli torte. Broccoli mousse with venison fillets on puff pastry base.

Tourte de ris de veau *page 64*
sweetbread torte, a specialty made from a pork tenderloin forcemeat and sweetbreads.

Tourte de saumon *page 83*
salmon mold with pike forcemeat.

Trimmings
waste and odd pieces of meat produced when meat or fish is trimmed.

Trout
large sea trout in particular are popular for pâté fillings or using whole.

Truffles *page 109*
an expensive fungus. The best of the truffle family are the black Périgord winter truffles. Only in the winter do they develop their full flavor. Périgord truffle is the botanical name; they have the same name when found outside Périgord, for example in Provence or Spain.

V

Varenyky
Ukrainian turnovers with cheese, sauerkraut or plum filling. Cooked in salted water and served with melted butter and sour cream.

Variety meat
innards, particularly of veal and lamb (can include beef – for example tongue), popular used in pieces in pâtés.

Vatrushki *page 166*
Russian cheese tartlets.

Veal
together with pork the most popular meat for pâtés. For fine forcemeats the loin is best.

Veal and ham pie *page 159*
traditional English pie. Typical of this pie is the inclusion of diced veal and ham and not as a puréed forcemeat. Filled with hard-cooked eggs and baked in pastry in a loaf pan.

Veal tartlets *page 142*

Velouté *page 148*
velvety white sauce (*velours* = velvet) made with flour, butter and strongly-flavored light veal broth. Boiled for 30 minutes, then skimmed. Thick reduced cream added and sauce strained through cheesecloth. Depending on the recipe, can be made with chicken, veal or game broth.

Venison pasties *page 160*
English, pastry rounds filled with diced venison marinated in groundnut oil and port wine with root vegetables, covered with second pastry round and baked.

Vintner's pie
puff pastry cases filled with chopped snails mixed with snail juice and chestnut purée and flavored with brandy.

Visishki
Russian fish pies. Chopped sea or freshwater fish is bound in a basic fish sauce, wrapped in small turnovers of yeast dough and deep-fried.

Vol-au-vent *page 151*
large puff pastry patty shell baked blind, then filled with fine forcemeat. Attributed to Carême. Requires about 1¼ lb puff pastry.

Vol-au-vent cardinal
filling of lobster, mushrooms, truffles in white wine, pike balls, brandy and cream. All mixed separately in béchamel sauce mixed with lobster juice and Hollandaise sauce and arranged in layers in the patty shell.

Vol-au-vent president-style
filling of fried sole fillets, sprinkled with lemon juice and parsley, topped with pike balls cooked in fish broth and then with shrimp and béchamel sauce with truffle purée.

Vol-au-vent Toulouse-style
filling of sweetbread and veal meatballs, boiled with root vegetables, with diced sweetbreads and mushrooms braised in butter, covered with velouté and topped with a slice of sweetbread.

W

White bread *page 34*
one of the best ways of lightening fine forcemeats, especially those made from fish and vegetables, without affecting the flavor. Must be high quality and fresh and of light, airy consistency. Usually moistened with cream and egg white.

Wild boar
has an ideal flavor (particularly the back) for forcemeats. Combines the advantages of the meat of domestic pigs with a delicate game flavor.

Wild boar pie with venison fillet *page 51*
pâté de marcassin au filet de chevreuil.

Wine
any wine used for cooking should always be best quality. This alone has the fine flavor necessary for aspic jellies and marinades.

Won-tons
Chinese dish. Meat or seafood filling wrapped in pasta-type pastry. Can be cooked in *congée* (a rice mixture) for breakfast, in the soup for supper, or as a snack – fried or steamed.

Y

Yeast pastry *page 15*
made from 4 cups flour, 2 (.6 oz) cakes compressed yeast, 1 cup lukewarm milk, ¼ cup butter, 2 eggs, 1 teaspoon salt. Can be used for both hot and cold dishes.

Yorkshire pie
fried onion and beef braised with carrot, tomato and leek, seasoned with salt and pepper, transferred to a pie dish, covered with suet pastry and baked.

Z

Zamponi *page 126*
Italian stuffed pig's feet. Scalded pig's feet are hollowed out to the toes and soaked. Stuffed with forcemeat of pork loin, fat, seasoning, thyme, marjoram, smoked tongue, diced veal fillet and pistachios, sewn up, wrapped in strips of linen and cooked in beef broth. Particularly good smoked.

Molds and Other Utensils

The would-be pâté maker should not be put off by the number of implements and pans available. You can make forcemeats for pâtés or terrines in any kitchen with the normal range of utensils. But an efficient grinder with a sharp blade and a cutting disk with the smallest possible perforations is essential, or an electric food processor with a sharp blade. It is important to have some experience of your oven and its temperature variations before starting on pâté making. Other utensils are by no means essential, but there are a variety of minor technical aids which will make your work much easier. A thermometer, for instance, to allow you to regulate the temperature of poaching broths or a meat thermometer which can help determine exactly when a pâté is cooked. The same is true of the many different dishes and molds. You could make do with an ordinary cake pan, but a pâté mold which folds open guarantees that the pâté will come out of the mold with the pastry intact.

1 Wood-framed sieve with metal mesh for sieving ground meats. A metal mesh is essential to cut through the meat fibers.

2 Chinois for straining broths and sauces.

3 Set of metal bowls for mixing forcemeats.

4 Rubber dough scraper.

5 Metal dough scraper, also useful when sieving forcemeats.

6 Rubber spatula, an essential aid for scraping out bowls with hot contents.

7 Rectangular cutters. A set of two different sized cutters (as for round cutters) for cutting out croustades.

8 Small cutters for making funnel openings and decorations.

9 Cutters for tarts and decorations. Plain and fluted round cutters allow for a variety of different decorations.

10 Tartlet tins, plain or fluted. With diameters of 3–5 in.

11 Open gutter mold.

12 Gutter mold with lid. Used for cooking dishes in a water bath and also for mousses (pâtés with aspic). Pâtés made in a mold of this shape are easy to slice.

13 Pastry brush, for brushing pâtés with egg yolk. Choose a wide brush with natural bristles.

14 Straight-edged pastry wheel.

15 Fluted pastry wheel (jagger).

16 Pastry crimper for decorating pâtés.

17 Fluted oval pâté mold (pâté en croûte mold). This traditional French mold consists of two side pieces, held together with clips, and a base. The mold comes apart, making it very easy to remove the pâté.

18 Hinged pâté molds. They consist of four side pieces and a base. The hinged joints make it very easy to remove the pâté.

19 Long loaf pan. The tapered sides make it easy to line with pastry and help the pâté to unmold cleanly.

20 English pudding basin in porcelain. The rim at the top allows for tying the cloth with which the filled basin is covered.

21 Round ovenproof molds for terrines baked without a lid.

22 Terrines of enameled cast iron with lid. Guaranteed to produce good results.

23 Timbale molds or custard cups. Range from $\frac{1}{2}$–1 cup volume, round or oval, but always slightly tapering to make for ease of unmolding timbales or mousses.

24 Earthenware terrine, in heavy glazed pottery for country-style terrines.

25 White porcelain terrines, oval or rectangular.

26 Rectangular porcelain terrines, open and with lids. The particularly thick walls guarantee that the filling will cook evenly.

27 Decorative game terrines (mock pâté en croûte). The shape of these terrines echoes the classic piecrust and the lid illustrates the possible contents.

28 Timbale milanaise pot, quite deep, intended for spreads.

Technical Terms Explained

A

aiguillettes, long thin strips of meat or poultry.

allumettes, matchstick-sized pieces.

à part, served separately, e.g. a sauce.

à point, at the right time, just right (of cooking time).

B

bain-marie, or water bath, a container partially filled with hot water in which delicate dishes such as sauces are cooked, kept warm or warmed up.

bard, partially or fully to cover meat, vegetables, fish, poultry with slices of fat or bacon. Meat fillets used whole in pâtés or pies are often barded.

barquette, boat-shaped tartlets with various fillings.

batterie de cuisine, kitchen equipment.

blanch, to pour over, or briefly immerse in, boiling water. Vegetables or fungi are often blanched to remove unpleasant flavors and impurities. Place vegetables in simmering salted water, boil for a few minutes and refresh in cold water. Some meats, e.g. sweetbreads, are also blanched. Cover the meat with plenty of cold water, bring to a boil and then refresh in cold water.

bake blind, to bake pastry cases without filling. To help keep their shape they are first lined with parchment paper or foil and filled with dried peas or beans. Remove paper and beans after baking.

boil to clarify, to cook sauces and soups slowly, continually removing foam and fat until completely clear.

bone, to remove all bones from meat, poultry or game, without damaging the skin so as to preserve the original shape.

bouquet garni, bunch of flavorings composed of various herbs, vegetables and seasonings. Used to improve flavor of broths or sauces.

braise, to simmer or steam pre-sealed meat in a highly seasoned liquid

braisière, cooking pan with tight-fitting lid for braising and steaming.

brioche, yeast cake.When applied to pastry refers to unsweetened yeast pastry.

brunoise, finely diced vegetables.

C

cannelated, fluted, e.g. pans or molds.

cannelons, stuffed rolls of pastry.

carcass, bird's rib cage.

carrée, front end of back (rib) of veal, lamb and pork (rack).

charcutier, pork butcher.

charlotte, round, cylindrical mold.

chaudfroid, meat dishes in savory aspic sauce, served cold.

chemise, outside coating.

chemiser, to line a mold evenly with aspic jelly or with some other mixture before adding the filling.

cimier, back section of loin of game.

clarify, to remove anything that makes a broth or aspic jelly cloudy. Adding egg white and finely chopped meat binds and removes impurities.

cocottes, or custard cups, small, ovenproof, porcelain or earthenware cooking dishes, in which food is both cooked and served.

colle, dissolved gelatin.

collé(e), mixture containing gelatin.

color, to brown or give color to.

consommé, strong, clear meat broth. Heat ground beef, diced root vegetables and a little egg white with cold, defatted meat broth and simmer for about 2 hours; strain, bring back to a boil and season.

contrefilet, rib of beef, roasting beef.

couenne, rind, skin.

couleur, brown sugar color.

court-bouillon, highly seasoned broth for cooking fish.

crêpes, thin, egg pancakes.

crustaceans, shellfish.

cuisse, thigh, leg.

cul, hindpart.

culotte, tailpiece of beef.

cure, to keep meat by salting or covering with pickling liquid. Curing keeps the red color of the meat and increases its flavor.

custard, egg cream.

D

dariole, small, smooth-sided cup mold.

deep-fry, to fry until golden in deep hot fat.

defat, to remove fat from broths, sauces and soups by skimming from the surface.

dégorger, to soak in water; specially applied to soaking blood from brains, sweetbreads, hearts or liver.

demi-glace, strong brown gravy, basic brown sauce.

dry, to drain or wipe dry.

E

entrée, warm or cold dish served as part of a long meal to precede the main course.

entremet, small dish served between the main course and the dessert.

essence, highly reduced broth, concentrated gravy.

F

feuillantines, small puff pastry cakes.

ficeler, to tie up with string.

filet d'eau, few drops of water.

fines herbes, finely chopped herbs, usually parsley, chervil, chives and tarragon, for sauces or soups.

flavor, to season a dish with an aromatic liquid.

fleurons, small, half-moon-shaped puff pastries used to garnish various dishes.

fond, extract produced by cooking meat, poultry, fish or vegetables. Basis of sauces.

fond d'artichaut, artichoke hearts.

fond blanc, white veal or chicken broth.

fond de gibier, game broth.

fond de volaille, poultry, chicken broth.

forcemeat or farce, filling for pâtés, terrines, meats, poultry, fish or vegetables, consisting of very finely chopped or puréed meat, fish, vegetables, fungi etc, seasoned and bound.

forcemeat balls, dumplings.

fricandeau, part of leg of veal.

fricassée, white stew of veal, lamb or chicken.

friture, deep fat for frying meat, poultry or fish and vegetables. Food to be fried is placed in a wire basket in hot fat. Also called frying fat.

frivolités, unusual small titbits.

fumet, essence, particularly game.

G

gardemanger, cook specializing in cold dishes (including pâtés and terrines).

garnish, to decorate a dish. The garnish is often included in the name of a dish.

gelatin, pure, tasteless bone extract in powder form used for setting liquids and light dishes.

gibier, game (hare and game birds).

glace, highly reduced, unsalted broth of veal, chicken, game or fish, used to improve sauces or glaze meats. Glace is boiled until it will set completely when cold, so that it can be cut.

glaze, to cover food with *glace*.

graisse, fat produced by boiling broth.

gratiner, to brown under the broiler to produce a crust.

grease, to coat a mold or pan with fat to make it easier to remove the contents at a later stage.

grind, finely chop or pass through grinder.

H

hang, to make meat juicier and add flavor by keeping for a time hanging in the air.

J

jelly, various clarified, solidified liquids.

julienne, fine strips of vegetable or truffle, included in or accompanying dishes.

jus, pure meat juice or roasting juices which set when cool.

L

lard, to insert small pieces of fat into meat.

lardon, small strip of pork fatback.

lier, to thicken.

line, to cover a mold with thin slices of fat or thinly rolled pastry.

M

macerate, to soak a food in a seasoned liquid in which it will be served.

mask, to cover with sauce or aspic jelly.

meat thermometer, instrument for determining precisely when a pâté, terrine or galantine is cooked.

mêler, to mix.

mie de pain, white bread crumbs without crust.

mijoter, to simmer or braise over a very low heat.

mirepoix, finely chopped root vegetables, onion and lean bacon lightly fried with thyme and bay.

mirlitons, filled puff pastry tarts.

mitonner, to boil slowly in liquid.

monter, to beat butter into a sauce or soup, to thicken it.

mousseline, mousse in small molds.

N

napper, to mask, or cover foods with aspic jelly or sauce.

P

panada, binding or thickening agent for forcemeats.

paner, to dip first in flour, then in bread crumbs (breading).

pâte feuilletée, puff pastry.

pickle, to put meat, poultry or game in seasoned acidic liquids to make them more flavorsome and mature, or to help them keep.

pickling liquid, highly seasoned, acidic liquids (vinegar, buttermilk, lemon juice, wine) which preserve or mature pieces of meat.

poach, to cook slowly without allowing to boil.

pound, to reduce meat, fish, seasonings, herbs, etc in a mortar.

primeurs, early or spring vegetables, early fruit, young wine.

purée, thick cream or pulp.

Q

quenelle, dumpling, small balls of meat or fish forcemeat.

R

ragoût, dish of chopped meat, fish or vegetables in a highly seasoned sauce. Used as filling.

râper, to rasp, to scrape meat out of the skin or off gristle.

reduce, to boil liquids such as broths, soups, sauces to the right consistency, or even until thick. Evaporates the liquid content and improves flavor.

refresh, to plunge hot foodstuffs into cold water to stop cooking.

rémoulade, highly seasoned mayonnaise with chopped herbs, anchovy fillets, capers and gherkins.

rissolé(e), fried or baked until brown and crisp.

rissole, to cook until brown and crisp.

roll out, to roll a rolling pin over pastry to make it of even thickness.

roux, lightly cooked flour and butter mixture, basis for many sauces and soups.

S

salmis, brown stew of game bird.

sauce chasseur, huntsman's sauce.

sauce à la creme, cream sauce.

sauce mornay, cheese sauce.

sauce mousseline, foam sauce.

sauce suprême, fine white chicken sauce.

sauce villeroi, white coating sauce.

saucer, to cover with sauce.

sauter, to fry small pieces of meat, poultry or fish in little fat over high heat.

seal, to quick fry meat fillets, liver, fish to prevent moisture being lost later.

sieve, to pass through a strainer or sieve (hair or conical) or cheesecloth.

skim, to remove curdled egg white or fat from the surface of broths, sauces or gravies with a slotted spoon.

soften, to fry lightly in fat without allowing the food to colour.

soubise, white onion purée.

spinach juice, liquid from spinach leaves used to color sauces. Squeeze out boiled spinach leaves in a cloth, heat the juice slowly, stirring from time to time and removing any bits of leaf that rise to the surface with a sieve, and then strain through a fine sieve.

suprême, a dish made with the best part of the animal, prepared in a specially fine way.

sprinkle, to cover a pan or mold with a thick layer of flour, bread crumbs, sugar or chopped almonds, for example. The pan or mold is first thoroughly greased with fat.

steam, to cook in water without the food coming into contact with the liquid. To steam you need a pan with a rack or trivet.

strain, to pour a liquid through a sieve or cloth.

stuff, fill with seasoned mixture (forcemeat).

T

thicken, to bind a dish with an agent such as cornstarch.

tourner, to cut to shape, e.g. garlic cloves or olives, to cut notches in mushroom heads.

tranche, slice.

trim, to remove fat, skin and gristle from meat or fish and cut to shape.

truss, to bring whole boned poultry back to its original shape with the help of a needle and thread.

U

unmold, to tip a dish out of the mold in which it has been cooked or left to set.

V

velouté, basic white sauce.

W

water bath, *see* bain-marie.

Index